The Logic of Price

Joseph P. McKenna

University of Missouri – St. Louis

The Dryden Press
901 North Elm Street
Hinsdale, Illinois

Copyright © 1973 by the Dryden Press
All rights reserved
Library of Congress Catalog Card Number: 73-1256
ISBN: 0-03-089-002-0
Printed in the United States of America
56789 090 9876543

Preface

Economics emphasizes an analytical approach to the social organization of mankind in the ordinary course of making and spending its living. It must therefore be practical and theoretical, particular and general, concrete and abstract, all at the same time.

Many economists prefer microeconomics, largely because it touches so many aspects of our lives and gives insight into so many different kinds of problems. However, if we are honest, we must admit that beginning students seldom share our enthusiasm. They seem to prefer macroeconomics, which enables them to understand discussions in the newspapers and the stories behind the headlines. (There is also a certain glee in being able to second-guess the President and his Council of Economic Advisers.)

Much of the appeal of macroeconomics is, it seems to me, that the applications come ready made; they are in the headlines of today's paper. In contrast, microeconomics applications often masquerade as problems in politics, sociology, or something else. Recognizing them as topics to be approached with economic tools requires an additional step.

Faced with this problem, some teachers have simply decided to teach the tools and leave the applications to the students. Others have so emphasized the problems that only minimal exposure to the tools has resulted. In this book, I have tried to avoid both errors. Each chapter is introduced with a parable which implies the economist's approach to a problem, but without detailed techniques. Then the specific tools appropriate to the topic are introduced, followed by an application which usually does utilize the tools of the chapter. In addition, various suggestions throughout each chapter suggest additional areas of application. Some of the chapters are followed by appendixes which add certain factual background. Finally, the whole book has been kept relatively short in order to permit individual instructors to provide other examples of the economic approach.

Some people may question the inclusion of indifference curves and production isoquants in an elementary text. They are here because of my conviction that the most important concept in all of economics is the trade-off and its implications. It is therefore important for students to understand the tools which economists use to deal with this concept. They have therefore been included in the text and then used and re-used in later chapters to deal with other problems. Thus indifference curves are used for labor supply and saving, as well as consumption, and production isoquants for factor demand as well as product supply.

My debts to all my colleagues in developing these ideas are substantial, but that to Elizabeth M. Clayton is especially strong. In preparing the manuscript, I received great assistance from Miss Vickie Landrum. I have also impressed my children into service, especially Celeste the typist, Kevin the draftsman, and Timothy the proofreader.

Joseph P. McKenna
University of Missouri — St. Louis
January 1973

Contents

		Introduction: Economic Reasoning	**1**
Part One		**Demand and Supply**	**5**
	1	Demand	**7**
	2	Supply	**30**
	3	Demand and Supply	**52**
	4	Consumers and Demand	**74**
		Appendix: The Nature of Households	**100**
	5	Firms and Supply	**109**
		Appendix: The Nature of Firms	**126**
	6	Resources and Costs	**132**
		Appendix: The Nature of Resources	**152**
Part Two		**Markets**	**159**
	7	Competitive Markets	**161**
	8	Monopolistic Markets	**184**
	9	Imperfectly Competitive Markets	**203**
		Appendix: Big Business	**224**
	10	Government and Markets	**231**
		Appendix: The Nature of Governments	**247**
	11	Resource Markets	**254**
		Appendix: Labor Unions	**279**
	12	The Market System and Economic Welfare	**284**
		Index	**294**

Introduction
Economic Reasoning

Problems of economics are everywhere: in newspapers, in Congress, in everyday life. However, the economist's method of looking at problems is much less common. This book is primarily an introduction to that method.

The essential characteristic of economic reasoning is a comparison of the benefits from any action with its costs. In order to acquire consumer goods, households must pay for them, thereby giving up goods which they might have bought instead. In order to obtain revenues from selling goods, firms must pay for materials and services to make them. In order to provide public services for their citizens, governments must pay those who provide them. To obtain the funds, governments either levy taxes, forcing their citizens to forgo other goods and services, or give up alternative governmental activities.

The essence of all economic decision is the choice of one alternative over others which are less desirable. It is based upon the hard reality that it is not possible to have everything we want; we must choose the most desirable and forgo the least.

All of us are familiar with this reality in our own

lives, but we sometimes forget its importance when looking at broader problems. Politicians often speak of the "need" or "desirability" of certain actions; but the real question is whether a particular action is better than the alternatives, public or private, which must be forgone to provide it. Gate-crashers may believe that rock concerts should be free, but promoters would be unwilling to hire artists and facilities to provide free concerts. The demand that they be free is, in effect, a demand that there be no concerts, a result which has occurred in many communities. Each of the short parables which introduce the chapters of this book is an example of the way that certain cost conditions produce certain results.

In order to deal with particular problems, economists have found that it is useful to simplify reality somewhat. For example, we usually assume that the sole aim of a firm is to maximize its profits, although we know that firms, and the men who run them, are often motivated by other goals. Nevertheless, profit is so important to firms and their survival that we are usually led to a surprisingly accurate description of their behavior by this simple assumption. Similarly, we often speak as if consumers made their choices among only two goods instead of thousands and as if firms produced single products. These simple assumptions make it possible to draw certain conclusions about behavior which still apply in the more general case.

One particular assumption is essential in most of economic reasoning: we pretend that a single event occurs and examine its effect while everything else remains unchanged. This assumption that *other things remain equal* makes it possible for us to concentrate our attention on one thing at a time. In the real world, of course, many things happen at once. However, if we examine them one at a time, we can then usually combine their effects into a single net result; whereas if we try to deal with them all at once, we are apt to become lost in the complexities of the situation.

The actual form of analysis which economists use varies between individuals and times. Economists of the nineteenth century usually used only verbal discussion; a common method in current use is algebraic equations. A very common technique, which we will use extensively in this book, involves the use of diagrams to describe relationships. It is therefore necessary for students to understand the elements of plotting a graph.

A graph provides a way of picturing the relationship between any two quantities. In the first chapter, we will meet a demand curve, which relates the quantity of something which will be purchased to the price which is charged. For example, suppose that a certain theater has calculated that 900 people would attend if the ticket price were $2.50, 1,400 if the price were $2.00, and 2,000 if the price were $1.50. These points can be plotted on a graph, as in Figure I.1.

To plot the first point, we move horizontally (along the attendance axis) to 900 and then vertically (in the price direction) to $2.50. Alternatively, we could draw a line upward at 900 and horizontally at $2.50. The required point is the intersection of these two lines. The second point is plotted at 1,400 and $2.00, the third at 2,000 and $1.50. These three points are then connected with a smooth curve. In many cases in this book, only the curve will be given, but particular points can be read off the curve if desired.

Many examples of such graphs will appear throughout this book, but the principles underlying them are the same. In most cases, they serve to describe the limitations within which choice must be made; outputs are associated with costs, increased sales are made only at lower prices, and so on. The underlying economic reasoning is always the same: benefits are measured against their costs to determine their worth and their desirability.

**Figure I.1
Simple Graphing**

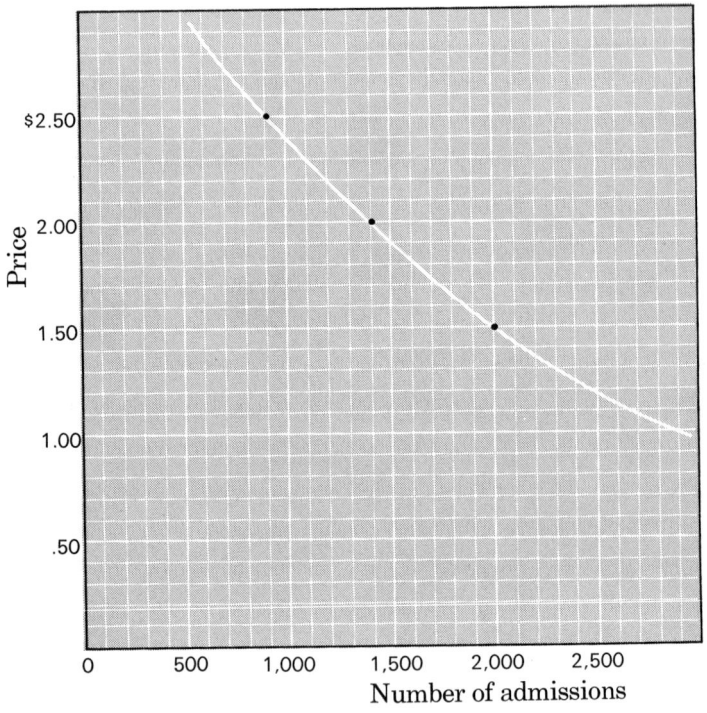

THE LOGIC OF PRICE

PART ONE

Demand and Supply

This section deals with conditions which determine the prices and quantities of goods in our society. In every case, we will assume that prices are determined by the impersonal forces of the market, but are not significantly affected by the actions of individual firms. (In Part II we will consider firms which are important enough to affect their own prices.)

Chapter I deals with demand and Chapter 2 with supply. These are combined in Chapter 3. Chapter 4 looks behind demand at consumer decisions. Chapter 5 shows the relation between costs of firms and supply, while Chapter 6 goes behind costs to examine firms' decision about resource use. Appendices to Chapters 4, 5, and 6 give some factual information about households, firms, and resources in the American economy.

Chapter 1
Demand

At Megalopolis University, the parking problem is a perennial aggravation. The parked cars of students, faculty, and staff cover acres of the campus. Students have traditionally been charged $25 per semester for parking, while the faculty, who get the lots closest to the classroom buildings, have paid $10 per month.

In a recent report, a committee of the local chapter of the American Association of University Professors condemned this system as discriminatory. The professor of political science who chaired the committee argued that the present system was undemocratic and should be replaced immediately by free parking for everyone, with free access to all lots by all persons. This report was supported by an editorial in the student newspaper and by a mass student rally on the mall.

Yielding to the pressure, the administration announced that henceforth all parking would be free. New parking stickers were issued to all members of the university community, and all parking lots were thrown open on a first come, first serve basis.

The result was chaos. The chief of campus security

estimated that the number of cars arriving on campus had increased 62 percent the first morning the new system went into effect. Lots close to the buildings were full at 7:15 a.m., and all lots were packed by 8:10. Many students missed their classes and spent the morning driving around looking for parking spaces. The 450 students gathered for the Psychology 1 lecture never heard it, for the professor in charge had been unable to find a place for his car and had returned home. The Biology 1 lecture was given, but only because the professor, who felt that Nobel prizewinners were entitled to park, had left his car in the driveway, thereby hopelessly blocking 425 other cars.

The next day the chancellor appointed a special committee on parking, headed by a professor of economics. The committee immediately announced new parking prices, ranging from $25 per month for the most desirable lots down to $5 for the less desirable lots. Students, faculty, and staff were given the opportunity to purchase stickers for the lots of their choice, and new parking stickers were issued. Within a week parking conditions were back to normal and congestion had dropped to a manageable level. The new pricing system was condemned as unjust and undemocratic by the AAUP committee, denounced by editorials in the student newspaper, and opposed at a mass rally on the mall.

The Demand Curve

Economists have long observed that people are apt to buy more of anything at low prices than at higher ones. If there is a limit to the amount of a product which is available, there will be some price at which the amount which buyers want to purchase is the same as the amount available. At higher prices, some of the supply will not be purchased; at lower prices, there will be too many buyers to satisfy. The example above illustrates this principle and also indicates that the price at which the number of buyers just equals the amount available may not bear any particular relationship to our views on justice or equity.

In order to deal with such problems, we use a tool called a *demand curve*. The demand curve represents the quantity of any good or service which buyers would be willing to purchase at each alternate price. (In practice, we only examine the prices which we think might actually occur. It is not very interesting to know how many new automobiles would be bought at $100 each.)

The demand curve is merely a way of summarizing information we already have in order to make better use of it. Implicit in the single curve are all of the many forces which affect demand. We will discuss these forces in somewhat more detail below, but it is useful to remind ourselves of a few of them here. First, notice that we have emphasized purchases. It makes no difference how much an individual wants something unless he has the money to buy it. On the other hand, money is unimportant if the individual has no desire for the product involved or wants other things even more. Only the combination of money to buy and the desire to spend it on a particular good constitutes demand in economic thought. Remember this the next time you hear someone talk about "America's need" for more teachers or nurses. Much of this "need" is not translated into demand and therefore will not be met by the economic system.

Second, we have emphasized alternative prices. The demand for parking might be for 3,000 spaces at $15 per month or for 5,000 spaces at $5 per month. This does not mean, however, that after 3,000 spaces have been sold for $15, an additional 2,000 can be sold at $5, for these are alternative, not successive, possibilities. For this reason, we use the conjunction *or* in referring to successive points on demand curves, never *and*.

Finally, every demand curve has strict time dimensions in two different senses. The present demand curve is based upon present incomes, the present number of buyers, and the present alternatives available. In the case of university parking, we would hardly expect the same demand curve next year when there are more students or ten years from now after a new rapid transit system is established. In addition, every demand curve represents the quantity of the product which will be purchased in a given period of time. In the example of parking spaces, we are probably interested in the average number of parking spaces which will be used *per day*. If we were discussing meat purchases, we might be interested in the number of purchases per week or per month. If we were to refer to the pounds of meat consumed per year, the numbers would be much larger, but we would still be talking about the same demand.

Table 1.1
Demand for Parking Spaces (hypothetical)

Price (dollars per month)	Quantity (spaces per day)
$20	2,000
15	3,000
10	4,000
5	5,000
0	6,000

Table 1.1 shows the various alternatives which are possible for parking spaces. (We have simplified matters and assumed that all parking spaces are equal in desirability, so that we will not need to distinguish according to location.) We now observe that 3,000 parking spaces would be demanded at $15 per month, or 5,000 at $5. If the parking spaces were made free, 6,000 spaces would be demanded. (Of course, there might be less than 6,000 available, so the demand might not be satisfied.)

We may naturally wonder where all of the cars would come from. If 3,000 cars could bring in the students, faculty, and staff when prices were $15 per month, why would it take twice as many if parking was free? The answer is that there are alternatives to driving to the university, but these alternatives represent something of a nuisance to those who adopt them. Some who live near the campus may walk; others who live slightly further away may ride bicycles. Some may use public transportation — bad as it may be — and a greater number of car pools may be formed. A few students might even drop out of school if parking is too expensive. Each of these alternatives represents a possibility; but for most people they are possibilities which will be used only if necessary. None of them is quite as convenient as simply getting into the car and going. (We should remember also that driving a car is not free, even if parking is. Therefore, not every student or faculty member would drive even if the price of parking were zero. We would expect 6,000 cars to be less than the number of members of the university community.)

Similarly, when we consider the demand for *any* product or service, there will be various alternatives which people might adopt. In general, they either find another way to satisfy the same purpose or they leave the want unsatisfied.

The foregoing discussion casts some light on the general question of the shape of the demand curve. In Table 1.1, we see that the quantity and the price move inversely—that is, quantity demanded falls as price rises and vice versa. This is a characteristic of most demand curves, and is sometimes called a *law of demand*. This inverse movement comes about because the incentives to do without or to find alternatives increase as prices rise and decrease as they fall. We can therefore say that, as far as demand is concerned, price serves a *rationing* function, discouraging or encouraging the use of the product. (Notice that in the parking example, price performed all of the rationing in the final system. In the initial system, some lots were rationed by use of rank, giving them only to faculty and staff. Price is an important rationing device in our society, but not the only one. For example, college admissions are rationed to those who pay the tuition *and* have the suitable grades and test scores.)

Like many other laws, the law of demand does have some "loopholes." The most important of these occurs in a few goods whose principal value is that they are so expensive that ownership conveys a certain snob appeal regardless of the actual merits of the product. Synthetic furs can be just as handsome and just as warm, and are certainly more durable than real ones. If the two sold at the same price, very few people would want the real furs; yet they choose them at the higher price. As another example, would more or fewer diamond rings be sold if diamonds cost only $10 per carat instead of $500?

The same information which has been summarized in Table 1.1 is shown in graphic form in Figure 1.1. This is done simply by plotting the alternative price-quantity combinations of the table on the graph and then drawing a smooth curve between them. (Those who are unfamiliar with curve plotting should review

**Figure 1.1
Demand for Parking Spaces**

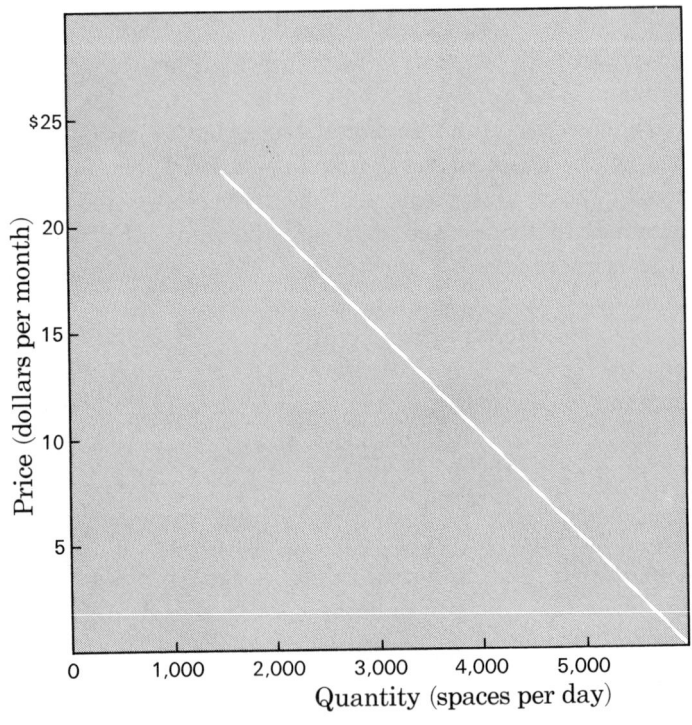

the discussion in the Introduction.) The smooth curve implies that the same relationship which exists for the points of the table also applies for the intervening points as well. The inverse relation between price and quantity is reflected in the fact that the curve slopes downward to the right.

The choice of a table or a graph is largely a matter of preference. Usually, it is easier to grasp a relationship by looking at a picture than by looking at the table. It is also easier to show changes in demand by drawing another curve than by constructing a new table. (You will probably find that your instructor prefers curves for classroom use because he can draw them faster than he can write all of the figures for a table.)

Table 1.2
Market Demand for Ground Beef,
Four Buyers
(Hypothetical)

Price per pound	Quantity demanded, Mr. A	Quantity demanded, Mr. B	Quantity demanded, Mr. C	Quantity demanded, Mr. D	Total quantity demanded per month
$1.40	5 +	10 +	4 +	0 =	19
1.20	10 +	15 +	9 +	5 =	39
1.00	15 +	25 +	15 +	9 =	64
.80	20 +	40 +	22 +	12 =	94
.60	25 +	60 +	30 +	14 =	129

Individual and Market Demand

So far we have been considering only the demand in a market where each individual purchases only one unit at a time. Although there are many cases where this is typical, there are also many where it is not. For example, if we considered the demand for a particular food—say ground beef—we would expect that almost all consumers would want to buy some quantity each month at almost every price. In Table 1.2, we have listed the demand schedules for our separate buyers and the total demand for the entire group. In each case, we take the quantity demanded by each buyer at a given price, and add them to find the quantity demanded in the market for that price. The same process is shown in graphic form in Figure 1.2.

When a particular group of buyers are purchasing from particular sellers, we call the process of interaction a *market*. Sometimes the market may be concentrated in a single place—such as the market for university parking places or the market for stocks at the New York stock exchange. More commonly, however, a market covers a wider area; we often speak, for example, of a metropolitan labor market. Since it is sometimes very difficult to define the boundaries of a market, we will discuss the problem again in later chapters. At this point, we will merely say that a market consists of all those buyers competing for the same goods. (In Chapter 2, a market is all those sellers competing for the same customers; and in Chapter 3, it consists of the groups of buyers and sellers dealing with each other.)

Table 1.3
Market Demand for Ground Beef,
One Thousand Buyers
(Hypothetical)

Price per pound	Quantity demanded, Mr. A	Buyers like Mr. A	Quantity demanded, Mr. B	Buyers like Mr. B	Quantity demanded, Mr. C	Buyers like Mr. C	Quantity demanded, Mr. D	Buyers like Mr. D	Total quantity demanded per month
$1.40	(5 ×	400) +	(10 ×	300) +	(4 ×	200) +	(0 ×	100) =	5,800
1.20	(10 ×	400) +	(15 ×	300) +	(9 ×	200) +	(5 ×	100) =	10,800
1.00	(15 ×	400) +	(25 ×	300) +	(15 ×	200) +	(9 ×	100) =	17,400
.80	(20 ×	400) +	(40 ×	300) +	(22 ×	200) +	(12 ×	100) =	25,600
.60	(25 ×	400) +	(60 ×	300) +	(30 ×	200) +	(14 ×	100) =	35,400

Most markets have more than four buyers, so the process would be more complicated. Let us imagine that there are actually 1,000 buyers, of whom 400 are like Mr. A, 300 like Mr. B, 200 like Mr. C, and 100 like Mr. D. In that case, it would be necessary to multiply the quantity purchased by each buyer at a given price by the number of buyers like him before adding to obtain the market total. Such a process is shown in Table 1.3. In general, a

**Figure 1.2
Market Demand for Ground Beef**

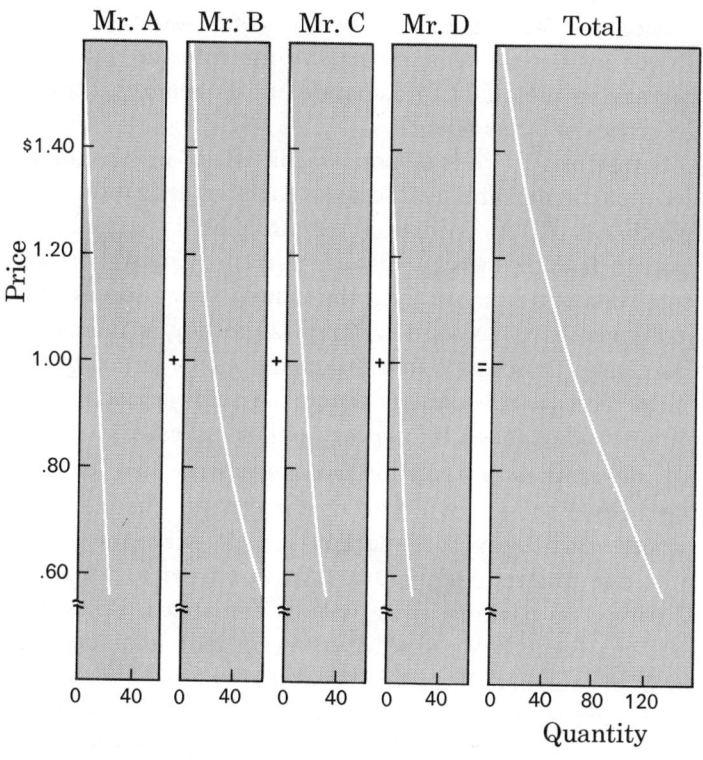

Demand

market demand curve can always be obtained by adding the individual demands (if we know them) in one of these two ways.

One additional reason why market demand curves are downward sloping is illustrated by the numbers in Tables 1.2 and 1.3. Notice that Mr. D does not buy any beef if the price is above $1.20. Prices lower than this one entice him into the market, thereby increasing the quantity demanded in the market, apart from the increases of other buyers.

Sometimes there is a "bandwagon effect" in consumer demand for a particular product, because each buyer is influenced by the purchases of other people. (Such an effect is particularly important in fashion merchandise.) When this bandwagon occurs, the total demand is more than the simple summation of individual demands; each person's willingness to buy is increased by the purchases of others. Such a demand curve is apt to show very large increases in quantity demanded at lower prices, as increased quantity demanded influences further increases.

The market demand for parking spaces has its slope solely because of the entry of new customers into the market at lower prices. Each individual market demand curve for parking looks like the diagram of Figure 1.3. At all prices above a certain amount, no parking space will be demanded. Below that price, one space will be demanded. Different individual demand curves will, of course, differ in the price at which the quantity increases from zero to one. The total curve of Figure 1.1 is the sum of thousands of such curves, indicating different buyers entering the market at different prices.

Determinants of Demand

Every demand curve represents a relationship between price and quantity. It shows that as price changes, there is an inverse change in the quantity demanded. Price is not, however, the only influence upon demand. Whenever any other factor changes, there is a shift in the whole demand curve, indicating a different quantity at every price. In order to avoid confusion, we reserve the term, *a change in quantity demanded*, for a movement along the curve as price changes. We refer to a shift in the whole schedule as *a change in demand*. In Figure 1.4, a movement

**Figure 1.3
Individual Demand for Parking**

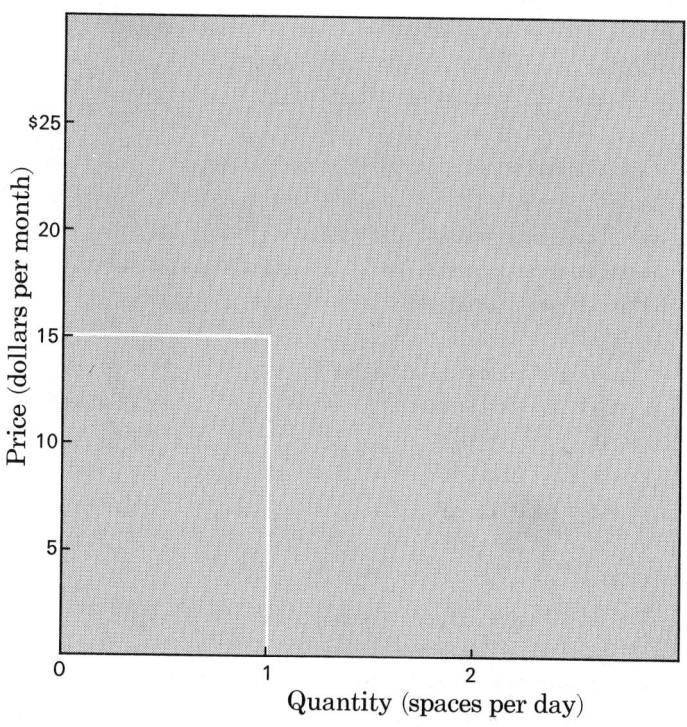

Demand

from P to Q is *an increase in quantity demanded*, representing the effect of a decrease in price from $1.00 to $0.80. The change from D_1 to D_2 is *an increase in demand*, for there will be a greater quantity purchased at every price. A movement from Q to P would, of course, be *a decrease in quantity demanded*, and a shift from D_2 to D_1 would be *a decrease in demand*.

Shifts in demand may come about for many reasons. These can be summarized under five general categories:

1. Changes in the number of consumers.
2. Changes in the incomes of consumers.
3. Changes in consumer tastes.
4. Changes in the price and availability of related goods.
5. Changes in expectations of future conditions.

Let us consider each of these in turn.

1. *Number of consumers.* We have already suggested that the demand for campus parking spaces would change if there were more or less students. Similarly, we saw that a market demand curve is the sum of the individual curves in the market. Naturally the market curve shifts if the number of individual curves changes.

Sometimes such changes in a market demand may result from new highways, making it possible for different consumers to enter a given market. Sometimes they may come about from the normal demographic changes in society; for example, the teenage market is much larger than it was ten years ago. Sometimes the changes may be the result of a single event, such as the establishment of an army camp near a small town. Sometimes, they are the result of many small changes—such as the individual decisions of many families to move to California.

2. *Incomes of consumers.* As consumers' incomes rise, there will be an increase in their general purchases of various goods; but the increase will not be spread uniformly through all commodities. The purchase of some commodities will increase by more than the proportion by which income has increased. The purchase of other commodities will tend to increase, but by a smaller proportion than income. Finally, the purchase of some goods will actually decrease as incomes rise. These goods are

**Figure 1.4
Changes in Demand**

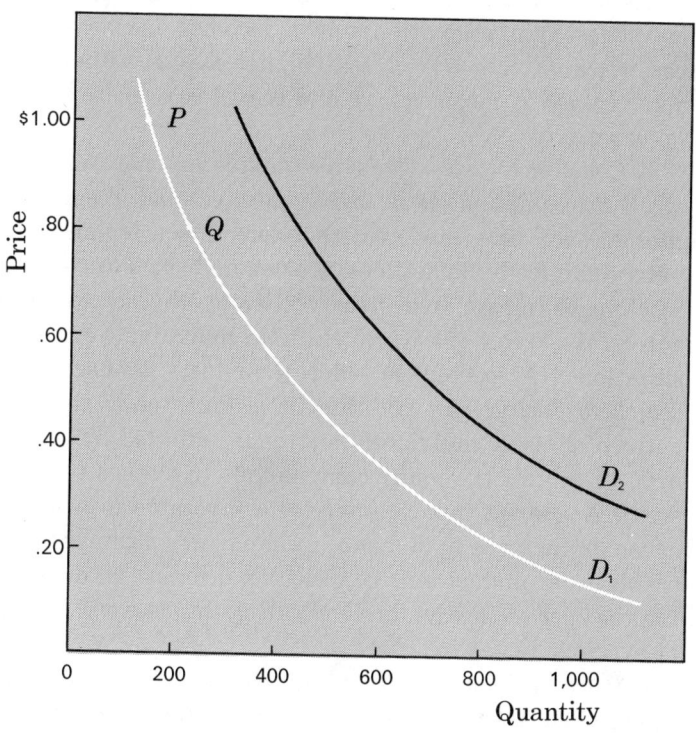

Demand

known as *inferior goods.* For example, as incomes rise, families tend to buy less oleomargarine and more butter, or they buy less hamburger and more sirloin. Hamburger and oleomargarine are therefore inferior goods for such families. Some goods may increase substantially at one stage of rising incomes, then increase less than proportionately as incomes rise more, and finally become inferior goods at still higher stages. Other goods will appear only as incomes rise, and therefore come to be known as *luxury goods.*

3. *Consumer tastes.* Consumer tastes are naturally the basis of all consumption. It is to be expected that these tastes will change over time, and will therefore affect demand curves for individual goods. Sometimes, the demand curves may be affected by changes in fashion or by advertising; other times the changes will be the result of natural shifts in individuals or their family situations. (As people get older, their taste for hard rock music seems to decline.) In addition, it is quite clear that the taste pattern of every individual is strongly affected by those around him. (Think of the many campus fads in clothes that you have seen.) A change in consumer taste favorable to a product will cause an increase in demand; a change in consumer taste unfavorable to a product will represent a decrease in demand, shifting the curve to the left and indicating that less will be demanded at every price.

4. *Price and availability of related goods.* With respect to any one product, there are two classes of related goods which are important. The first of these classes consists of goods which may be *substituted* for the one under consideration. In this sense, pork is a substitute for beef, rapid transit is a substitute for automobile transportation and parking as well. In general, if a substitute product, such as pork, becomes more easily available, or if its price goes down, the result will be a shift of the original demand curve for beef to the left; that is, there will be a decrease in demand for beef. Conversely, an increase in price of a substitute good or a decrease of its availability will lead to an increase in the demand for the good under question.

The other kind of related good is called a *complementary* good. Complementary goods tend to go together, as ham and eggs, scotch and soda, tires and gasoline, or fish and chips. As the price of complementary goods goes down, the effect is to make the whole combination less expensive, and therefore lead to an increase in demand for the goods under consideration. On the other hand, if the price of complementary goods goes up, the price of the combination also rises, and the effect is a decrease in demand.

In a certain sense, all goods are both substitutes and complements for each other. They are substitutes because all of them compete for the same income, and every dollar which is not spent on one is available to be spent on another. On the other hand, they are complements because each of us has in his mind a pattern or model of what is the appropriate combination of goods and how he should spend his income. We have all said at some time that one of our friends spends his income unwisely because of the way he purchases some things. Clearly, this might simply be because his tastes differ from ours; but we tend to assume that most of the people in our own group should have tastes which are similar to ours because they have all been conditioned by the same forces. It is in this sense that all goods tend to be complements, for they correspond to a particular pattern.

5. *Expectations of future conditions.* What we do today obviously depends upon what we expect tomorrow. If prices of certain goods are expected to be lower in the reasonably near future, we might postpone their purchase. On the other hand, if we expect prices to go up, it is apt to be worth our while to purchase now and stockpile. Naturally, the question of whether to postpone purchases or not depends on how postponable the satisfaction or service which the goods will render is. It is obviously not feasible to postpone the purchase of food even if we know the prices will be lower next month. We could more easily postpone the purchase of a new car until then. In the same way, whether or not we buy ahead depends on our ability to store and to keep the products involved. It would make very little sense to purchase an orchid corsage right now because it might be more expensive at prom time.

It is not only our expectation of price changes which influences our purchases. It is quite possible that we expect changes in other factors which we have already discussed. If we expect our income to be higher later, it may be possible to postpone many purchases until then, or to borrow money to buy them. (Students are quite familiar with this process.) Similarly, if we expect a lower income at some future time, it might be preferable to save our money against that possibility and to make fewer purchases now. (People nearing retirement are quite conscious of this problem.) Sometimes we can also foresee changes in our taste patterns. For example, we know that certain kinds of fads may be attractive now, but will seem less desirable later. Therefore, if we can postpone their purchase, we often do without the purchase entirely.

We have seen that there are many possible causes for a shift in demand, whether it be an increase or a decrease. In contrast, there is only one reason for a change in the quantity demanded: a change in price. As prices rise, the quantity demanded falls; as prices fall, the quantity demanded rises. The reason for this difference is that the quantity demanded is, by definition, only the change which takes place as we move along a given demand curve; therefore it assumes that all of the factors discussed above are fixed and only the price has changed.

Elasticity

We have already seen that the quantity demanded usually increases as the price declines. It is clear, however, that how much the quantity increases for a given change in price will vary substantially for different products. It is therefore necessary to have some kind of measure of how responsive the quantity change is to changes in price. At first glance, it might seem that we could use the slope of the demand curve as the measure of the responsiveness of the quantity changes to changes in price. However, it is clear that this slope will depend on the units in which the product is measured. For example, we have previously noticed that we can measure the quantity purchased per week, per month, or per year. Depending upon which of these we use, we can get very different slopes, and yet we have really described the same demand situation. It is therefore better to measure changes in percentage terms. Such a measure is called elasticity, and is given by the formula:

$$\text{Elasticity of demand} = \frac{\text{Percentage change in quantity}}{\text{Percentage change in price}}$$

Since the percentage changes are obtained by dividing the absolute amount of change by the original amount, we can restate the formula as follows:

$$\text{Elasticity of demand} = \frac{\text{Change in quantity}}{\text{Quantity}} \div \frac{\text{Change in price}}{\text{Price}}$$

If the elasticity coefficient is large, we say that a demand curve is *elastic*. If, on the other hand, it is small, we say that the demand curve is *inelastic*. As the boundary line between these two conditions we use an elasticity measure of one, a special case called *unit elasticity*. In this case, the percentage change in quantity demanded is exactly equal to the percentage change in price. On an elastic demand curve, the percentage change in quantity is larger; and on an inelastic demand curve, the percentage change in price is larger. Two demand curves are shown in Figure 1.5. It is clear that D_2 is much more elastic than D_1. If, for example, we look at the change in price from $0.50 to $0.40, a 20 percent fall, we see that quantity demanded increases by 56 percent on D_2, but only 12 percent on D_1. We can therefore say that the elasticity of demand at this point on D_2 is 2.8, but only 0.6 on D_1.

An alternative way of measuring elasticity of demand is simply by looking at total revenue as price changes. If the percentage change in quantity is greater than the percentage change in price—that is, if the demand curve is elastic—we would expect the total revenue to rise as price falls. In other words, total revenue moves in the same direction as the quantity. For an inelastic demand curve, we would expect that the total revenue would follow the price, which is the larger of the two percentages. Inelastic demand curves show a greater total revenue at higher prices; elastic demand curves show a greater revenue at lower prices. If we look again at Figure 1.5, we see that both demand curves show

**Figure 1.5
Elasticity of Demand**

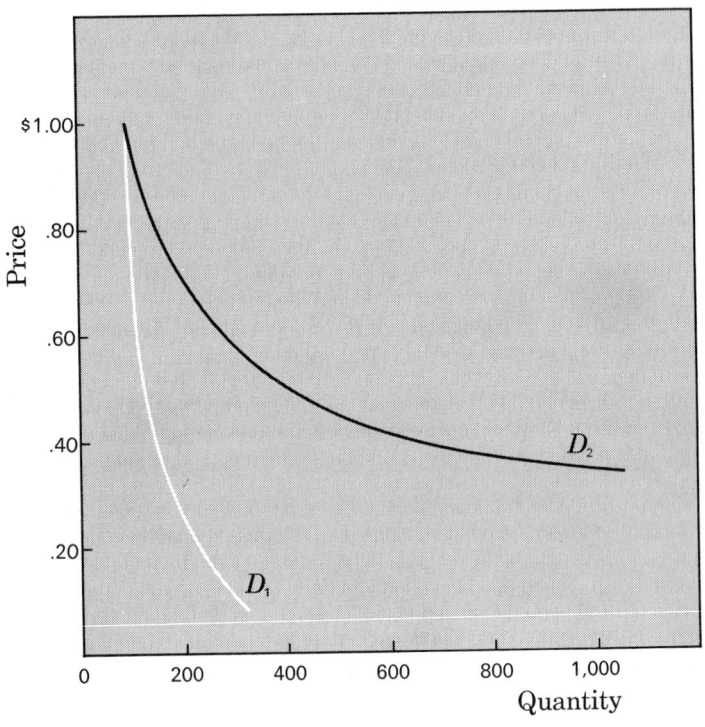

a total revenue of $100 at a price of $1.00. At a price of $0.50, however, D_2 shows a total revenue of $200, the quantity of 400 times the price of $0.50. We can conclude that D_2 is an elastic demand curve. At the same price on D_1, total revenue is about $70, the quantity of about 140 times the $0.50 price. Thus D_1 is an inelastic demand curve.

Both of the methods which we have been using to measure elasticity are relatively crude. Let us illustrate by looking at D_2. If we observe the decrease in price from $1.00 to $0.90, a cut of 10 percent in price, we see that quantity increases 23 percent for an elasticity coefficient of 2.3. If we cut the price from $1.00 to $0.80, a 20 percent cut, the quantity increases 56 percent for an elasticity measure of 2.8. For the 30 percent cut to $0.70, the quantity increases 104 percent and the elasticity coefficient is 3.5. For the price decrease to $0.60, the elasticity is 4.4; and for the price cut to $0.50, the elasticity is 6.0. To avoid this difficulty, economists have agreed that elasticity of demand should ideally be calculated only on very tiny, even infinitesimal price changes. Had we done this, we would find that D_2 has an elasticity of 2.0 and D_1 an elasticity of 0.5, not only at this point, but everywhere along the curve. This limitation to infinitesimal changes need not bother us, however, for we will not need precise numerical measures of elasticity. Our concern will be only with the general concepts of elastic and inelastic demand. We can use the numerical computation method given above as a crude measure or simply check the effect on total revenue of a given price change.

Not all demand curves have the same elasticity throughout their lengths. We should therefore speak of a curve as inelastic or elastic at a particular point. When we do use the phrase, "elastic demand curve," it is usually a short way of saying that the demand curve is elastic in the general region in which we are interested. Most curves are elastic in some regions and inelastic in others. As an exercise, one can easily prove by careful calculation and measurement that a straight-line demand curve is elastic in the top half and inelastic in the bottom half.

As an illustration of these principles, Table 1.4 presents the data for a demand curve and shows the calculations of the elasticity coefficient for each of the price intervals given and the effect upon total revenue.

**Table 1.4
Elasticity of Demand**

Price	Quantity demanded	Total revenue	Change in revenue	Elasticity coefficient
$1.00	4,000	$4,000	Increase	$\frac{4,000}{4,000} \div \frac{.20}{1.00} = 5.0$
.80	8,000	6,400	Increase	$\frac{6,000}{8,000} \div \frac{.20}{.80} = 3.0$
.60	14,000	8,400	Increase	$\frac{8,000}{14,000} \div \frac{.20}{.60} = 1.7$
.40	22,000	8,800	Decrease	$\frac{10,000}{22,000} \div \frac{.20}{.40} = 0.9$
.20	32,000	6,400		

An Illustration: Medical Care

In recent years, there has been an increasing public awareness that many people in our society are unable to obtain adequate medical service because they are unable to pay the cost. Accordingly, Congress has adopted various plans under which the government has provided funds to provide medical care. The first of these was Medicare, which added a medical care program to social security benefits for persons over sixty-five. This program was adopted in 1966. A second program, called Medicaid and adopted in 1969, was designed to aid welfare clients by grants to the states. The net effect of these programs has not been total success; both programs have been more expensive than forecast, and rising medical costs have made medical care more difficult to obtain for middle- and lower-middle-income families. The tools of this chapter help us to understand why.

The supply of doctors in the United States is severely limited by the number of places in medical schools. Because most students apply to several schools, it is difficult to estimate accurately how many applicants might wish to enter medicine but are unable to do so. However, the number is certainly quite large. Because medical schools are so expensive to operate, universities are slow to expand existing ones and even slower to establish new ones. Thus the number of doctors at any particular time is almost fixed, and it grows very slowly.

Similar conditions exist with respect to hospitals. Hospital charges often cover only operating expenses, and the hospitals must rely on special community fund-raising for the expansion of facilities. Thus the number of hospital beds is also relatively fixed.

The government programs discussed are not designed to alter these conditions; instead they provide funds to add to the demand for medical services. The impact of these programs is shown in Figure 1.6. Without any government programs, the demand for medical services would be represented by D_1, and the price at which the quantity demanded would equal the available supply is P_1. This price would tend to be established in the market.

With the addition of government medical programs, the demand curve shifts to the right, to D_2. Notice that the size of the shift is greater at the higher price levels than at lower ones, because, although the elderly and the poor would have purchased some medical service at all price levels, they would have purchased less at higher prices. Therefore, the higher the prices, the more important are the government programs. The quantity demanded on the new demand curve would equal the supply only at a higher price, P_2. Thus we should not be surprised that medical costs have risen almost twice as fast as other prices since 1966.

Another impact of the new programs can also be seen in Figure 1.6. The total amount of medical service available is the same, regardless of the demand. At the higher price, P_2, a significant amount of the demand is in the government supported area, the difference between D_1 and D_2. The nonsupported patients have been forced by higher prices to cut back on their purchases of medical care, indicated by the fact that the quantity demanded on D_1 is much less at price P_2 than at P_1. Such a result was inevitable; if government policies make more medical care available to some groups, and the total is fixed, less will be available for others.

More recent testimony before congressional committees has emphasized the problems of the "medically indigent"—those persons who have enough income for their ordinary needs, but

**Figure 1.6
Market for Medical Services**

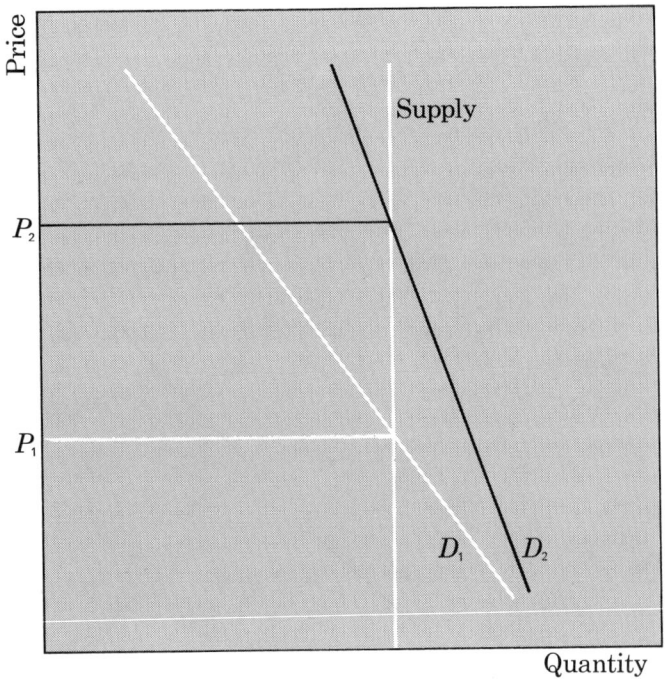

Demand and Supply

not enough to pay the higher costs of medical care. Accordingly, several plans have been proposed to broaden federal support for medical costs. Figure 1.6 demonstrates that these plans cannot achieve their goal of providing adequate medical care for everyone. If the plans cover only a part of the population, a new class of medical indigents will appear among the lowest income groups not covered. If the plans cover the entire population, some nonprice method of rationing service will be required, for there is simply not enough medical care to go around.

If it is really desired to provide more adequate medical care in our society, it is quite clear that actions which are designed to increase the quantity of care available will have a more beneficial impact than any action which concentrates on demand. It might still be necessary to provide funds to the poor to permit them to purchase medical care, but more care would be available. Without an increase in total availability, better medical care for one group can be provided only at the expense of some other group.

Chapter 2
Supply

Like most other school systems, Centerville School District has a salary schedule which depends upon the degrees earned by teachers and the number of their years of experience. No distinctions are made for area of specialization, except for physical education. English and history teachers are paid on the same scale as mathematics and physics teachers. Naturally, coaches are paid more.

Last year the school system received a routine accreditation visit from the regional association. (Even after school systems are accredited, they are revisited periodically to insure that standards are being maintained.) The report of the visiting team praised the curriculum innovations which had been adopted in some areas, especially in the literature and American history courses. On the other hand, there were suggestions that the chemistry course and the entire mathematics sequence were far behind the standards which prevailed in the better school systems. Although the report did not actually say so, there was a strong implication that the teachers in these areas were incompetent.

The school board was quite upset by the report

and held several closed-door sessions with the superintendent. The superintendent admitted that the charges were true, but said that he had been unable to hire good mathematicians or scientists. Several of the local manufacturing firms were offering $5,000 a year more than the school system, using such people as aides to their professional scientific staffs. Consequently, only the dregs of the market were available to the school. On the other hand, many students who had majored in history and English found few alternate employment opportunities. As a result, the school usually had more applicants in these fields than it could use and chose the best ones.

The chairman of the board, a successful local businessman, suggested offering higher salaries in math and science. "After all," he said, "I have to pay more for computer programmers than for secretaries, even though my secretary is twice as bright as my average programmer. It ought to be the same in the schools." His proposal was accepted, and a new salary schedule was adopted. The proposal was denounced as unfair by the local president of the American Federation of Teachers. Many teachers charged sex discrimination, since more of the science teachers were men and most of the English teachers were women.

Nevertheless, the school board stuck to its position, and the superintendent did a very fine recruiting job. Within a year, a series of exciting innovations were made in the math and science curricula. The opposition died down somewhat, but there was still some unhappiness and some teachers were talking about organizing before the next school board election.

The Supply Curve

In the last chapter we saw that consumers will normally buy more of a product if the price is low than if it is high. In this chapter we see that suppliers will provide more of the product when the price is high than when the price is low. Again, there is one price at which enough will be supplied to provide almost any desired quantity. At prices lower than that one, less than the desired quantity would be supplied and there would be a shortage; at higher prices, more would be supplied and there would be an excess. In the school example above, the same price produced a shortage of one kind of labor and a surplus of a different kind because the supply conditions for the two were different. There need be no relationship between our concepts of equity and justice and the price which provides the quantity required in the market. Equal wages might or might not be fair, but they would not always be effective in attracting the desired quantity of each kind of labor.

Just as we used a demand curve to represent the conditions surrounding purchase, so we use a *supply curve* to represent the conditions surrounding sale. The supply curve depicts the quantity of any good or service which would be offered for sale at each alternate price.

Like the demand curve, the supply curve is merely a way of summarizing information we already have in order to make better use of it. Behind it are all of the forces which affect supply. Several of these forces will be discussed below, but it is useful to remind ourselves of some of them here. First, we now emphasize an offering for sale. This means that there must be both an *ability* to provide the desired product and a *willingness to do so*. It is obviously of no concern to us at what price someone might be willing to sell automobiles unless he has the production capacity to provide them. In the same way, if we are considering the supply of skilled labor, we would consider only the willingness of those who have the necessary training and skill, not of people in general. Remember that the demand curve depended upon both a willingness and an ability to buy.

Second, the supply curve represents alternative quantities that would be available at alternative prices. These are not successive offerings, but only alternatives. The conjunction *or* is appropriate in referring to successive points on supply curves, never *and*.

Finally, like a demand curve, a supply curve has strict time dimensions in the same two different senses. A supply curve is based upon present capital equipment, present skills, and present ability to produce. Naturally, we would not expect the same conditions to apply at some later time. In the school example, supply would certainly be different after more mathematics teachers had been trained or if local manufacturers stopped hiring mathematicians. In addition, like the demand curve, every supply curve represents a quantity of the product which would be sold or offered for sale during a given period of time. In the example of the services of teachers, we are usually interested in the number of man-years of service that would be offered—that is, the number of workers who would be available per year. If we were discussing the supply of meat or vegetables, we would be interested in the quantity which would be offered for sale during a given week or month. If we were to measure the pounds of meat supplied per year, the numbers would be larger, but we would be talking about the same supply conditions. For many agricultural products, a year is the appropriate supply measurement, because of the natural dependency of agriculture upon the annual crop season.

Table 2.1
Supply of Mathematics Teachers

Salary* (9 month year)	Number of teachers
5,000	0
6,000	30
7,000	60
8,000	100
9,000	160
10,000	180
11,000	190

*Starting salaries without allowance for experience or advanced degrees.

Table 2.1 shows the various supply alternatives which are possible at a given time. In this case, we have examined the supply of mathematics teachers in a given area, one obviously larger than a single school district. We now see that the number of teachers offering their services increases as the price goes higher and decreases as the price goes down. The number of teachers available goes to zero long before the price which is offered them does so. The reason, of course, is that if salaries of teachers were too low, most teachers would find some alternative employment.

It is the possibility of alternative employment which accounts for a large portion of the slope of this supply curve. Naturally, the number of people who are qualified to be mathematics teachers does not change simply because of the change in price, but the number of them who are willing to teach does depend upon the price. At lower prices, a great many mathematics teachers will find themselves working in businesses as engineering aids or in the growing computer field. Many of them prefer teaching, however, and will teach if the sacrifice is not too great. Therefore, as the wages in teaching begin to approach those in alternative occupations, we can expect that there will be a substantially increased quantity of labor supplied. (As a test of your understanding of these principles, analyze for yourself the shape of the supply curve of English teachers, remembering that there are fewer alternatives available to them than to mathematics teachers.)

The same information which is summarized in Table 2.1 is also shown in graphic form in Figure 2.1. This is done by plotting the alternative price-quantity combinations of the table on the graph and drawing a smooth curve through them. This supply curve slopes upward to the right, while the demand curve of Figure 1.1 slopes downward.

We saw in the last chapter that there is generally an inverse relationship between price and quantity demanded, and that the quantity demanded increases as the price falls. In Table 2.1 we see that the relationship between the price and the quantity supplied is direct—that is, quantity falls as price falls, and rises as price rises. The direct relationship is shown in Figure 2.1 by the upward slope and is characteristic of most supply curves, although, as we will see shortly, not of all of them. This direct relationship—often described as a *law of supply*—comes about because prices received by suppliers provide an incentive to the suppliers to forgo their alternative possibilities. We can therefore say that, as far as supply is concerned, price serves an incentive function, encouraging or discouraging the supply of the product and the forgoing of alternatives. Remember that price serves a rationing function in demand. (Although price is an important incentive in the supply of any good or service, it is not the only one. Many professions attract people because of the prestige as well as the money.)

So far we have been considering the supply of a particular

Figure 2.1
Supply of Mathematics Teachers

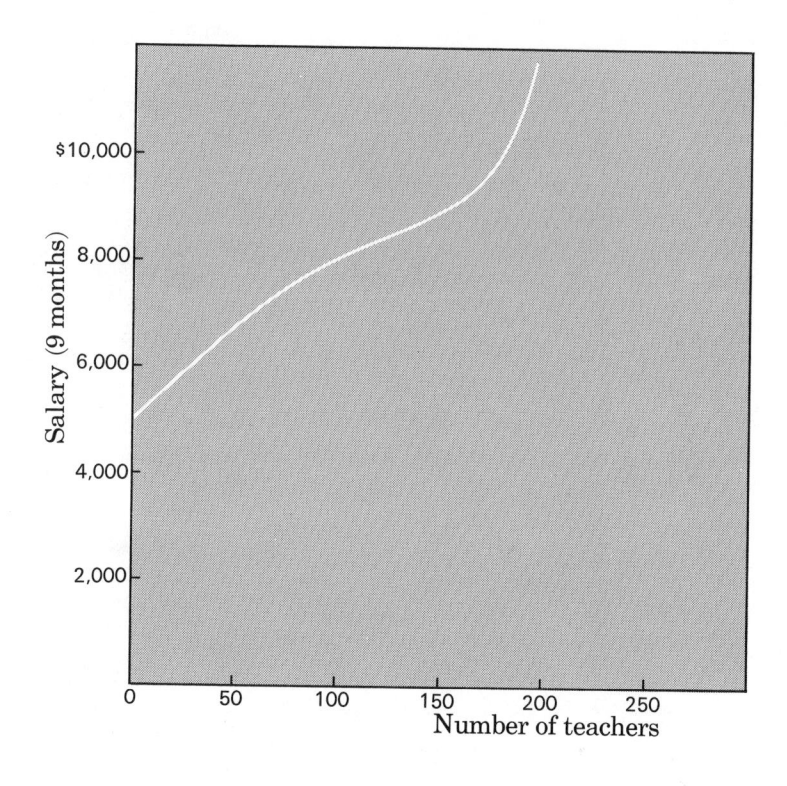

**Figure 2.2
Immediate Supply**

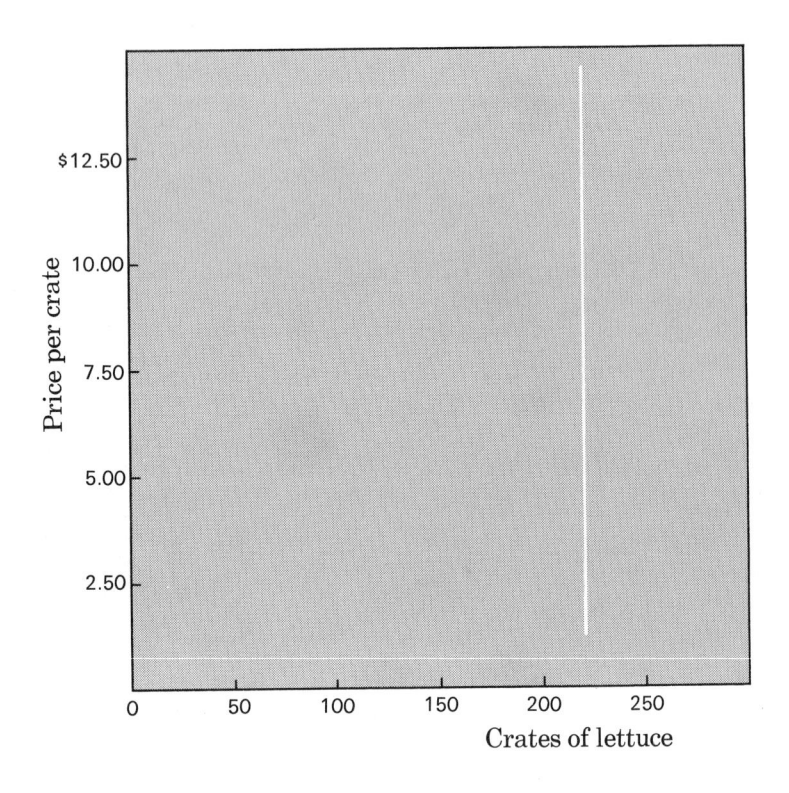

kind of labor. In this case, changes in the quantity supplied depend upon the incentives of the workers to accept this job and forgo others. In much of this book, we will be more concerned with the supply of products; changes in the quantity supplied will then be more closely tied to costs of production. These costs, however, are related to alternative uses which either the firm or society can find for the resources which the firm needs for production. We will return to this problem in Chapters 5 and 6.

The law of supply has more "loopholes" than the law of demand. These loopholes are closely associated with the time period over which we are considering the supply curve. If we are considering a very short period of time, the supply of a product or service might be absolutely limited. Furthermore, if the product is quite perishable, it might be sold even though the price should go quite low. An example of this kind of situation could occur in a produce market at any particular time. On a given day, various farmers might bring in loads of lettuce expecting to sell them at certain prices. If prices should go up, that still does not make it possible for them to provide any more lettuce on that particular day. On the other hand, even if prices should fall very low, we would expect that they would continue to sell even though they would be unhappy at the conditions under which they were doing so. Such a supply curve is shown in Figure 2.2. In addition to the example of the daily produce market, one would expect that the supply curve of certain kinds of labor in very short periods is apt to be of this type—at least until such time as existing contracts can be changed. For example, it is usually difficult to obtain new teachers in the middle of a semester.

The second major exception to the generally upward sloping supply curve is at the opposite end of the time scale—that is, quite a long period of time. Over a long period, we would expect a very substantial number of entrants into any market if only the price exceeded the amount which they could earn by the best alternative use of their resources. Similarly, over a long period of time, we would expect everyone to leave the market if the price was below the amount that could be earned in the best alternative use. For this reason, the long-run supply curve is apt to be practically horizontal, indicating a zero supply below a certain price and a supply as large as the market could possibly

Supply

**Figure 2.3
Long-run Supply Curve**

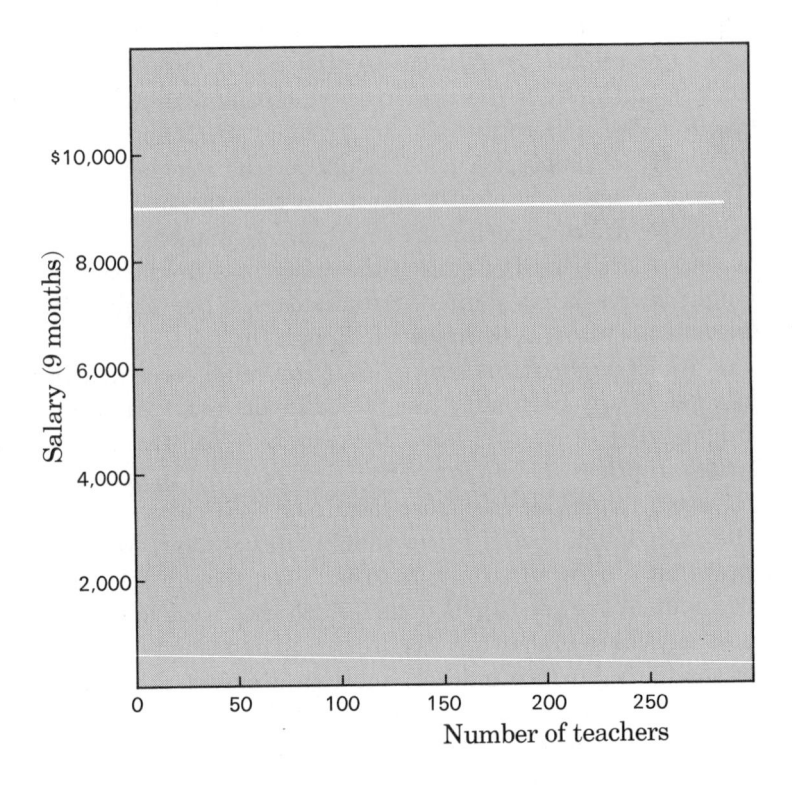

use at or slightly above that price. Such a reaction would naturally require enough time for new capital equipment to be acquired and — possibly — built. In the case of skilled labor, it would require time for training new people in the trade. Such a supply curve, usually called a *long-run supply curve*, is shown in Figure 2.3. In Chapter 8 we will see the relationship between this long-run supply curve and the general short-run conditions of supply which are more typical.

Individual and Market Supply

Like the demand curve, the supply curve really represents the sum of all the individual supply curves in a particular market. With respect to the supply of such things as labor, the supply curve may measure the number of workers available per year. It is clear that the individual supply curve would be about like Figure 2.4, indicating no supply below a certain price and a supply of one worker above that price. The entire market supply would represent the sum of many such supply curves, with different workers shifting into this occupation at different wages.

Table 2.2
Market Supply of Ground Beef, Four Firms

Price per pound	Quantity supplied Firm A		Quantity supplied Firm B		Quantity supplied Firm C		Quantity supplied Firm D		Total quantity supplied per month
$1.40	280	+	260	+	240	+	240	=	1020
1.20	240	+	230	+	180	+	200	=	850
1.00	200	+	190	+	120	+	130	=	640
.80	160	+	140	+	50	+	0	=	350
.60	120	+	80	+	0	+	0	=	200

In the more general case, the individual supply curve will be upward sloping like the supply curve of Figure 2.1. This will occur because each individual producer of an item will be more willing to concentrate on producing that item at higher prices than at lower ones. Even in the case of labor, the individual curve

**Figure 2.4
Individual Supply Curve**

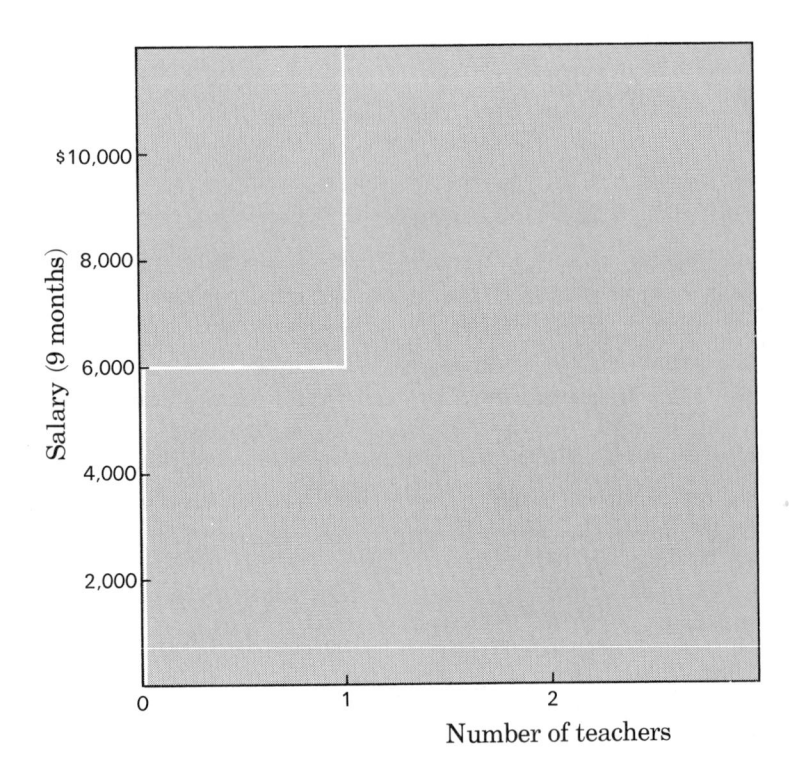

**Figure 2.5
Market Supply of Ground Beef, Four Firms**

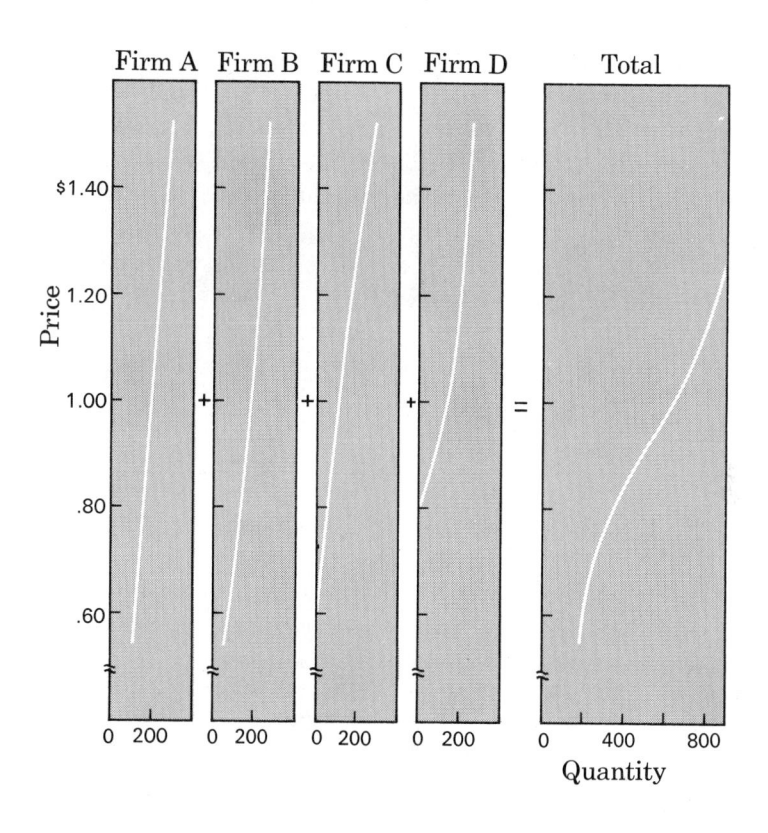

Supply

might be upward sloping if we considered hours per week or other suitable time periods. The market supply curve would then represent the sum of these several upward sloping supply curves. It should be noted, of course, that some suppliers might not enter the market at all until the price is above a certain point. In Table 2.2, we have shown the data for the individual supply functions of four separate firms; we have also shown the market supply curve, assuming that these firms are the only ones in the market. We find the market supply by adding the quantity that would be supplied by each of the four firms at each price; we then record the total as the market supply at that price. The same process is shown in graphic form in Figure 2.5.

Table 2.3
Market Supply of Ground Beef, One Hundred Firms

Price per pound	Quantity supplied Firm A	Firms like A	Quantity supplied Firm B	Firms like B	Quantity supplied Firm C	Firms like C	Quantity supplied Firm D	Firms like D	Total quantity supplied per month
$1.40	(280 × 40)	+	(260 × 30)	+	(240 × 20)	+	(240 × 10)	=	26,200
1.20	(240 × 40)	+	(230 × 30)	+	(180 × 20)	+	(200 × 10)	=	22,100
1.00	(200 × 40)	+	(190 × 30)	+	(120 × 20)	+	(130 × 10)	=	17,400
.80	(160 × 40)	+	(140 × 30)	+	(50 × 20)	+	(0 × 10)	=	11,600
.60	(120 × 40)	+	(80 × 30)	+	(0 × 20)	+	(0 × 10)	=	7,200

In most markets there will be more than four sellers, so the process is slightly more complicated. Let us imagine that there are actually 100 sellers of whom 40 are like Firm A, 30 are like Firm B, 20 are like Firm C, and 10 are like Firm D. In that case, it would be necessary to multiply the quantity supplied by each buyer at a given price by the number of sellers like him before adding to obtain the market total. This process is shown in Table 2.3. In general, a market supply curve could always be obtained by adding the individual supplies, if we know them, in one of these two ways. The similarity to the process of obtaining a market demand curve will be obvious.

We now see another reason why market supply curves are usually upward sloping. Notice that Firm D does not offer any of the product if the price is below $1.00. Prices lower than this one keep him out of the market. At higher prices he enters the market, causing an increase in the quantity supplied apart from the increases offered by other sellers. In Chapter 5 we will return to the question of why individual supply curves slope upward.

Determinants of Supply

Every supply curve represents a relationship between price and quantity. It shows that as prices change, there is a direct change in the quantity offered for sale. Price is not, however, the only influence upon supply. Whenever any other factor changes, there is a shift in the whole supply curve, indicating a different quantity at every price. To avoid confusion, we reserve the term *a change in quantity supplied,* for a movement along the curve as price changes. We refer to a shift in the whole schedule as *a change in supply.* In Figure 2.6, a movement from P to Q is *an increase in quantity supplied,* representing the effect of an increase in price from $1.00 to $1.20. The change from S_1 to S_2 is *an increase in supply,* for there will be a greater quantity supplied at every price. A movement from Q to P would be *a decrease in quantity supplied* and a shift from S_2 to S_1 would be *a decrease in supply.*

Shifts in supply may come about for many reasons. These can be summarized under five general categories:

1. Changes in the number of sellers in the market.
2. Changes in costs of resources.
3. Changes in the techniques of production.
4. Changes in the prices of other goods which the seller could supply.
5. Changing expectations of future conditions.

Let us consider each of these in turn.

1. *The number of sellers in the market.* We have already seen that the market supply curve depends upon how many sellers of each type there are in the market. Naturally, the market supply curve shifts if the number of individual curves which go to make it up increases or decreases.

**Figure 2.6
Change in Supply**

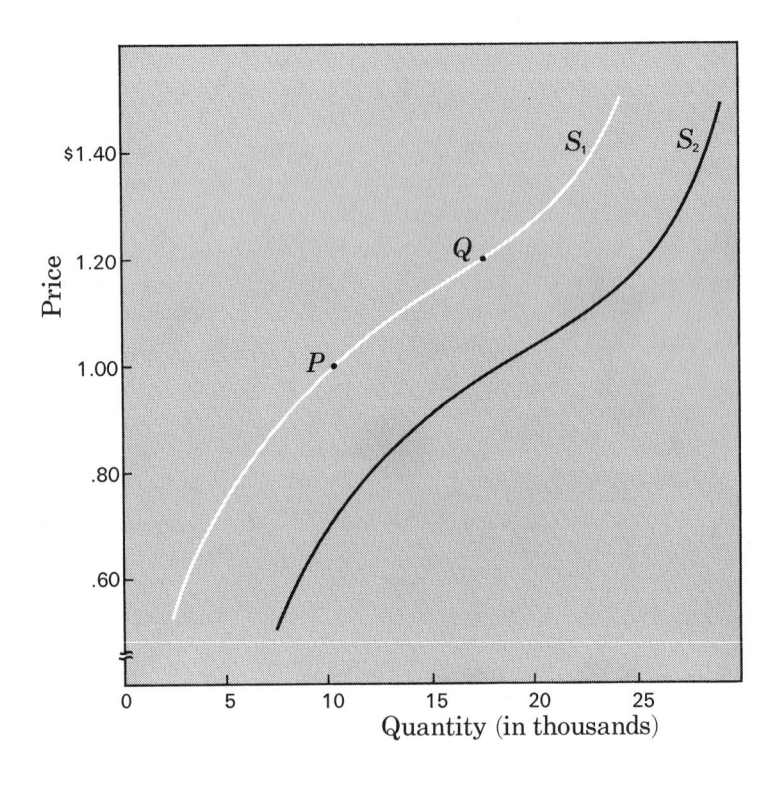

Sometimes, such changes in market supply, like changes in market demand, may occur because of transportation shifts which make it possible for new sellers to enter the market. Other times, they may be the result of the simple entry of new firms into the market because they see profit-making opportunities. We saw in Chapter 1 that changes in the number of consumers are apt to be the result of natural changes. Changes in the number of sellers, however, are much more apt to be the direct result of profit-seeking activity. (We will see in Chapter 7 that such changes are an important part of the distinction between short-run and long-run supply.)

2. *Cost of resources.* Naturally, the willingness of a seller to provide a certain product will depend upon the cost of producing it. The cost of production is clearly the result, among other things, of the cost of the materials and resources which go into the product. We could therefore expect that there will be a close relationship between the supply of ingredients and the supply of the product itself. The higher the costs of resources, the higher the price that would be necessary to induce a given seller to offer a certain amount of the product.

Although we do not usually think of the costs of production when discussing labor, the costs of training are an important influence upon the supply of *skilled* labor. In the illustration at the end of the last chapter, we noticed that the higher cost of running medical schools has limited the increase in the supply of medical care.

3. *The techniques of production.* Just as the prices of materials are an important part of the supply conditions for any producer, so are the techniques by which he combines these materials into a particular product. Usually, changes in production technique have the effect of lowering the cost of production. (If the changes did not have this effect, they would not be apt to occur, since few sellers are interested in ways of increasing their own cost.) One would therefore expect that changes in technology are rather apt to lead to an increase in supply, indicating that a greater quantity would be offered in the market at each price. Thus, changes in resource prices may lead either to an increase or a decrease in supply, but changes in technology almost always lead to an increase.

4. *Prices of other products.* Every seller is continually choosing between the products which he is producing and others which he might produce in their place. Similarly, workers are apt to consider alternative occupations. We saw that consumers view products either as substitutes or as complements. Sellers, on the other hand, view most products as substitutes. It follows that higher prices on other products will decrease their willingness to continue production of their present line, for the higher alternative prices probably mean that the seller could make more profit producing something else. Similarly, lower alternative prices will make him more willing to expand present activities. (We should remember that higher prices for substitute products make consumers more willing to buy. We notice now that they make sellers less willing to sell.)

Although products are usually substitutes from the viewpoints of sellers, there are a few cases where they are complements. These occur when the technical conditions of production force the producer to provide two products at the same time. For example, cotton seeds and soybeans are pressed, producing simultaneously an oil which can be used for cooking and a meal which is used for cattle feed. Clearly, both oil and meal are produced at the same time. In this case, a higher price on the complementary product will increase the willingness of the producer to supply the particular product under consideration. A lower price on the complementary good would make him less willing to supply the combination. Meat packing offers another example of complementary production.

5. *Expectations of future conditions.* We saw in Chapter 1 that consumers often delay their decisions in the expectation that future conditions will be changed. Similarly, producers may do the same if the conditions of storage permit. For example, a farmer is not likely to sell his current wheat stock if he expects the price to be higher later on in the year. If, on the other hand, he expects prices to fall, he may sell immediately, even if the current price is somewhat low. Suppliers might also choose to produce large quantities of a product at the present time if they expect the price of their raw materials or their labor to rise in the future. It is true that certain of these expected changes might cause producers only to accumulate inventories of raw materials; but some

resources, especially labor, cannot be stored and can only be used to make the product at the present time. A stock of finished goods may be the only way to accumulate an inventory of labor.

In some cases, certain expectations may be self-defeating. If producers expect prices to rise in the future, they may increase production in order to be ready for the higher prices. Because of the increased production, however, the higher prices may not come about.

Elasticity

It is useful to have a measure of how much the change in quantity reacts to changes in prices. The measure which is used for supply is the same as that used for demand, the *elasticity*. Elasticity of supply is defined in exactly the same way as elasticity of demand:

$$\text{Elasticity of supply} = \frac{\text{Percentage change in quantity supplied}}{\text{Percentage change in price}}$$

Again, this same equation may be rewritten in a slightly different form:

$$\text{Elasticity of supply} = \frac{\text{Change in quantity supplied}}{\text{Quantity supplied}} \div \frac{\text{Change in price}}{\text{Price}}$$

We should remember that the measure of elasticity is only that given at a certain point; and when we say that a supply curve is elastic, we really mean that it is elastic in the neighborhood of a certain price. Many supply curves will be elastic in some areas and inelastic in others. In particular, since most supply curves show some region where no quantity will be supplied, they tend to be quite elastic just above that price and somewhat less elastic further up. For complete accuracy, it would be desirable to measure elasticity of supply only with very tiny changes in price in order to avoid the confusions which might result from using price changes of varying size, but none of our discussions will depend upon a precise measure of elasticity. This argument is essentially the same as that given with respect to the elasticity of demand. Elasticity of demand is very important in economics because of the relationship between total revenue and elasticity. There is no comparable relationship with supply, so precise measures of supply elasticity are less important.

The ordinary supply curve may have widely varying elasticities over its range. In contrast, the extreme cases which we discussed earlier indicate the extremes of elasticity. The very short-run supply curve of Figure 2.2, where the quantity is absolutely fixed, shows an elasticity of zero. One can calculate this by seeing that the percentage change in quantity is zero for any given percentage change in price. In contrast, the perfectly flat long-run supply curve of Figure 2.3 has an elasticity which is effectively infinite, because a tiny percentage change in price causes a very large percentage change in quantity.

We can therefore describe the different reactions of supply in different periods of time in terms of the relative elasticities of demand. Over a very short-run period, the elasticity of supply is almost zero because it is not possible to change the quantity available immediately. Over a moderate period of time, the supply curve has an intermediate elasticity, indicating that a greater quantity will be supplied at higher prices and less at lower ones. Over a very long-run period of time, when it is possible to shift almost all resources, we see that the elasticity is infinite, because it is possible to increase the quantity supplied to almost any desired level as long as the price is high enough to make this product more profitable than alternative activities.

An Illustration: Equal Pay for Women

One of the principal complaints of the Women's Liberation movement has been that women are paid less than men, even for the same work. The passage of the Civil Rights Act of 1964 made direct discrimination on grounds of sex illegal, but many forms of discrimination persist. Most prevalent of all is the informal classification of certain types of jobs as "women's work," paying less than "men's jobs." Among the most common of these are clerks' and typists' jobs and, among professional jobs, elementary and secondary teaching posts.

Such discrimination is usually explained from the demand side—that is, by the attitude of employers. At the simplest level of explanation are the charges of "male chauvinism" and emotional prejudice, often justified. These would account for a lower demand curve. Some employers admit such discriminatory demand, but justify it on the basis that time and money spent training women may be wasted; they may quit to have children or to follow their husband's jobs. (Employers have been known to complain that they cannot satisfy the demands of liberated women without antagonizing some of their "unliberated" women employees, who do not want overtime work, who refuse jobs requiring travel, etc. "How can I refuse to discriminate when most of the women demand discrimination?" was one complaint.)

Despite the truth in both explanations based on demand, it is clear that the present pattern of widespread discrimination could not have developed without the special characteristics of the supply curve of female labor. It is therefore worthwhile to examine these supply conditions.

The first characteristic of supply has been that, at least until very recently, most women thought of themselves as secondary earners. Unmarried women living at home and working wives considered their wages supplementary to a basic income provided by husbands and fathers. Even women "on their own" thought only of supporting themselves. In contrast, wages for men's jobs were evaluated by most prospective employees in terms of funds which could support a family. Women therefore were willing to work at much lower wages than men. The supply curves for labor for men and women tended to be like those of Figure 2.7. (Interestingly, wages for students in college communities show much less discrimination, although wages are usually low for both men and women. In this case, both sexes are usually supporting only themselves and often work to supplement basic income received from home.)

A second factor affecting women's wages has been the concentration of women in a limited number of occupations. Some occupations exclude women because of their demands for physical strength, although growing mechanization steadily decreases the number. Some occupations have excluded women largely through the prejudice of those already in the field and, in many

**Figure 2.7
Labor Supply by Sex**

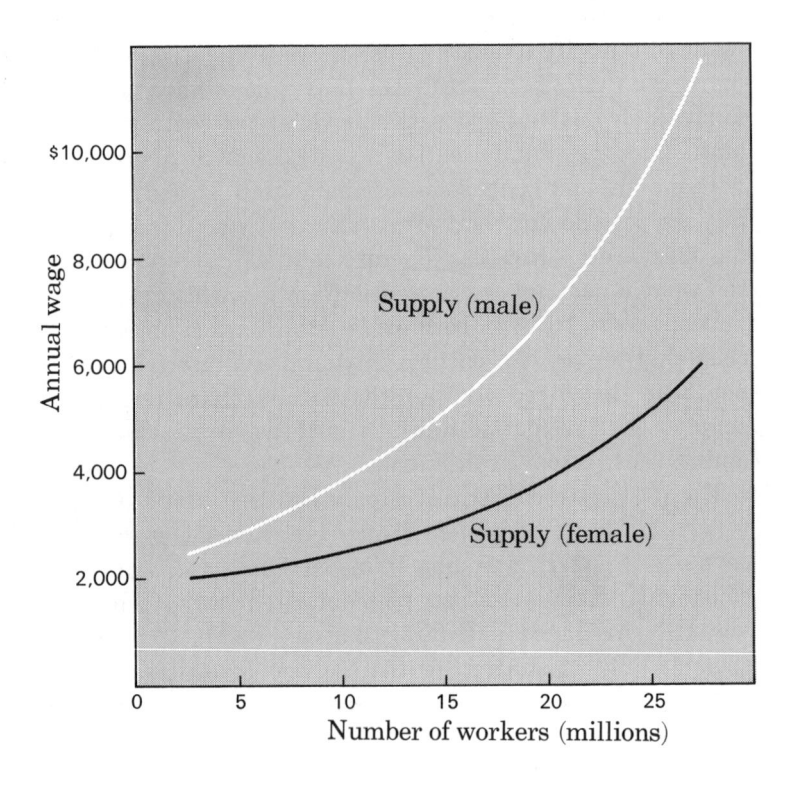

cases, those operating the institutions where they are trained. For example, medical schools bear much of the burden of excluding women from medicine. Finally, women themselves have tended to avoid certain areas. For example, few women major in physics or chemistry. (This last is often alleged to result from a cultural domination by men, who imply that nice girls are not interested in such things.)

As women are kept out of some activities, they tend to crowd into others. As a result, the supply curve shifts to the right and employers can hire any given number of workers for lower wages than they otherwise could. The concentration of college women in schools of education is an important part of the explanation of lower salaries for teachers and lower incomes for women.

Thus the goal of equal pay for women will not be achieved solely by actions designed to break down discrimination by employers; it will also take action by women themselves to refuse to accept low wages and to scatter themselves through all occupations as widely as men. The problem is not merely a biased demand; there is a supply aspect as well.

Chapter 3
Demand and Supply

Boom City is a thriving small city in the midwest. In the last ten years its population has increased 74 percent, largely because several large manufacturing plants have been established in the community. The principal problem which growth has brought is that housing is very scarce. Although there has been a great amount of new building, it has not kept up with the population expansion.

During the ten-year period, there were numerous reports of substantial rent increases — increases which the tenants grumbled about but nevertheless paid, for they had few alternatives. The grumbling reached the city council, which held hearings, determined that rents were actually rising, and passed a comprehensive rent control law. This law provided that rents must remain fixed at the level of a recent base period, except for adjustments to reflect demonstrated increases in costs. Further adjustments were permitted for significant improvements in the facilities, but not, of course, for routine maintenance. Rents in new buildings were to be determined at the level of base rents in comparable facilities.

In the years following the passage of the rent control law, the housing shortage seemed to get worse. The population continued to grow, but there was little new building. Several apartment builders complained that profits were too low on the new buildings, and some of them actually ceased local operations and moved to other cities.

The quality of the existing rental housing began a slow decline. Landlords felt, correctly, that few tenants would actually move if redecorating or other maintenance was postponed. There was, however, a flurry of "facility improvement," which would permit higher rents. One tenant reported that his landlord had installed a second bathroom (and increased the rent $10 a month), but had still not repaired the broken toilet in the first bathroom two months after it had been reported.

On the demand side, tenants actually seemed to be using more space. In the days before rent control, families which became smaller as children married tended to seek smaller residences. This tendency had now stopped, partly because the rents on their existing quarters were quite reasonable, but primarily because other apartments were very difficult to find. Almost all apartment owners reported long waiting lists for vacancies.

New families moving to town were at a special disadvantage. Some of them managed to find housing, usually by bribing apartment managers. Others moved into surrounding towns, commuting fifty miles each way to and from work. Some gave up, and left Boom City forever. The employment managers of local firms reported increasing difficulties in obtaining workers.

Lately a special committee of the chamber of commerce has forecast a substantial decline in the city's growth rate. The leading political question in town is whether the rent control law is to be continued. Almost every political and civic group in town has passed a resolution on one side of the question or the other; and a few have passed resolutions on both sides, depending upon who was present at a particular meeting.

Equilibrium Price

In the examples of Chapters 1 and 2, we were considering circumstances in which the quantity supplied or the quantity demanded was fixed. We now wish to consider cases where both the quantity supplied and the quantity demanded change as price changes—that is, cases where both supply and demand curves are sloped. Such an example is shown in Table 3.1. It can be seen in this table that at all prices above $1.00, the quantity supplied exceeds the quantity demanded. At all prices below $1.00, the quantity demanded exceeds the quantity supplied. Thus, the two are equal only at the price of $1.00, which is called the *equilibrium price*. It is called an equilibrium because such a price, when reached, will tend to persist as long as the basic supply and demand curves are unchanged.

Table 3.1
Supply and Demand

Price	Quantity supplied (per week)	Quantity demanded (per week)	Surplus or shortage (per week)
$1.40	13,000	5,000	surplus 8,000
1.20	12,000	7,000	surplus 5,000
1.00	10,000	10,000	0
.80	7,000	14,000	shortage 7,000
.60	3,000	19,000	shortage 16,000

Let us consider the possibility of an alternate price, say $1.40. At this price, the quantity demanded is only 5,000 per week; but the quantity supplied is 13,000, leaving a surplus of 8,000 units. (Actual sales would only be 5,000, the lower of the two.) If these sales took place in one week, by the next week it would be quite clear to sellers that they could not sell the full 13,000 at that price. They would therefore tend to offer their products at a lower price, say $1.20. They would also cut their production back to 12,000 units. Similarly, buyers would become aware that they could get all of the product they wanted for less than $1.40 and would cut their bids. At the lower price, they would also be willing to buy more. Prices would decline in the second and third weeks until a price was reached which eliminated the surplus. Such a price is $1.00. At that price, sellers would have cut back the quantity supplied from 13,000 per week to 10,000, and buyers would have increased the quantity demanded from 5,000 per week to the same 10,000.

In many cases, of course, this process could take place much more rapidly. Both buyers and sellers could discover quite quickly that a greater quantity was being supplied than demanded, and prices could adjust very rapidly to these conditions. In any case, it is clear that as long as the price is above $1.00, there is a downward pressure on prices as sellers try to make sure that they are not left with an unsold product.

Had we started at a price below equilibrium, say $0.80, we would have seen a shortage, caused by the fact that the quantity demanded, 14,000 per week, is much greater than the quantity supplied, 7,000. In this case, sellers would be tempted to raise prices, knowing that they could still sell their products at higher prices. Similarly, buyers fearful of being left out of the market would offer higher prices—or at least readily agree to them. Therefore, as long as price is less than $1.00, there is a steady upward pressure on prices. We now see why $1.00 is described as the equilibrium price: it is the only price at which no pressures arise to shift the price to different levels. At this price, the forces of demand, which tend to raise prices, and the forces of supply, which tend to lower them, are exactly balanced; so the price would remain at this level for as long as these supply and demand conditions persist.

We saw in Chapter 1 that price has the function of rationing a particular quantity of goods among the various buyers. In Chapter 2 we saw that it also has the function of providing incentives to sellers to provide more of the product. We now see that price is performing both these functions simultaneously—rationing the buyers down to a quantity of 10,000 per week from the 14,000 or 19,000 they might wish to buy if the price were lower, and, at the same time, providing incentives to producers to supply the 10,000 units of the product rather than the lesser units they would supply at lower prices. If the price were above the equilibrium price of $1.00, the incentives to produce would be too high compared to the rationing function which the price is performing. Therefore, a greater quantity would be supplied than would be demanded. It is only as the price declines toward $1.00 that these forces are brought back into equality.

The same situation can be portrayed graphically in Figure 3.1. In the diagram, as in the table, it can readily be seen that at all prices above $1.00, the quantity supplied exceeds the quantity demanded. Prices are therefore pushed downward from these levels. At all prices below $1.00, the quantity demanded exceeds the quantity supplied and a shortage ensues. This shortage has the effect of driving prices upward. A process of competitive bidding — either by buyers driving the prices up or by sellers driving the prices down — will always tend to eliminate either shortages or surpluses of any commodity.

Perhaps the best example of the process by which competitive bidding eliminates a shortage occurs in an auction of rare art works. In such a case, only one Rembrandt is for sale. Several buyers representing museums or individual collectors appear, each prepared to pay a certain price in order to obtain the painting. At the beginning of the bidding, when the price is relatively low, many buyers may be competing. As the price rises, however, it passes the highest point that certain buyers are prepared to pay, and they drop out of the competition. Finally, the price gets so high that only one buyer is left, and no one bids against him. At that stage, the quantity of Rembrandt paintings demanded has fallen to 1, the same as the quantity supplied, and the sale is made. Notice that at lower prices, the quantity demanded was much greater than the quantity supplied — that is, there were several buyers, each of whom wanted the one painting available. It is only by the process of competitive bidding that the market is brought back into equilibrium.

We have therefore seen that if left to themselves, prices in competitive markets will tend to reach the equilibrium price. However, many markets are not left to themselves, and there are numerous examples of government attempts to control prices. Such price control may be designed either to hold prices down, as in the example given at the beginning of this chapter, or to keep prices up, as happens in attempts to establish minimum wages. The effects are similar in both cases. Normal movements of price are no longer permitted to find the equilibrium which would equate the quantity supplied and the quantity demanded. Instead, a permanent shortage or surplus results, unless some nonprice system of rationing or incentives is developed. In the

**Figure 3.1
Supply and Demand**

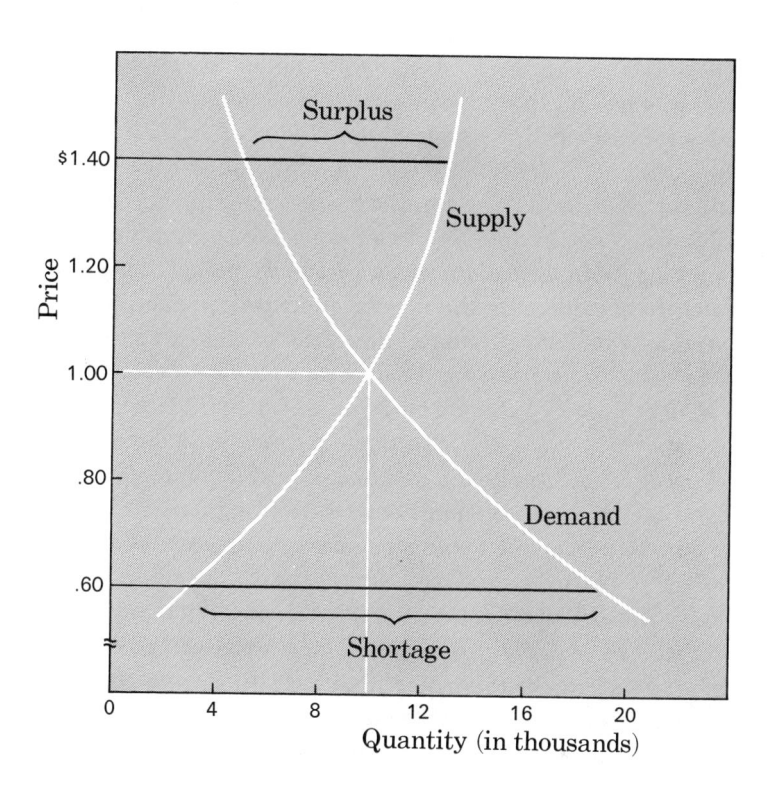

example of rent controls, price was not permitted to perform either its incentive function or its rationing function, and the result was a substantial housing shortage in the area.

In cases where minimum prices or minimum wages are established, the effect is often merely to produce unemployment among those whom the law is designed to help. The reason is that the established minimum wage is above the equilibrium wage at which the quantity supplied and the quantity demanded would be equal. At this higher wage, more unskilled workers are available than desired. Whether the higher unemployment is a reasonable price to pay for the higher wages of those who are actually working is a political question which we cannot solve here. However, it is clear that the unemployment does exist. It is not surprising that governments have increasingly turned to other programs to help low-paid workers.

The amount of the shortage or surplus which will result from a departure from the equilibrium price will depend upon the elasticities of supply and demand. If both demand and supply are quite elastic, a very small departure from the equilibrium price is apt to produce a very large shortage or surplus. On the other hand, if both demand and supply are quite inelastic, a rather large departure in price might result in only a relatively small surplus or shortage. In the case of controlled prices, the extent of shortage or of unemployment resulting from controls would depend upon the relative demand or supply elasticities. One might imagine that politicians would be quite willing to accept small unemployment in exchange for the substantial increase in wages of unskilled workers which would result from a minimum wage, if supply and demand were both relatively inelastic. On the other hand, if supply and demand were quite elastic, they would be less willing to accept the rather large unemployment which would result from trying to achieve a given increase in wages.

Changes in Supply or Demand

If there is a change in either supply or demand, there will naturally be a change in the equilibrium price and quantity which would result from the free play of the competitive market.

Exactly what that change would be depends upon the particular shift which caused it. Let us take each of these in turn.

Increase in supply.

If there is an increase in supply, such as might result from technological improvements, the new intersection of the supply and demand curves will be to the *right* of the old one. Such a case is shown in Figure 3.2. The new price will be *lower* and the new quantity greater than before. Whether the total revenue—the price times the quantity—will be greater or less depends upon the elasticity of demand. If the demand is elastic, the total revenue will be greater; if the demand is inelastic, the total revenue will be less.

The process by which the new price and quantity come about is similar to that previously discussed. As the supply curve shifts, the quantity supplied at the old price increases, causing a surplus. As sellers observe this situation, they begin cutting prices; even at lower prices, they are willing to sell more than consumers are actually buying. Price rationing eases until the price falls enough to re-establish a balance between supply and demand.

Decrease in supply.

The effect of a decrease in supply, such as would result from high resource prices, would be the opposite of the one above. This decrease, which is shown in Figure 3.3, will lead to a *higher* price and a *lower* quantity. Again, the total revenue will depend upon the elasticity of demand. If the demand is elastic, the total revenue will be less; if the demand is inelastic, the total revenue will be more.

Increase in demand.

If there is an increase in demand, caused, say, by an increase in consumers' incomes, the effect would be an *increase* in price and an increase in quantity. Such a shift is shown in Figure 3.4. Since both price and quantity have increased, there will naturally be an increase in total revenue. We can say that if the supply is elastic, there will be a larger percentage of change in the quantity; and if the supply is inelastic, the greater change will be in price.

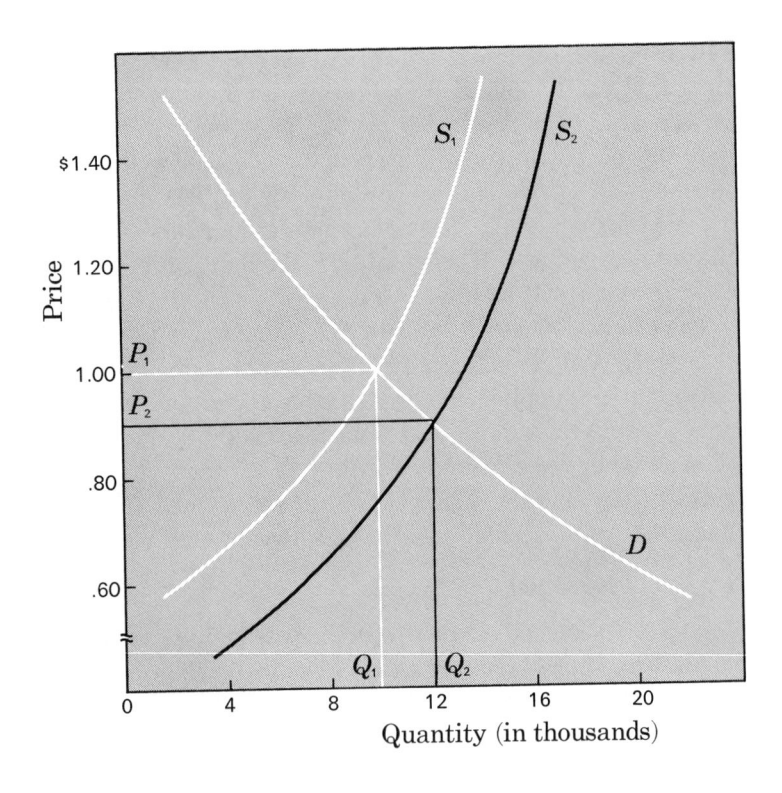

**Figure 3.2
Increase in Supply**

**Figure 3.3
Decrease in Supply**

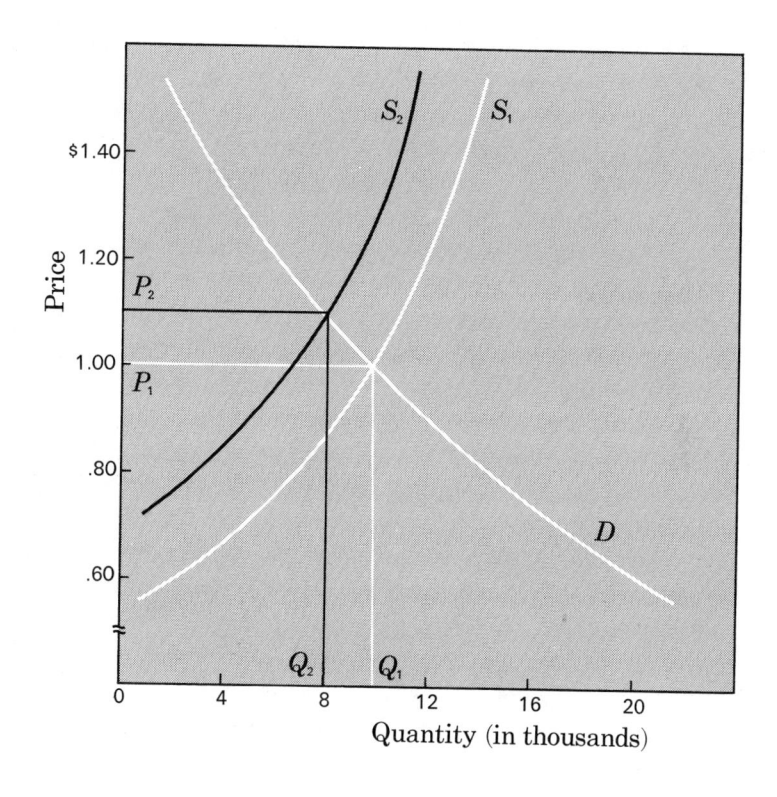

**Figure 3.4
Increase in Demand**

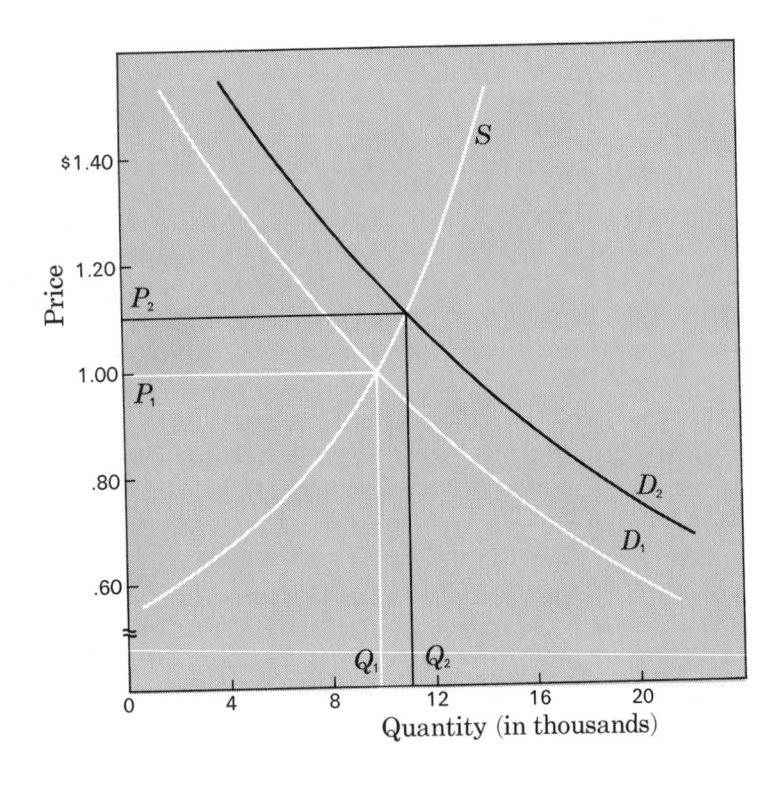

Decrease in demand.

If there is a decrease in demand, as shown in Figure 3.5, the effect will be a *decline* in *both* price and quantity and a decline in total revenue. Again, if the supply is elastic, the greater change will be in the quantity; if the supply is inelastic, the greater change will be in the price.

The four cases given above enable us mechanically to find the results of changes in supply and demand. We saw in Chapter 1 that changes in demand come about because of changes in the number of consumers, the incomes of consumers, tastes, the price and availability of related goods, and expectations of future conditions. We saw in Chapter 2 that changes in *supply* come about because of changes in the number of sellers in the market, the cost of resources, changes in the techniques of production, the prices of other goods, and expectations of future conditions. By combining the techniques given here with the causes listed in Chapters 1 and 2, we can see ways to analyze the effects upon price and quantity of a great number of possible changes in the society at large. Many examples of these relationships could be given, but here we will mention only one. In the illustration at the end of Chapter 1, it was stated that the increase in demand for medical services had caused a substantial increase in medical costs but almost no change in quantity supplied. However, new programs designed to produce more trained personnel would tend to lead to increased quantities and, possibly, decreased prices. As a summary check on your understanding of the material thus far in this book, see if you can demonstrate the truth of the following statements:

Higher incomes will raise beef prices.

Cheaper pork will decrease beef prices.

Increased diet consciousness will increase beef prices and lower pork prices. (Most people believe that beef contains less fat than pork.)

New antibiotics for cattle will decrease beef prices.

Rising population will increase beef prices.

The Surgeon General's report on the medical hazards of smoking will decrease cotton prices (unless the government takes action to maintain them.)

Expected inflation will raise wheat prices now.

**Figure 3.5
Decrease in Demand**

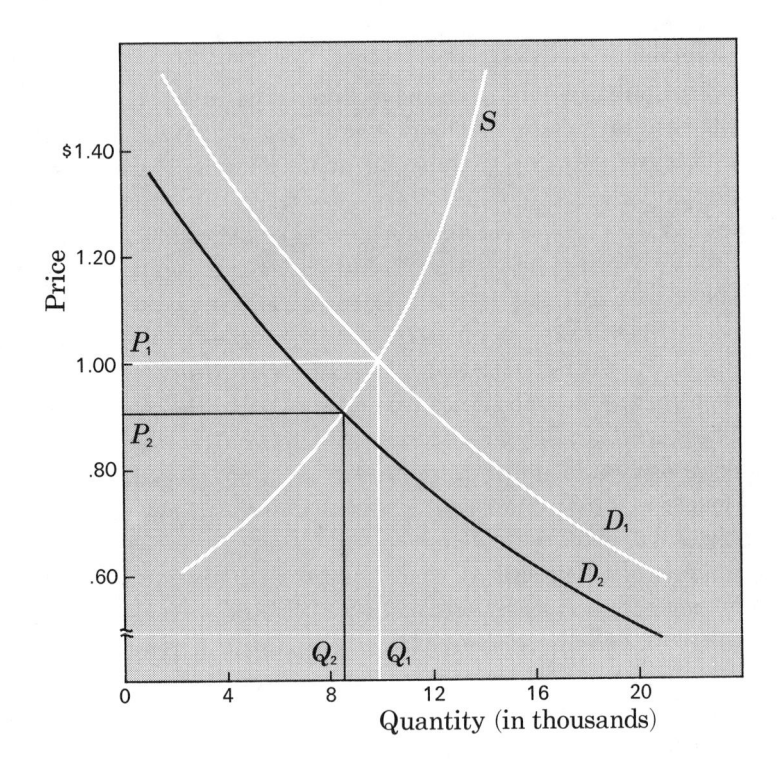

Changes in Both Supply and Demand

When there is a shift in both supply and demand, it is not always possible to be sure what the effects will be on both price and quantity, but it is always possible to tell what will happen to one or the other. In many cases, if additional information can be obtained—as, for example, if one knows something about the shape of a particular demand or supply curve—it is possible to say what the effect will be on both price and quantity.

Both change together.

If supply and demand both increase, the result will certainly be an increase in quantity. Such a change is shown in Figure 3.6. The old intersection of S_1 and D_1 at the quantity of Q_1 is replaced by the new intersection of S_2 and D_2 at the quantity Q_2. Since both supply and demand curves have moved to the right, it is clear that their intersection must also move to the right. In this particular diagram, the price has fallen very slightly from P_1 to P_2; but this is accidental, due to the way this diagram has been drawn. It would easily be possible to imagine the price having risen, as would have been the case if the demand had risen slightly more than it did.

The opposite case, a decrease in both supply and demand, would result in a decrease in quantity; but again, it would have an uncertain effect upon the price. One can examine the results of such a decrease by following the same argument as in Figure 3.6, but by imagining demand falling from D_2 to D_1, and supply falling from S_2 to S_1.

We thus see that when both supply and demand increase, there is an increase in the quantity which will be sold in the market. When both supply and demand decrease, there is a decrease in the quantity sold. In general, nothing can be said about the change in price without additional information.

A discussion of a particular case in which both supply and demand would increase is given in the problem on legalized marijuana at the end of this chapter.

Opposite changes.

If supply increases and demand falls, the result would be as shown in Figure 3.7. In this diagram, the demand

Figure 3.6
Increase in Both Supply and Demand

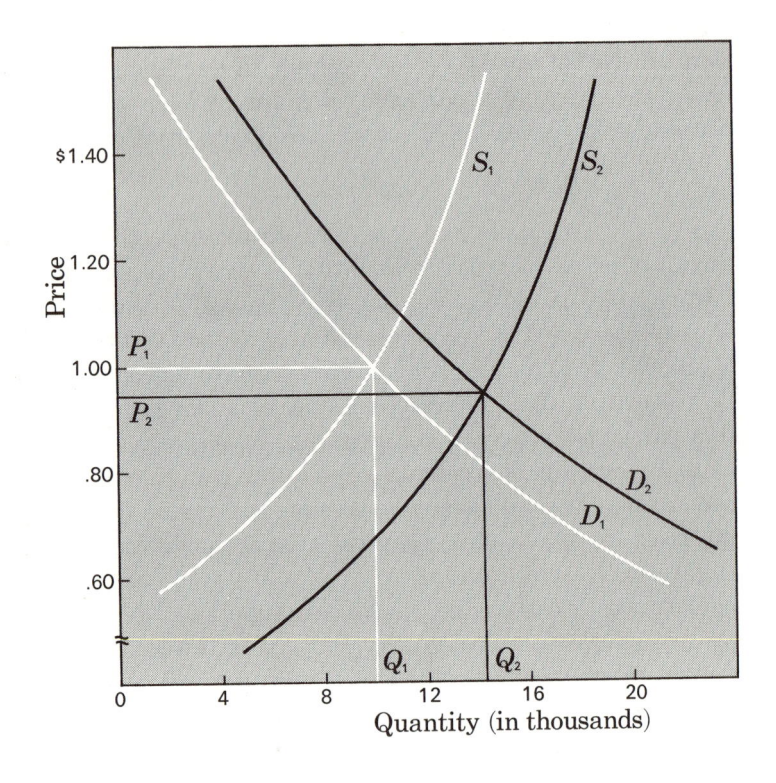

Figure 3.7
Decrease in Demand, Increase in Supply

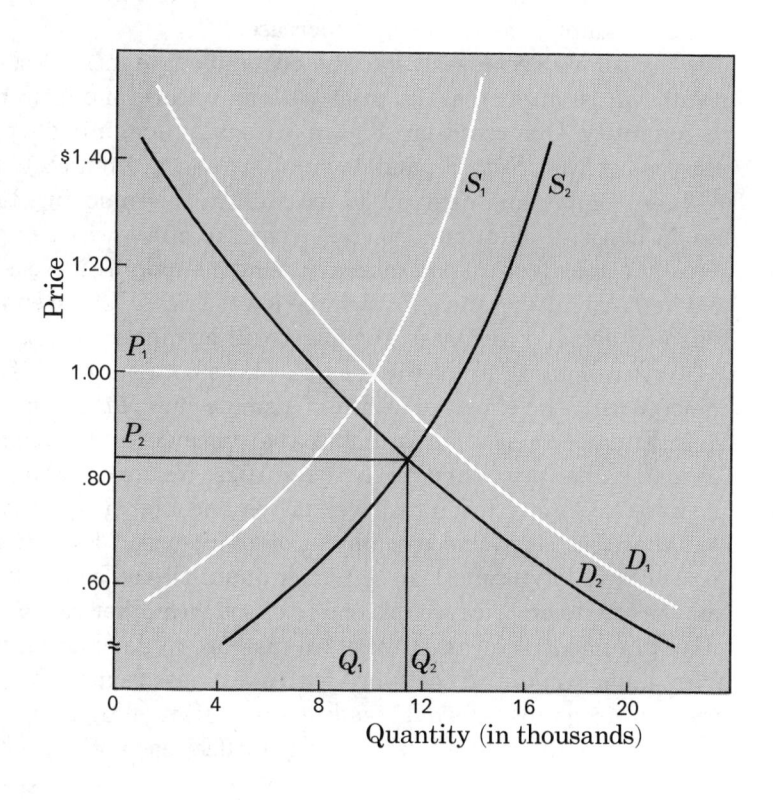

Demand and Supply

has dropped from D_1 to D_2 at the same time the supply has increased from S_1 to S_2. The result is clearly a decrease in price from P_1, the old intersection, to P_2. It is not possible to say with certainty what will happen to the quantity, although in this particular example, we see a slight increase.

If the supply decreases while the demand curve increases, the result will be an increase in price with an uncertain effect upon the quantity. One could use Figure 3.7 again, imagining supply decreasing from S_2 to S_1, and demand increasing from D_2 to D_1.

Where supply and demand do not shift in the same direction, but in opposite ones, one can tell what the effect will be upon price but not always upon quantity. Where supply is increasing and demand falling, the effect will be lower prices. Where supply falls and demand increases, the effect will be higher prices.

One can analyze all of these cases where both curves shift by remembering the effects of a shift of a single curve and then combining them. We saw, for example, that an increase in demand leads to higher prices and higher quantities. We also saw that an increase in supply leads to lower prices and higher quantities. It is therefore clear that a combination of increased demand and increased supply would lead to higher quantities on both counts, but the effects on price would tend to offset each other. Using the same argument, we can see that an increase in demand (higher price, higher quantity) combined with a decreased supply (higher price, lower quantity) would lead to a net effect of higher prices, but with the quantity effects tending to offset each other.

An Illustration: Legalized Marijuana

In recent years, there has been increasing talk of legalizing the sale and use of marijuana. The major questions involved are not economic, and we have nothing to add to their discussion here. There are, however, some important economic effects which should be considered before drawing any conclusions on other bases.

The most important effects of legalization would be that both demand and supply curves would shift substantially to the right. Clearly many potential sellers and buyers are kept out of the market only because it is illegal. Let us look at supply and demand changes separately, and then put them together.

The present marijuana industry is a very primitive one. Much of the marijuana is imported from Mexico and other countries, usually in small quantities to escape customs inspections. Some marijuana is grown domestically, again on a small scale. It is cured and "packaged" in small quantities in kitchens, cellars, and other such makeshift "factories." It is sold through a loosely organized network of pushers, most of whom handle relatively small volumes. Markups at all levels are quite high to compensate for the risks of arrest which must be taken. Prices are relatively high—usually the equivalent of fifty cents a joint or more—and quality is often low and highly variable.

In contrast, one would expect a legal marijuana industry to resemble the tobacco industry quite closely. (It has been rumored, but denied, that one major tobacco firm has already registered the trademark "Acapulco Gold.") Marijuana is probably less difficult to grow than tobacco. It now grows as a nuisance weed in several areas of the plains states. To obtain marijuana, large firms would either contract with growers or establish organized auction markets. Manufacturing could be highly mechanized and costs kept quite low. Distribution could go either through the present tobacco dealers or through liquor package stores. The principal uncertainty would be taxes. One would expect the new supply curve to be quite elastic at a retail price near the present level of tobacco cigarettes, about fifty cents for a package of twenty. The quality would also probably increase and become quite standardized as companies tried to establish their new brand names. The shift in supply is shown in Figure 3.8, where S_2 represents the new supply and S_1 the old one.

It is more difficult to analyze the demand for marijuana. (The sources of data which can be used in most industries obviously do not apply.) Clearly the current high prices must limit the consumption somewhat, but a marijuana "high" can be reached by consumption of only a few joints. Therefore one would not expect the demand curve to be highly elastic. For simplicity, both demand curves of Figure 3.9 have been drawn with an elasticity of 0.5, largely for lack of any better information. (Cigarettes have a very low price elasticity, whiskey an elasticity near unity. It

**Figure 3.8
Marijuana Supply**

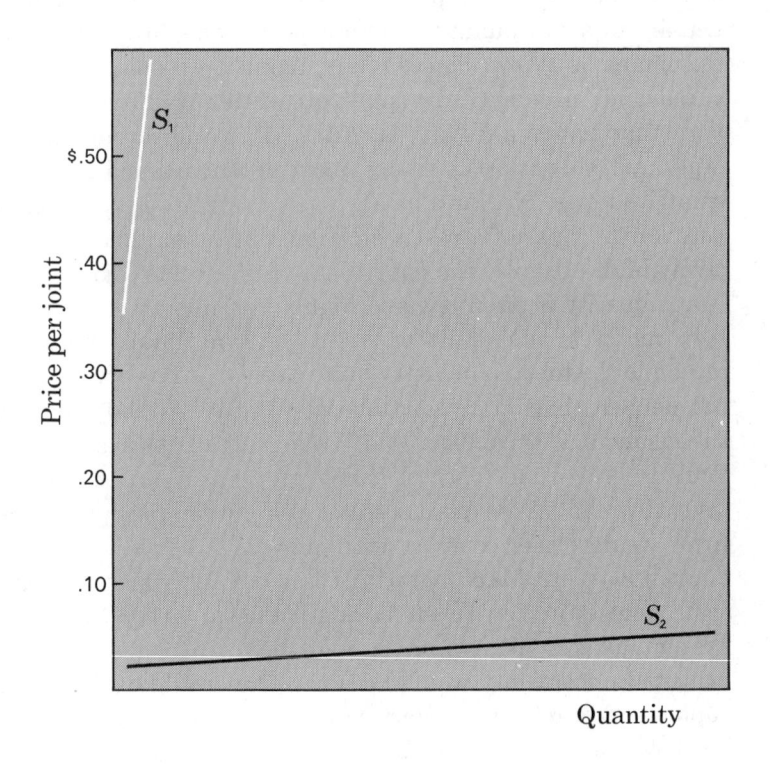

Quantity
Price per joint
$.50
.40
.30
.20
.10
S_1
S_2

**Figure 3.9
Marijuana Demand**

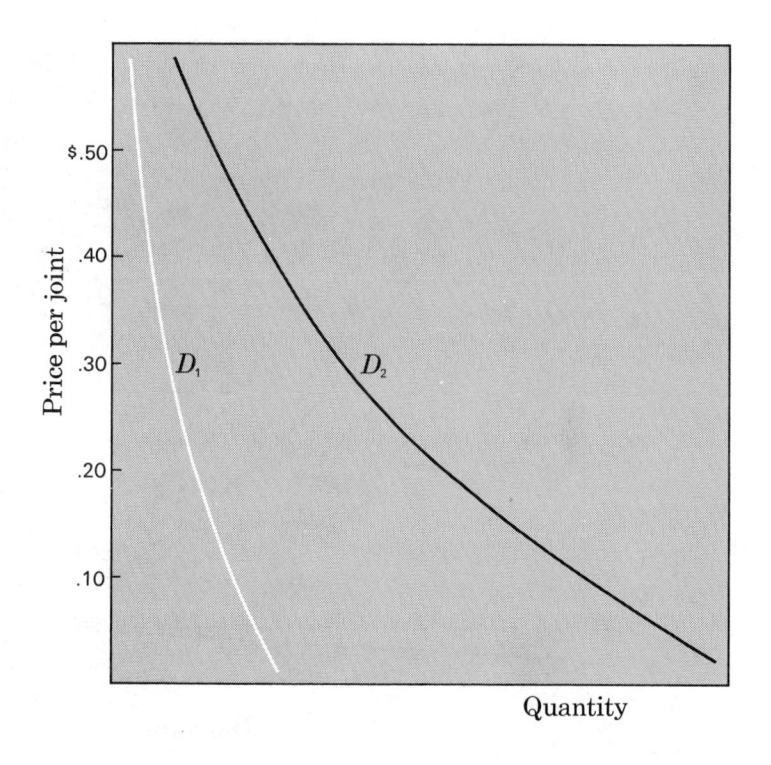

Demand and Supply

**Figure 3.10
Marijuana Supply and Demand**

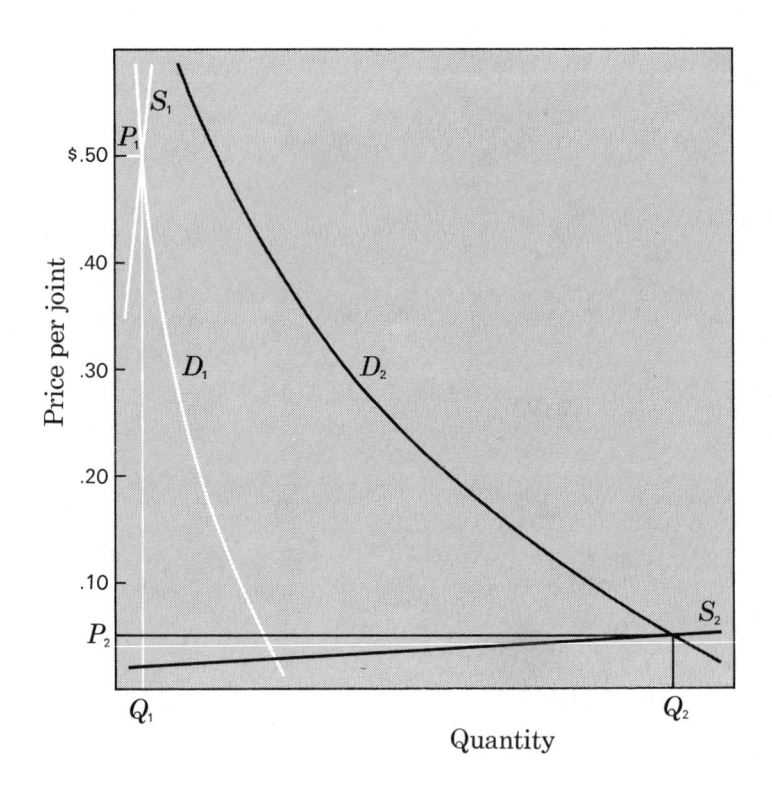

is probable that the marijuana demand would most resemble that of whiskey.) The major limitation on demand is undoubtedly the illegality, so that legalization would shift the demand substantially. The demand curve for legal marijuana, D_2, is shown at four times the quantity demanded at every price as the demand curve for illegal marijuana, D_1. This increase is probably conservative.

Both sets of supply and demand curves have been combined in Figure 3.10. When these curves are combined, we see that we must compare the intersection of S_1 and D_1, shown at a price of P_1 and a quantity of Q_1, with the intersection of S_2 and D_2, shown at P_2 and Q_2. The price decline is very large, more than 90 percent. The quantity sold is almost twenty times as large. A part of this increase comes about because of the lower price, but an even greater proportion occurs because the demand curve has shifted. It should be remembered that we assumed rather inelastic demand curves and a rather modest shift in the demand curve. If the demand is more elastic or the shift is greater, the quantity actually sold would increase even more.

For most products, the combination of lower prices and larger quantities would be considered a social gain, but many people would not come to the same conclusion about marijuana. We said at the beginning of this discussion that the basic decision on whether to legalize marijuana is not economic in character, but it would be absurd to make the decision without taking into consideration the large change in prices and quantities which would result.

Chapter 4
Consumers and Demand

Harriet J. Housewife is known in her neighborhood as a very efficient homemaker. She always seems to know how to do the best for her family, despite rising prices and higher taxes. She buys powdered milk in 50 lb. bags and reconstitutes it, rather than buying milk at the stores. (Her cost is about a nickel a quart; store prices are many times that.) Her friends usually ask her advice on purchasing appliances, for she seems well informed on the performance of different brands, their prices in different stores, and the reliability of service available. She even carries a slide rule to the grocery store to calculate prices in cents per ounce, because she has found that there is no easy way to select the most economical package of detergent, toothpaste, or instant mashed potatoes; it isn't always the "economy size."

She is a good cook, but a thrifty one. She had to be in the early days of her marriage, when her husband was still in college. At that time, she acquired at least 100 different recipes for hamburger, as well as fish, macaroni, and spaghetti. These are still her "dollar stretchers." She also takes full advantage of the specials which are currently being featured at the supermarket, and reacts to each change in price.

Recently she has noted that there has been a decline in the price of better cuts of beef and pork. When she mentioned the price change to her husband, he remarked, "I suppose this means we will be eating less hamburger for a while."

Her answer surprised him. "Actually, we will probably eat more. I'll be buying more of the better meat, but I'll actually be spending less on it than I have been. I'll use the money I save to buy a little more hamburger, and we won't have as many meals where the meat is skimpy or nonexistent as we've been having lately. It's beans we'll be eating less of."

Income and Substitution Effects

Behind every individual demand curve stands the behavior of a consumer unit, which economists call a household. As we will see in the appendix to this chapter, households are of many types. They come in sizes ranging from a single individual living alone to a large family, sometimes of several generations. Their incomes range from almost nothing to very large amounts. Nevertheless, there are certain characteristics of all households which make them similar and which determine their behavior in consumer markets. We will concentrate on these similarities rather than on the differences between households.

A household is any consumer spending unit and may consist of either a family or a single individual. In the case of the unmarried worker living with his parents, however, the question of whether to treat him as a separate household or part of the larger one may prove difficult. If most of his income goes into the family pool, he would be considered a member of the family household; if he pays a sum for room and board and keeps the rest for himself, he would be treated as a separate household.

The basic goal of the household is its own welfare, a general catch-all term which includes physical satisfaction, social status, and all other dimensions of the good life. To avoid having to define all of the exact details that go to make up welfare, economists use the term *utility*. Utility is the measure of the consumer's welfare, *as he himself sees it*. It is therefore a complex of all those things that a consumer desires, weighted the way the consumer himself evaluates them.

We can then say that households maximize utility. In view of the definition we have just given of utility, however, what we are really saying is that households try to do what they want to do. If automobile buyers choose flashy cars with a long wheel base, bright colors, excess power, and extra accessories, we cannot conclude that they are not seeking utility; it merely means that they are buying a complex of things in their car which may include transportation but is certainly not limited to it. Our concern is not with the question of what pattern consumer utility actually takes. That is primarily a question for psychologists and marketing managers. As economists, we are more concerned with taking the utility valuations as given and concentrating on the effects which those valuations will have on market processes—on the quantities and prices which actually prevail.

A consumer has a wide range of various combinations of goods which he could buy in order to seek his highest utility, but a consumer's decisions are not based only upon what he would like. He must maximize his utility subject to an important constraint: his ability to buy. The basic rule which he must always follow is that the total amount he spends on various goods must not exceed the total amount which he has available for spending. (The amount available is not always the same as his income. He may, after all, borrow money; but in many circumstances, he may also wish to save money.) The sum of all possible combinations of the various goods which the consumer could buy, within the limitation of the money which he has to spend, is called his *opportunity set*. Naturally, there are a very large number of possible combinations of goods which are within the opportunity set. In fact, if goods were completely divisible, there would be an infinite number. If the amount of divisibility is limited, the number is still very large. The goal of the household or, what amounts the same thing, the person who is making decisions for the household, is to try to choose from among all of the possible combinations available the one which will lead to the highest possible level of utility or welfare for the household unit.

Normally, it is not possible by any simple device to choose the single best combination within the opportunity set. Usually households operate by a series of trial and error decisions, improving the welfare position by every change. For example, it would be easy to imagine that a family could spend its entire budget for fruit on apples. However, a little experimentation would probably indicate that welfare would be improved by spending a dollar less on apples and a dollar more on oranges, to provide a little variety. Perhaps it would also be desirable to shift a second dollar and a third in the same direction. However, the time would come when the shifting of extra money from the purchase of apples to the purchase of oranges would no longer increase welfare, but would instead decrease it. At that stage, one would say that the opportunities for utility improvement by shifting from apples to oranges had been exhausted. Since there are a large number of possible combinations and directions of shifts, it is clear that few households will ever exhaust all the possibilities; but, with experience, each will tend to find a pattern of living which is reasonably close to the optimum level and which avoids the cost of continual shifting and decision-making.

If a household's income rose and prices did not, there would be a need for a new series of decisions to determine how to allocate the increased income among the various possibilities which were available in the increased opportunity set. If income fell, decisions would be required to conclude which items of consumption could be given up with the least loss of utility. In each case, the household might conceivably make all of the changes, either up or down, in one commodity, and then shift a dollar here or a dollar there to find a new combination which approached the optimum. More likely, the household would tend either to change consumption of all goods a little and then adjust further, or simultaneously change and shift.

When discussing the shift between apples and oranges above, we suggested that it would be possible to give up a dollar's worth of apples and add a dollar's worth of oranges. It is clear, however, that a dollar's worth of apples may constitute very different amounts at different times of the year and in different years. The same, of course, would be true of oranges. One would therefore expect that the shift between apples and oranges would depend upon the prices of the two fruits. If apples cost $0.25 a pound and oranges were three pounds for $1.00, shifting a dollar's worth of purchases would mean giving up four pounds of apples in exchange for three pounds of oranges. We thus see that the opportunities for shifting are determined by the ratios of the prices of the two goods. The desirability of shifting would depend upon the relative utility which one could obtain from a pound of oranges as compared with a pound of apples.

By putting together the two proportions, we can say that a household would achieve its best position at the point where four pounds of apples produced exactly the same utility as three pounds of oranges. At that stage, the internal valuation ratio — the relative utilities — would just match the market valuation — the relative prices. If the household were to continue adding oranges and subtracting apples, it would find that the extra oranges would be slightly less valuable and provide slightly less utility than the previous ones, and that the additional apples given up would be more valuable than the previous ones. Therefore, an additional shift toward more oranges would probably get the household into a region where the utility valuations were not three pounds of oranges for four pounds of apples, but, perhaps, three pounds of oranges for only three pounds of apples. In that case, it would certainly not pay to give up four pounds of apples, a dollar's worth, and receive in exchange only the three pounds of oranges which that dollar could buy.

When we are talking about the utility to be gained or lost by adding one more unit of a particular product, we call it the *marginal utility* of that product. You will meet the term *marginal* many times in economics. In general, marginal refers to the extra something which results from an extra unit. Notice that what we have been concerned with here is finding the relative *marginal utilities* of two consumer goods and then matching them with the relative *costs* of those goods. As long as the two ratios — prices and marginal utilities — are not the same, the household can improve its utility by shifting goods somewhat.

When the price of one commodity changes, the ratio of prices will certainly change and therefore a new combination of goods will provide the best combination. In general, we can say that if the price of one particular commodity falls, it would pay the household to purchase more of that commodity and less of something else. (Notice that, in the example above, Harriet's husband suggested that the family would be buying more better cuts of meat and less hamburger.) This is an example of the *substitution effect* of a price change. It always leads to an increase in the purchase of the commodity whose price has gone down, and a decrease in the purchase of the commodity whose relative price has risen.

The substitution effect is only half of the story. As prices change, the effective value of our income also changes. In the example given, Harriet's family could buy all of the same foods it had been purchasing in the past and still have money left over. This extra money could be spent on an improvement in the general quality of the family's food purchases. In most cases, the effect of such an increase in effective income is to increase the quantity of all of the commodities which the family will buy. (In the example given, notice that the family increased its purchases of both hamburger *and* better cuts of meat.) This particular shift in purchase patterns, which results when lower prices increase the real income of a household, is called the *income effect*.

We saw in Chapter 1, when we were discussing the effects of higher incomes upon demand, that an increase in income leads to an increase in the purchases of most commodities, but that some commodities tend to increase more proportionately as incomes rise. We saw also that there are some commodities which are considered inferior goods, whose consumption actually falls as incomes rise and households begin to purchase something better to replace them. (Notice that Harriet suggested that the family would be eating fewer beans in the future.)

In summary, we can say that the effect of a price change on the purchase of two commodities can be broken down into an *income effect* and a *substitution effect*. The substitution effect indicates that, as the price goes down, one will buy more of the commodity whose price has fallen and less of other commodities. The income effect implies that one will usually buy more of all commodities. The net effect of the two is almost always an increase in the purchase of those goods whose price has fallen and either a decrease of an increase of other goods, depending on whether the substitution effect or the income effect is stronger. (There is a special case which is sometimes called Giffen's paradox. It occurs with inferior goods which are an important part of the total budget of very poor consumers. In this case, if the price of the inferior good falls, the income effect may be more important than the substitution effect; and the net result of the lower price of the inferior good will be fewer purchases, rather than more. It is rather doubtful that Giffen's paradox is of any great importance in the modern world.)

Indifference Maps

We have noted that households match the opportunity set (what they *can* buy) against their utility pattern (what they would *like*). In order to analyze the pattern of consumer behavior somewhat more precisely, it is necessary to provide a method of describing these two sets of information and then combining them. For simplicity's sake, we will limit our discussion to a household which purchases only two commodities. Naturally, this is not a very typical description of the way that households really work, but it is necessary in order to draw diagrams on the two-dimensional pages of a book. Our conclusions will still apply to a many-commodity world. Let us start with the opportunity set.

We imagine a household which has a certain amount of money, say $5.00 per month, which it can use to purchase fruit. We further assume that the only fruits available are apples at $0.25 per pound and oranges at three pounds for $1.00. We can say that the opportunity set consists of all combinations of apples and oranges which satisfy the inequality:

$$P_o Q_o + P_a Q_a \leq B \tag{4.1}$$

In the above inequality, P_o and P_a represent the price of oranges and apples respectively; Q_o and Q_a represent the quantity of the two fruits to be purchased; and B represents the budget. If we then include the budget of $5.00 and the prices given above, the limitation becomes:

$$.33Q_o + .25Q_a \leq \$5.00 \tag{4.2}$$

We can find the boundary of the area represented by this inequality by simply taking the equality. We then see that it would be possible to buy as many as 20 pounds of apples per month if we bought no oranges. The total cost would be $5.00. We also see that it would be possible to buy fifteen pounds of oranges if we bought no apples. Again, the cost would be $5.00. It would also be possible to buy various combinations of apples and oranges, because every four pounds of apples we give up would permit adding an additional three pounds of oranges. Thus, the various boundary combinations which are possible are given in Table 4.1. We can easily see that every combination of apples and oranges given in the table costs exactly $5.00. Clearly, it would also be possible to buy a smaller quantity of one of the two fruits given and the same quantity of the other as shown in any combination in the table. The figures in the table represent maximum values.

Table 4.1
Opportunity Set

Pounds of apples per month	Pounds of oranges per month	Cost of apples (0.25 per lb.)	Cost of oranges (0.33 per lb.)	Total cost
20	0	$5.00	$0.00	$5.00
16	3	4.00	1.00	5.00
12	6	3.00	2.00	5.00
8	9	2.00	3.00	5.00
4	12	1.00	4.00	5.00
0	15	0.00	5.00	5.00

The same combination of opportunities is shown in Figure 4.1. It can be seen that the boundary line is the line representing either twenty pounds of apples and no oranges, or fifteen pounds of oranges and no apples, or any of the combinations between them. The white area represents all combinations which are possible, including all those on the boundary line and all those below the boundary line. Clearly, this opportunity set depends upon the particular prices of apples and oranges and the budget available for purchase of these goods. If any of these three were to change, the opportunity set would also change.

We must also find a way to describe the utility of a particular household. One of the difficulties with our definition of utility,

**Figure 4.1
Opportunity Set**

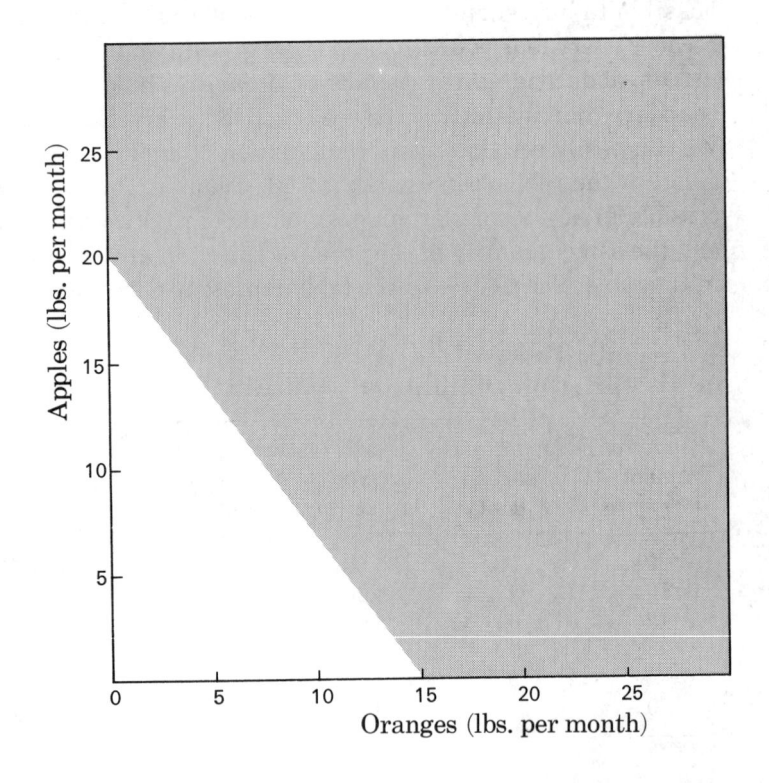

which states that it is whatever consumers try to maximize, is that there is no convenient unit of measurement. It is, however, possible to measure utility in the simple terms of more and less – just as we would measure temperature as warmer or colder, even without a thermometer. Let us consider a particular combination of the two fruits – say, twelve pounds of apples and six pounds of oranges per month. This combination is shown as point P in Figure 4.2. It is clear that any point in the quadrant numbered I would be better than the point P, because it would mean that the household would have more of both oranges and apples. It is also clear that any point in the quadrant numbered III would be worse, because it would involve less of both fruits. Points in the quadrants numbered II and IV are not so clear, because they involve more of one fruit and less of the other. However, one would expect that points very close to quadrant I are probably better than P and that points close to quadrant III are probably worse than P. In Figure 4.2, point R is probably better and point Q is probably worse. It follows that it is possible to draw a curve passing through point P and going in a general southeasterly direction which would divide all of the points which are better than P from all of the points which are worse. Such a curve has been drawn and labeled IC.

Points actually on the curve IC, being neither better nor worse than point P but equal to it in value, are said to be indifferent points, because a household would be indifferent to which of the points along IC it chose. For this reason, IC is called an *indifference curve*. The bend which is shown in IC is probably typical, because we would expect that, as a family acquired more oranges, it would take more and more oranges to compensate them for giving up a single pound of apples. We see, for example, that at the left end of the curve the family would be willing to give up several pounds of apples for a single pound of oranges. Gradually, the trading ratio declines; and, on the right hand side, we see that the family would give up a single pound of apples only for several pounds of oranges. The ratio of the number of pounds of oranges which just compensates for the number of pounds of apples is called the *marginal rate of substitution,* and represents the ratio of the marginal utility of the two commodities. (Notice the use of

**Figure 4.2
Indifference Curve**

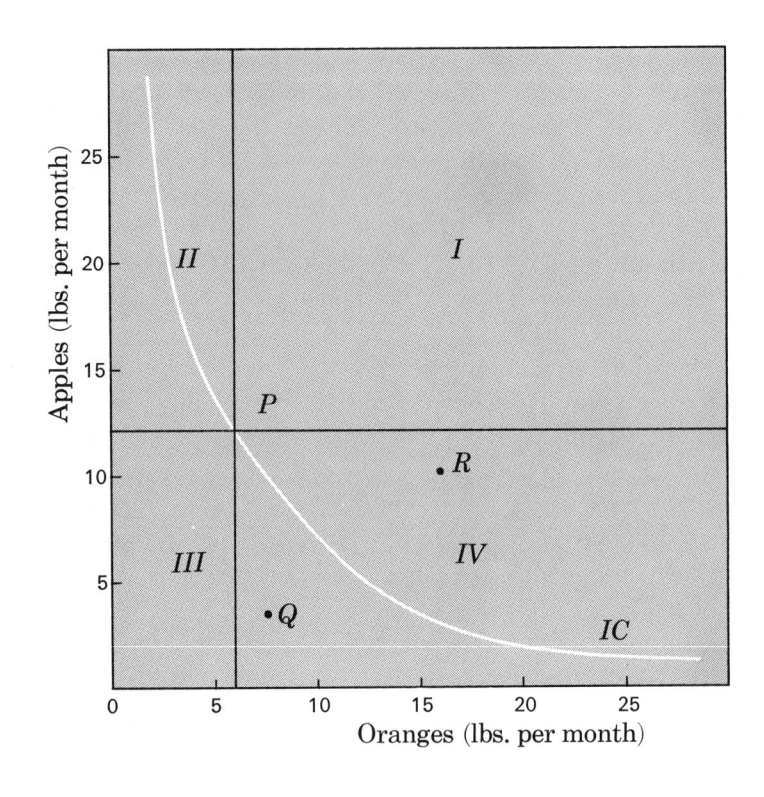

the word *marginal* as the rate of substitution for one more pound of apples.)

The marginal rate of substitution gives us an indication of the relationship between commodities. If goods are substitutes, the marginal rate of substitution will be relatively constant and the indifference curve will have only a slight curvature. If goods are perfect complements, they are usually sold only in sets (like right and left shoes.) Such complementary goods show a sharp break in the indifference curve at the right combination, for the marginal utility of excess quantities is slight. Most complementary goods are not perfectly so, and show a moderately sharp bend at the customary combination.

Most goods are, to some extent, both substitutes and complements. All goods produce utility and compete for income, and are, to that extent, substitutes. In addition, they all have elements of complementarity. In every social group, certain standard patterns of living are customary. For members of such groups, the ingredients of this standard pattern are complementary. The elements of substitutability and complementarity are blended, and the usual indifference curves (like that of Figure 4.2) have a curvature between the straight line of perfect substitutability and the sharp bend of perfect complementarity.

Naturally, the indifference curve in Figure 4.2 is only one of a possible set of indifference curves which we might have drawn. This one consists of all points which are equal in value to the original starting point P; but for each starting point which is either better or worse than P, we could have drawn a separate indifference curve. Therefore, we can say that the indifference curve of Figure 4.2 is simply a single example of a set of indifference curves such as those shown in Figure 4.3, which is called an *indifference map*. However, the map of Figure 4.3 does not include all possible indifference curves, since we could imagine drawing an additional curve between any two which are drawn here. Our indifference map, like any map, contains only enough features to permit us to recognize the whole pattern rather than every detail of the phenomenon which it maps. The different curves of the indifference map shown in Figure 4.3 do not have any numbers on them, because we do not have a measure for utility; but we can assume that the indifference curves in the upper right

**Figure 4.3
Indifference Map**

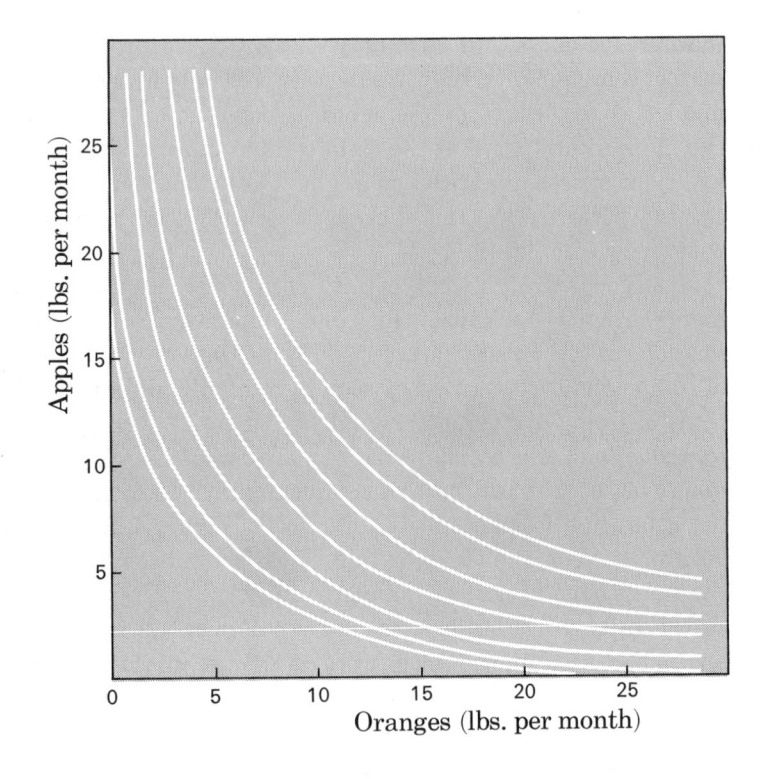

represent higher utility than the indifference curves in the lower left corner of the map.

In order to visualize the way in which a household makes its decisions between commodities, we must combine the opportunity set of Figure 4.1 with the indifference map of Figure 4.3. This has been done in Figure 4.4. We now seek to answer the question: What is the best possible combination available to this household which is still within the budget limitation? We can phrase this question another way by asking what point within the white area is on the highest possible indifference curve, because the indifference curves represent desirability and the white area represents possibility. Such a point is given at *P* where the budget line, which is the boundary of the opportunity set, is just tangent to an indifference curve. Clearly, every other point within the opportunity set is on a lower indifference curve than the one which goes through *P,* and is less desirable. Clearly also, every point on every indifference curve above the one through *P* is outside the opportunity set and, although more desirable, is not possible. Thus, point *P* represents a position where the household has done the best possible under the circumstances. (Although the entire white area is the opportunity set, the best point, *P*, is on the boundary. In the rest of the book, we will therefore always represent the opportunity set by its boundary line.)

We can observe an important characteristic of the optimum. At point *P*, the indifference curve is just tangent to the budget line. Since it is tangent, the two have the same slope at this point. The slope of the budget line represents the relative prices of the two commodities, apples and oranges. The slope of the indifference curve represents the marginal rate of substitution — the relative marginal utilities of the two commodities. At the optimum point, the two ratios are equal, indicating that the price ratio and the marginal rate of substitution are the same. This is the conclusion which we reached earlier in our discussion of household behavior.

Income and Price Changes

As income changes, the quantity of apples and oranges which will be purchased will change. In Figure 4.5, three

**Figure 4.4
Equilibrium**

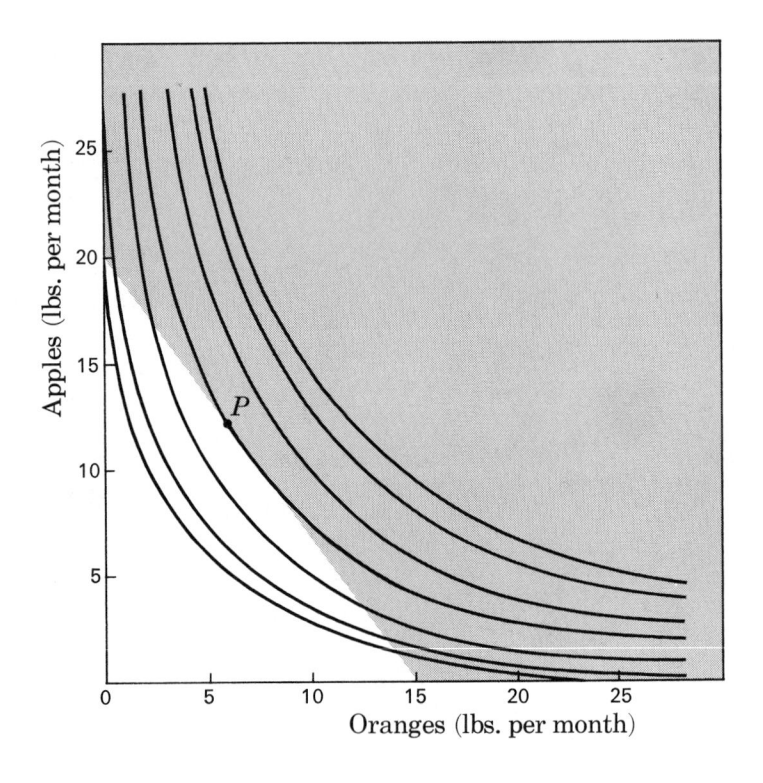

**Figure 4.5
Income Changes**

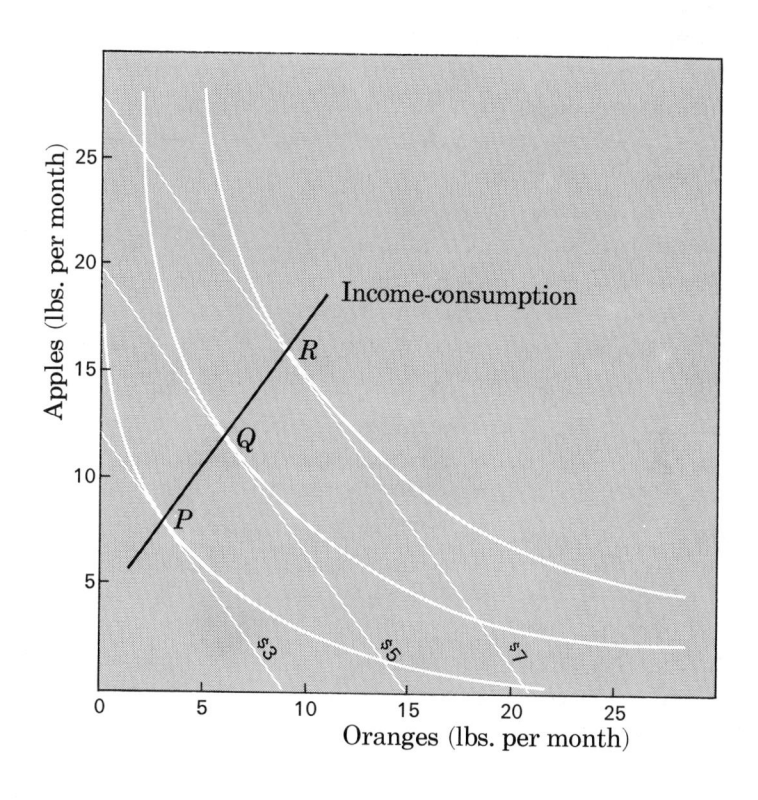

Consumers and Demand

different fruit budgets, $3.00, $5.00, and $7.00, are shown. The optimums, each determined in the same way as the equilibrium of Figure 4.4, are shown as points P, Q, and R. Since this family regards neither apples nor oranges as inferior goods, the quantity of each increases as income rises.

The points P, Q, and R are sometimes connected to form an *income-consumption* line. This line represents the way in which the family distributes changing incomes between the two goods. However, this income-consumption line is limited by the fact that it is calculated using a particular set of prices. Had the prices been different, a new income-consumption line would have resulted.

Another way to represent the reaction of consumer purchases to changing incomes is by using the *income elasticity*, modeled upon the price elasticity. The definition of income elasticity is:

$$\text{Income elasticity} = \frac{\text{Percentage change in quantity}}{\text{Percentage change in income}}$$
$$= \frac{\text{Change in quantity}}{\text{Quantity}} \div \frac{\text{Change in income}}{\text{Income}} \quad (4.3)$$

In Figure 4.5, we see that as income rises from $5.00 to $7.00, a 40 percent change, the purchase of apples increases from twelve to sixteen pounds per month (33 percent), and the purchase of oranges increases from six to nine pounds per month (50 percent). The income elasticity of demand for apples is ($\frac{0.33}{0.40}$), or 0.83; that of oranges is ($\frac{0.50}{0.40}$), or 1.25.

For inferior goods, the income elasticity is negative, because the quantity falls as income rises. It is common to describe goods with low income elasticities (under 1.00) as *necessities*, and those with high income elasticities (over 1.00) as *luxuries*. This designation corresponds to a precise definition of necessities as goods which one cuts less as income falls, and of luxuries as goods which expand with income. It does *not* correspond to ordinary usage, where we often use the term luxury to mean goods which we believe people *ought* to give up. By their behavior, smokers consider cigarettes a necessity; in their moralizing, nonsmokers consider them luxuries. When we use the terms, we should keep in mind which way we are using them. Behaviorally, medical care is a luxury; politically, it is often called a necessity. Many other examples of this confusion could also be given. (At the end of Chapter 3, we observed the difference in individual evaluation and social judgment on marijuana. Here we meet the same distinction in a different case.)

Let us examine the effects of a change in price of one of the commodities upon the behavior of this household. Let us imagine that the price of oranges falls from $0.33 a pound to $0.25 a pound, while the price of apples remains at $0.25 and the budget remains at $5.00. The family's new opportunity set would be determined by a new budget line higher than the old one. This higher budget line is shown in Figure 4.6 as B_2, with the old budget line at B_1. The new equilibrium position would be at point R with the family purchasing twelve pounds of oranges a month and eight pounds of apples, rather than the old combination of six pounds of oranges and twelve pounds of apples, indicated on Figure 4.6 as point P. In order to understand the process by which the new equilibrium point is reached, let us observe that the new budget line is different from the old one in two respects. In the first place, it has a different slope, caused by the different price ratio—now one to one, instead of the old four to three. Second, the new budget line is higher at all points except its tip. Let us divide these two differences and draw a third hypothetical budget line, indicated on Figure 4.6 as B_3. This line has the same *slope* as the new budget line B_2, but it has the same *level* as the *old* budget line B_1, indicated by the fact that it is tangent to the same indifference curve. We can therefore say that B_3 represents a set of alternatives which would permit the family to be just as well off at the new prices as it was at the old prices.

In Figure 4.6, we see that the equilibrium point along the budget line B_3 is at point Q, representing eleven pounds of oranges and six pounds of apples a month. We can now break down the movement from P to R into two sections: the first, a movement from P to Q in response to the changing price ratio; and the second, the movement from Q to R in response to the changing level of real income. The first of these (from P to Q) represents the substitution effect of the lower orange prices. The second (from Q to R) represents the income effect of the lower

**Figure 4.6
Income and Substitution Effect**

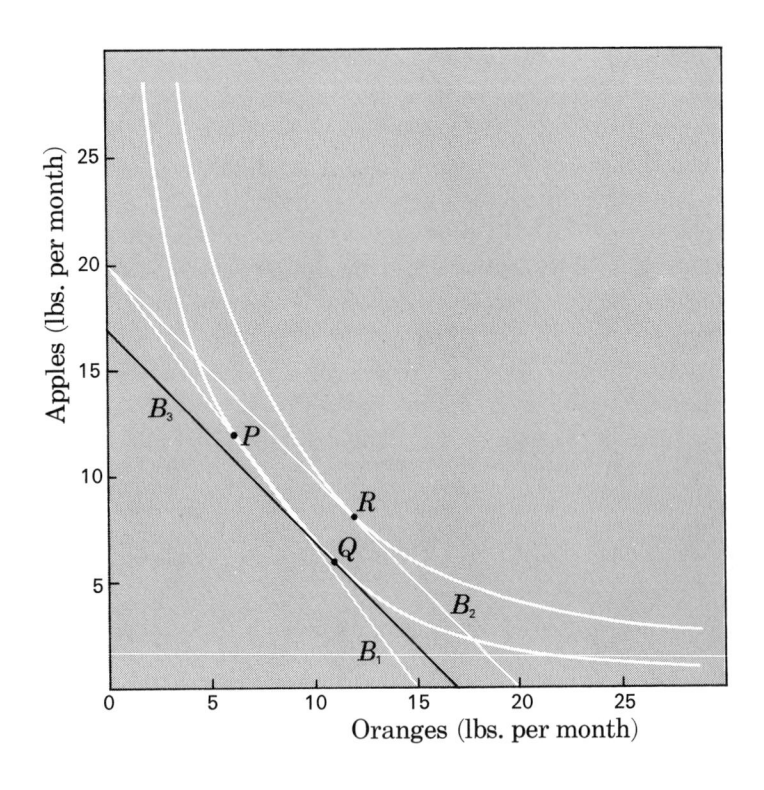

prices. We see that the shift from P to Q, in response to the changing price ratios, involves a decrease in the purchase of apples and an increase in the purchase of oranges, which have become relatively cheaper. The second shift, from Q to R, represents an increase in the purchase of both fruits as a response to the higher income level. When the two effects are combined, both of them contribute to an increase in purchase of oranges; but the substitution effect reduces the purchase of apples and the income effect increases it. In the particular example shown in Figure 4.6, the net result is a decrease in the purchase of apples; but it is possible that the income effect could have been larger, in which case there would have been an increase in the purchase of apples. (Notice that in the example given at the beginning of the chapter, the lower price on better cuts of meat led to increases in purchases of hamburger because the income effect was larger than the substitution effect.)

A description of the relationship between commodities is sometimes given by a third elasticity measure, the *cross elasticity of demand*, which is defined as:

$$\text{Cross elasticity} = \frac{\text{Percentage change in quantity of one good}}{\text{Percentage change in price of another}} \quad (4.4)$$

In the example of Figure 4.6, the quantity of apples purchased decreases from twelve to eight pounds per month (-33 percent), as the price of oranges falls from $0.33 to $0.25 (-25 percent). The cross elasticity of apples and oranges is therefore 1.33. In measuring cross elasticity, it is important to watch signs, because the elasticity will be positive if the substitution effect predominates and negative if the income effect predominates. We often say that substitute goods are those which have positive cross elasticity, and complementary goods are those which have negative cross elasticity. This does not always correspond exactly to our earlier definition in terms of curvature of the indifference curve, but it is accurate enough for most purposes.

The Demand Curve

Finding the household's individual demand curve is merely a matter of finding its equilibrium position at a number of different prices. We will assume throughout that the household's fruit budget is $5.00 and the price of apples $0.25 per pound. We now wish to see how many oranges will be purchased at each of several prices. Let us start with a price of $1.00 per pound. We see in Figure 4.7 that the highest utility comes with sixteen pounds of apples and only one pound of oranges, at the point where the $1.00 budget line is tangent to an indifference curve. We have therefore plotted the one pound against the $1.00 price in the lower half of Figure 4.7. When we repeat the process for a price of $0.50, we find that the best position calls for the purchase of fourteen pounds of apples and three pounds of oranges. We have therefore plotted three pounds of oranges against the $0.50 price. We repeat this process for successive prices of $0.33 a pound, $0.25 a pound, and $0.20 a pound; and in each case we plot the quantity of oranges which would be purchased against the price in the lower portion of the diagram. Finally, we connect these points to obtain the individual demand curve for oranges, other things being equal.

This last phrase is important. We must remember that we have calculated this demand curve on the assumption of a fixed $0.25 price for apples and a $5.00 fruit budget. If either of these were different, we would obtain a different demand curve for oranges. We have also assumed fixed tastes, represented by a single indifference map.

To give a more complete picture, we sometimes use total income and a composite demand for all other goods to determine the total purchase of oranges. This composite is usually measured in dollars and represents the best possible way of spending money for all goods except oranges. Naturally, we assume that the prices of all other products remain unchanged, as we focus our attention on the price and quantity of oranges.

We can connect the points of tangency shown in the upper half of Figure 4.7 to form a *price-consumption* line, which shows the way consumers change their consumption decisions as the price of oranges changes. Just as the income-consumption line assumed unchanged prices, the price-consumption line assumes unchanged income and an unchanged price of apples.

We can use this price-consumption line to say something about the elasticity of demand for oranges. We see that, as the price

**Figure 4.7
Demand Curve**

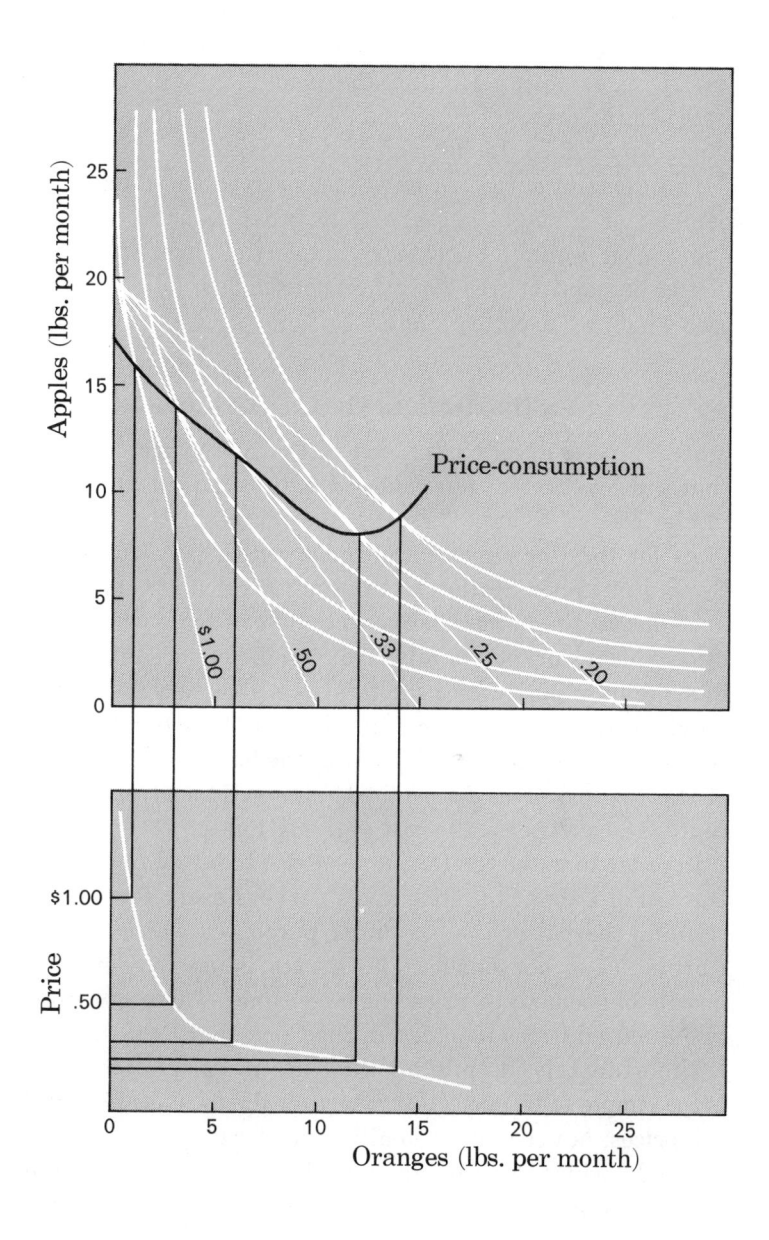

Consumers and Demand

of oranges falls from $1.00 to $0.50 and $0.33 to $0.25, the quantity of apples being purchased from the $5.00 a month budget is declining (the price-consumption line slopes downward). Since the price of apples is fixed, the amount of money being spent on them is also declining. The total expenditure on oranges is therefore rising as the price falls, so the demand is elastic in this range. Between the prices of $0.25 and $0.20, the price-consumption line slopes upward, so the demand curve is inelastic.

The demand curve we have just derived represents only the demand of a single household. In order to obtain the market demand, it would be necessary to add this demand curve to all of the demand curves for other households, following the process which we used in Chapter 1.

An Illustration: The Cost of Living

We very often see in the newspapers a statement that the government has released figures indicating an increase in the cost of living. These figures represent the latest quotations for the Consumer Price Index which is calculated by the Bureau of Labor Statistics. In order to calculate the Consumer Price Index, the bureau defines a bundle of goods which is bought by a typical worker's family. This bundle of goods is then priced in some base period and the total cost is determined. The same bundle is repriced every month. The cost of the bundle in the current month is divided by the cost in the base period, and the ratio of the two prices is determined. This ratio, converted into percentages, constitutes the cost of living index.

In order to make the Consumer Price Index more accurate, the Bureau of Labor Statistics takes surveys every few years to determine the pattern of consumer purchases which is typical of working class households. This survey is used to determine the bundle of goods to be priced at later times. There are more than two hundred items included in the Consumer Price Index.

Unfortunately, despite all this care in calculation, the index is too simple to be perfect. It measures the income effect of changing prices, but it makes no allowance for changes in the bundle of goods which consumers purchase in response to changing prices. In other words, it does not take into account the substitution effect and therefore always overstates the increase in the cost of living. In order to demonstrate this overstatement, let us calculate a simplified cost of living index based only upon apples and oranges. Let us assume that in the base period, the household purchased twelve pounds of apples at $0.25 per pound and six pounds of oranges at $0.33 per pound. The total expenditure would be $5.00 for these foods. Now let us suppose that the price of both apples and oranges rises to $0.50 a pound. According to the usual method, one would calculate the index as follows:

$$\begin{array}{l} \text{12 lbs. of apples @ \$0.50} = \$6.00 \\ \underline{\text{6 lbs of oranges @ \$0.50} = \$3.00} \end{array}$$

$$\text{Total} \quad \$9.00$$

The cost of living index would therefore be $9.00 divided by $5.00, or 180 percent. This is incorrect, because it does not allow for the fact that the consumer would shift and buy more oranges since the price of oranges has risen less than the price of apples. In Figure 4.8, the original point is indicated as *B*, the base combination; and last year's price line of $5.00 is shown passing through *B*. The new line of $9.00 at this year's prices is also shown, going through *B*, but at a different slope. However, it is clear that this line *crosses* the old indifference curve and would permit the family to find a better position than *B*, perhaps at a point like *P*. What is really required is a new line at the present price ratio, but one which just touches the old indifference curve. Such a price line has been drawn and is tangent to the old indifference curve at point *R*. This line represents a total expenditure of $8.50, not $9.00. At point *R*, the household will purchase six pounds of apples per month and eleven pounds of oranges. The total budget is therefore:

$$\begin{array}{l} \text{6 lbs. of apples @ \$0.50} = \$3.00 \\ \underline{\text{11 lbs. of oranges @ \$0.50} = \$5.50} \end{array}$$

$$\text{Total} \quad \$8.50$$

It is clear that the *true* cost-of-living index should be $\dfrac{\$8.50}{\$5.00}$ or

Figure 4.8
Cost of Living

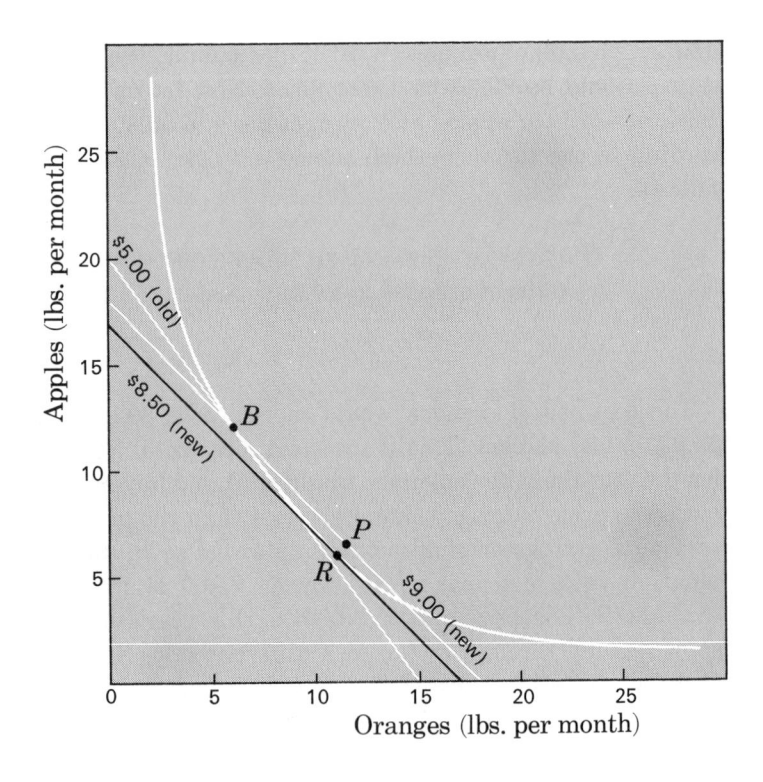

170 percent. Thus the usual method of calculating changes in the cost of living has overstated the price index by ten percentage points.

It is not clear exactly how much practical importance should be attached to this overstatement of the cost of living index. Clearly, the usual index indicates the income effect of price changes, but ignores the substitution effect. If the substitution effects which are omitted are quite large, the error in the index would also be quite large. If, on the other hand, the substitution effects are comparatively modest, it is probable that the error in the conventional index would also be modest. It is not possible to say in general exactly how much substitution does take place. We would presume that the amount of substitution is probably small and mainly confined to goods which are close substitutes for each other, such as apples and oranges, pork and beef, etc. If rent rises, one would expect an income effect, but no substitution effect. The same thing would apply to many other kinds of purchases for which it is difficult to make substitutions. On the whole, one would expect that the error in the cost of living index is modest and changes very slightly from month to month, or even from year to year. Consequently, we can still rely on the Consumer Price Index as a reasonably satisfactory measure of price changes over short periods of time. For longer time periods, it is more likely that substitution will occur and the error will be greater.

Appendix to Chapter 4
The Nature of Households

In this chapter, we have looked at the general process by which consuming units make their decisions and divide their income among various kinds of expenditures. In this appendix, we wish to examine some of the facts about households which can be derived from actual statistics.

The usual household is a family unit, with parents and children, making consumption decisions in common. (The actual decision-making power is sometimes exercised by the wife, sometimes by the husband, and sometimes by both jointly.) Some family units consist of only one parent and one or more children, and some of only a husband and wife. From the economic point of view, the essential characteristic is the combined decision for several people. According to the 1970 Census of the United States, there were 51 million such units, comprising 90 percent of the population.

At the other end of the scale are those individuals who live alone. Most of these are concentrated at the ends of the age scale, representing either young people in their pre-family years or the elderly in the post-family bracket. (Despite the different approach to life styles in recent years, it remains true that most people are members of family units at some time in their lives.) In 1970, there were 10 million of these single person households, comprising 5 percent of the population.

A small, but perhaps growing, portion of the population lives in groups of unrelated individuals, of which the youth commune is the most visible type but not the only one. Groups of single workers often live together to avoid the high costs of apartments and the dreariness of rooming houses. Such groups usually share a portion of their income and make decisions jointly, but tend to reserve some income for individual control. One common arrangement is where each member pays a proportionate share of the rent and food, but treats all other expenses as personal. The statisticians usually list the members of such groups as single individuals. Full pooling of funds and decisions, as in families, is quite rare. Where it does exist, the group should perhaps be listed as a family.

Finally, a significant portion of the population (3 percent in 1970) lives in institutions, including prisons, nursing homes, and some kinds of hospitals. In these units, decisions are made for the inmates by the directors, so that the usual household decision processes do not apply. Some of these institutions are profit-oriented and should be treated as firms; most are either governmental or nonprofit, and are run as bureaucracies.

Household Incomes

From the standpoint of consumption, the most important characteristic of a household is its income, which determines the resources it has available for spending. The sources of household income are shown in Table A4.1.

The largest source of household income is the wages and salaries paid to employees, accounting for 71 percent of personal income. This category includes payments of all kinds and sizes, from the amounts paid to part-time janitorial staff to the salaries of highly paid executives.

For statistical reasons, the income of proprietors is reported separately. This includes the income of all independent businessmen, such as shopkeepers, doctors, lawyers, and professional

Table A4.1
Sources of Personal Income, 1971

	Dollars (in billions)	Percent
Wages, salaries and other labor income	$607.8	71%
Proprietors' income	68.4	8
Rental income	24.3	3
Dividends	25.5	3
Interest	67.5	8
Total	$793.5	93
Plus Transfer payments	94.7	11
Less Social Security Contributions	31.2	−4
Total personal income	857.0	100

Source: *Economic Report of the President, 1972,* pp. 214-215.

consultants. Clearly, much of this income is payment for their labor, the same as wages and salaries. However, some of the income represents interest on invested funds, rent on property owned, and actual profits. Because there is no satisfactory way to separate these categories, it is reported in a single amount. We can be reasonably confident, however, that if we combine the labor part of this income with the wages and salaries of employees, we will find that more than three-fourths of personal income is derived from the sale of labor.

The amount of income which any given household receives from its labor obviously depends upon the quality and quantity of the labor which it has to sell. For example, all studies show a significant relationship between the level of education and the labor income. High school graduates usually earn about 25 percent more than those with only an elementary education. College graduates earn about the same amount more than high school graduates in the years immediately after college; but the gap keeps widening, since incomes of college graduates keep increasing up to retirement, while incomes of high school graduates tend to level off at about the age of forty.

These statistics are often quoted to demonstrate the economic advantages of a college education. But one must be very careful about drawing such inferences, because high school graduates and college graduates differ in more ways than merely four years of extra education. For example, the average college graduate had a much better high school record than the average student who quit after twelfth grade. Even in high school, these groups showed a different combination of native ability and application. We should therefore expect that at least some of the difference in income is the result of these characteristics, and not merely education. Education probably helps, but it is difficult to say how much. Perhaps one of the greatest advantages of education is the doors which it opens. Many occupations are closed to those persons without college degrees, even when the degree itself has little to do with job performance.

Household income is also affected by the quantity of labor which the household can offer. As we would expect, statistics demonstrate that households in which both husband and wife work have significantly higher incomes than those in which only the husband works. Of course, the typical contribution to income made by the wife is much lower than that of the husband. This difference results from a combination of factors: the generally lower wages paid to women, a significant number of part-time workers, and some tendency for working wives (and their employers) to consider the jobs more or less temporary.

Other categories of income depend upon the wealth a household owns rather than the labor service it offers. These categories include the receipt of rents, interest, and dividends, representing income from ownership of real estate, bonds, and stocks, respectively. (Dividends are not the only gain from ownership of stock. A corporation usually pays only a portion of its profits in dividends and reinvests the remainder in plant and equipment. Because of this reinvestment, the value of the stock rises and it can be sold for more than the purchase price.)

Because these kinds of income are tied to wealth, they are concentrated in those income groups which are able to accumulate wealth by saving — that is, spending less than their incomes. As we will see in the next section, households with higher incomes save a greater proportion of their incomes. We therefore find wealth more concentrated in the upper income brackets; and upper bracket incomes contain a larger portion of rents, interest, and dividends than lower bracket incomes.

Table A4.2
Percent of Households by Money Income (1962 dollars)

	1929	1941	1960	1970
Under $2,000	31%	27%	13%	15%
$2,000 to $3,999	39	29	19	15
$4,000 to $5,999	15	22	22	16
$6,000 to $7,999	7	12	18	15
$8,000 to $9,999	3	4	11	11
$10,000 to $14,999	} 5	} 6	11	14
$15,000 and over			6	14

Source: Data for earlier years from Herman Miller, *Income Distribution in the United States*, U.S. Census, 1966. Data for 1970 calculated by author from current Census reports.

Table A4.3
Distribution of Income by Fifths

	1929	1941	1960	1970
Lowest fifth	} 12.5%	4.1%	4.9%	5.5%
Second fifth		9.5	12.0	12.0
Middle fifth	13.8	15.3	17.5	17.4
Fourth fifth	19.3	22.3	23.6	23.5
Highest fifth	54.4	48.8	42.0	41.6
Top 5 percent	30.0	24.0	16.8	14.4

Source: Data for earlier years from Herman Miller, *Income Distribution in the United States*, U.S. Census, 1966. Data for 1960 and 1970 from *Income Distribution in 1970*, U.S. Census.

Two different ways of looking at the distribution of income in the United States are shown in Tables A4.2 and A4.3. Table A4.2 shows the percentage of families in each income bracket in each of four years: 1929, 1941, 1960, and 1970. (All of the figures have been adjusted to 1962 prices, to avoid the effects of inflation.) These figures show that even in the boom year of the "Roaring Twenties," one-third of all households had incomes of less than $2,000 and over two-thirds had incomes below $4,000. Only one family in twenty had an income over $10,000. By the beginning of World War II, slightly over one-fourth of all families were still below $2,000 and over half below $4,000. The percentage over $10,000 had increased slightly. By 1960, only one-eighth were below $2,000 and less than one-third were below $4,000. Four times as many families were over $10,000. The data for 1970 show a continuing rise into the higher brackets, with 28 percent over $10,000. However, 1970 also shows an increase in the lowest income bracket—a reflection of the widespread unemployment of the time. These figures show a substantial shift upward in all income categories. Incomes had more than doubled.

Table A4.3 shows the percentage of total personal income received by each fifth of the population (and by the top 5 percent) for the same years. These figures demonstrate that incomes have moved slightly toward the direction of equality. (If all incomes were equal, each fifth of the population would have one-fifth of the income.) The top fifth of the population has a significantly smaller share of total income in recent years, and all other brackets have gained. However, income still shows a substantial degree of inequality. The top 5 percent of households have about 15 percent of the income, while the bottom 20 percent have about 5 percent. Thus the average household income in the top bracket is more than ten times as high as in the bottom bracket. We can therefore summarize the two tables by saying that typical family incomes are rising, but that the poor have achieved most of their gains through the general growth of the economy, and not by increasing their share at the expense of the rich.

As indicated earlier, interest and dividends are a significant portion of income only in the higher income brackets. In most income brackets, the bulk of income is derived from labor services. In the bottom category, however, transfer payments—including welfare and social security—constitute a large portion of total income. These lowest categories are composed primarily of those who cannot sell their labor services, or cannot sell them for very much.

Table A4.4
Disposition of Personal Income, 1971

	Dollars (in billions)
Personal Income	$857.0
Less Personal tax	115.8
Equals Disposable Income	741.2
Less Consumption Expenditures	680.8
Equals Personal Saving	60.4

Source: *Economic Report of the President, 1972*, p. 212. Consumption expenditures include personal interest and personal transfers to foreigners, which are reported separately.

Uses of Income

Table A4.4 shows the uses to which consumers put their incomes. From this table, we see that about one-eighth of personal income goes to federal, state, and local taxes. (This is not the entire burden of taxes. Many taxes levied on businesses are reflected either in higher prices or in lower incomes of households.) Of the remainder, less than 10 percent is saved and the rest is spent for consumption.

Table A4.5 shows the distribution of consumer outlays. In this table, we see that services constitute a large portion of total expenditure, and nondurable goods almost as much. In poorer societies, nondurables (especially food and clothing) are apt to make up the largest portion of consumption, with housing expenses (especially rent) close behind. One sign of the generally high living standards in the United States is the large expenditure for "other" services, including education, recreation, personal care, and many other attributes of the "good life."

Another sign of our increasing affluence is the large expenditure on durable goods. One could argue that the purchase of durable goods is simply a form of saving, and that we should only charge the annual depreciation as a consumption expenditure. Such treatment is given to housing. The purchase of a house is treated as saving, and an imputed rent is included with the services. But our statistics still treat the purchase of other durables as consumption, thereby understating saving.

Table A4.5
Personal Consumption Expenditures, 1971

		Dollars (in billions)
Durable Goods		100.4
Automobiles and parts	46.2	
Furniture and household equipment	39.5	
Other	14.7	
Nondurable Goods		278.8
Food and beverages	136.6	
Clothing	57.0	
Gasoline and oil	24.3	
Other	60.9	
Services		301.6
Housing	99.7	
Household operation	39.3	
Transportation	19.0	
Personal interest	17.7	
Other	125.9	
Total		680.8

Source: *Economic Report of the President, 1972*, p. 207.

In this chapter, we discussed the income elasticity of demand for different goods. Many kinds of statistical analysis have been used to demonstrate that expenditures of different types vary with the level of income. Some of the oldest of these generalizations are called Engel's laws, after Ernst Engel, the statistician who first discovered them. (Do not confuse him with Friedrich Engels, Karl Marx's patron and coauthor.) Engel found that as incomes rise, the proportion of income spent on food declines. Since then, we have found that as incomes rise, expenditures on clothing and housing tend to stay about proportional while expenditures on services rise more than proportionately. The amount of saving also rises more than proportionately with income. We will postpone discussion of taxes until the Appendix to Chapter 10.

Sometimes we hear or read discussions of why people consume certain kinds of goods. Some, such as basic foods or warm clothing in cold climates, are consumed for the physical benefits which they yield. Others, such as paintings and decorations, are often acquired for the psychological pleasure they yield to their owner. Still others are purchased to impress one's neighbors.

Most consumption, however, contains elements of all three. An automobile serves the practical need of providing transportation, gives its driver a feeling of power, and can establish its owner among his friends as a man of substance. Each of us has his own views on which of these goals is more or less worthy; but an economist must accept the fact that all these forces create a desire for certain commodities—a desire which will be translated into demand if funds are available. Any evaluation of motives must be left to moralists, philosophers, and magazine writers.

Chapter 5
Firms and Supply

At Megalopolis University, as at many others, students are convinced that cafeteria prices in the student union are outrageous and that "they" are making huge profits at the expense of the students. The chancellor has provided rather detailed cost-accounting records to the student council to prove otherwise, but the most vociferous opponents are unconvinced. (Since the spokesman for the group is an English major, there is some suspicion that he was unable to understand the material provided.)

Recently, the local chapter of SDF (Students for Decent Food) decided to prove that food could be provided for less than cafeteria prices. They initiated a regular program of providing, on certain days, one hot dish at bargain prices. One day it was chili, another spaghetti, and so on. The food was — surprisingly — delicious, and certainly cost far less than the cafeteria charged for such food. After a series of such demonstrations (six in all), the organization announced that it had made a profit of $54, thereby proving its point. It also announced that it was discontinuing the program, but expected an immediate response from the university cafeteria. (One reason for discontinuance was that chapter members who had done the cooking had decided that a demonstration was fine, but cooking on a regular basis was a bummer.)

When the student newspaper interviewed Mr. Arthur Packer, the cafeteria manager, he insisted that the demonstration had proved nothing. "Those kids donated their labor, which is my principal expense. They used pots and pans from someone's home, and paid nothing for them. They provided only one dish, and not enough of that, so they were sold out each time and had no waste.

"I still had to prepare food for those they couldn't feed. Operating their way, it's easy to make a so-called profit, but it won't provide regular food service."

An editorial in the same issue condemned Mr. Packer's "self-serving analysis," and demanded a full investigation of food service by the student council. The council took up the challenge and appointed a special committee. At last reports, the committee was still working its way through the accounting reports which the chancellor submitted months ago.

The Measurement of Costs

The basic unit of production is the *firm*, which buys goods and services, combines them, and sells the resulting product. Its goal is a *profit*, the difference between the cost of the inputs and the value of the output. (Remember that the household, the basic consumption unit, seeks the maximization of its utility, a more broadly defined goal. Thus households and firms are different in their goals.)

Firms are even more varied than households, as we will see in the appendix to this chapter. They include everything from a single individual, such as a doctor who provides services to his patients, to huge corporations with many plants, many employees, and many products. The similarity among them, however, is that each acquires resources and combines them to produce an output which can be used to obtain revenue. Economic goods may be either commodities or services, and production occurs in any process which results in goods or services which can be sold. A grocery store is productive; it combines equipment, labor, and various foods (usually bought in large quantities) to provide retail food service. Here, the productive activity consists of providing food in a convenient place and in convenient quantities. The terms *firm, input,* and *output* apply to all economic activity in our society.

The basic decision of any existing firm is how much to produce — that is, what will be its scale of output. It is therefore useful for us to relate costs and revenues to output. If we knew the costs of selling every conceivable output and the revenue to be gained from selling each one, it would be a simple matter to determine the best scale. We would simply subtract cost from revenue to find the profit at each level, and then choose that output at which the profit was highest. The procedures which we will be using are simply variants on this basic principle.

The measurement of cost is a somewhat complicated problem, especially because economists often want to use a different definition from the ones commonly used by the firm itself. The simplest definition of cost is that it includes all money paid or payable in order to carry out a particular operation. This is the usual accounting definition. There are problems in measuring such cost, especially where a single payment must be divided to obtain the costs of different items of production. If a machine can run for twenty years, how much of its value should be treated as a cost in each particular year? Various answers have been given to this and other questions, but they need not concern us here.

This definition of cost is too simple for our purposes. Every economic action involves a choice between alternatives. The true cost of any action is what one has given up for it, which is not always the same as the cash expenditure. We therefore say that the proper measure of cost is *opportunity cost,* the value of the alternative that has been forgone to produce a certain output. In many cases, this may be the same as the market price, for all that one has given up to use a ton of coal is the price of that coal. As long as goods are bought in the market and readily available, this will be the case. In fact, the market price does reflect the *social* opportunity cost, for each buyer must outbid others to force them to pass up the opportunity of using the inputs.

For inputs which are not purchased currently in the market, price is no longer a satisfactory measure of cost. Among these nonmarket inputs are machinery and equipment which the firm has had for some time. Clearly, the price which the company paid for this machinery some years ago is not a good indication of what could be done with it now, especially if similar inputs are now more expensive. Opportunity cost is higher than original cost. This problem occurs especially in measuring depreciation charges and inventory changes, for these are the cases where the intervals between purchase and use are the longest. A second important difference between cash cost and opportunity cost occurs with those inputs which are provided by the owner. The man who works in his own firm does not incur a cash expense, but there is certainly an opportunity cost; he might otherwise be working for a salary. In the same way, any of his own money which he has devoted to the business might have been loaned out at interest. We call these nonmarket costs *implicit costs* and the market costs *explicit costs*. In order to understand decision-making in the firm, it is necessary to include both implicit and explicit costs. For this reason, cost as measured by the economist will usually be higher than cost as measured by the accountant, for the accountant typically measures only explicit costs.

Since our primary concern is the cost-output relationship, it is also useful to distinguish between those costs which change with output and those which do not. We call the ones that change *variable costs*, and the ones that do not *fixed costs*. Remember that this designation refers only to the variability with respect to output, not to the possibility of changes over time. In general, wages and raw materials are variable costs, whereas overhead items are fixed costs. A convenient rule is that fixed costs are those which would continue even if output were zero, and variable costs are everything else.

Figure 5.1 shows a typical cost curve. This curve starts at a level above zero, representing the fixed cost. It rises rather steeply at first, then less so, and then more steeply again. In the next chapter, we will see that this shape reflects certain common production relationships; but for now we will merely accept it.

The Best Output

So far, we have discussed only the question of cost. It is clear, however, that a firm can choose its best output only

Figure 5.1
Total Cost Curve

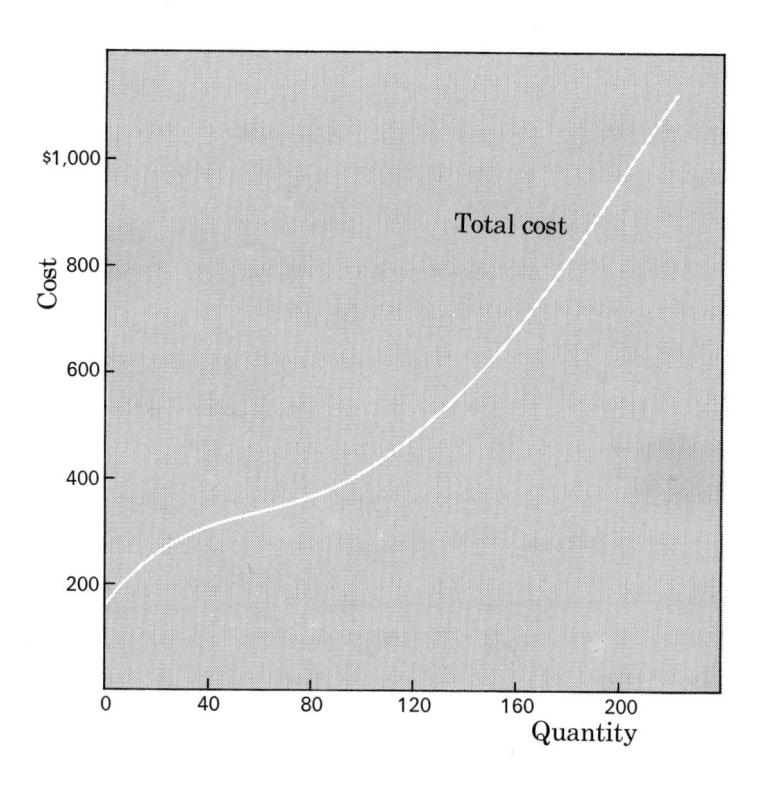

by comparing its costs with its revenues. Since we have assumed that the price is outside the control of the firm, its total revenue curve will be a straight line, representing the output times the price.

In Figure 5.2, we have combined the total revenue curve—at an assumed price of $5.00 per unit—with the total cost curve of Figure 5.1. A total profit curve has been calculated by subtracting cost from revenue at each output. It can be seen that the maximum profit point is at an output of 140 units per month, where the firm would make a profit of $130. We could also have found this point of maximum profit by looking for the place where the distance between total cost and total revenue is greatest, without actually calculating total profit.

In Figure 5.2, the firm made a profit. However, if the price had been lower, the total revenue curve might have been flatter and the best profit might still have been a loss. Would it still have been worthwhile for the firm to operate? The answer is a qualified yes. It would pay to operate at a loss, at least temporarily, if the loss is less than that which would result from not operating. Since the firm would lose its entire fixed cost by shutting down, it will operate at any smaller loss; that is, if

$$\text{Total Cost} - \text{Total Revenue} \leq \text{Fixed Cost} \quad (5.1)$$

Since total cost is the sum of fixed and variable cost, Inequality 5.1 can be rewritten:

$$\text{Fixed Cost} + \text{Variable Cost} - \text{Total Revenue} \leq \text{Fixed Cost} \quad (5.2)$$

$$\text{Variable Cost} - \text{Total Revenue} \leq 0 \quad (5.3)$$

$$\text{Variable Cost} \leq \text{Total Revenue} \quad (5.4)$$

In other words, as long as revenues cover the cost of operating, whether or not they cover the fixed cost, it pays to operate. Only if the revenues are less than the variable costs should the firm shut down. (This conclusion applies only in the short run. We will discuss the long run later.)

**Figure 5.2
Best Output**

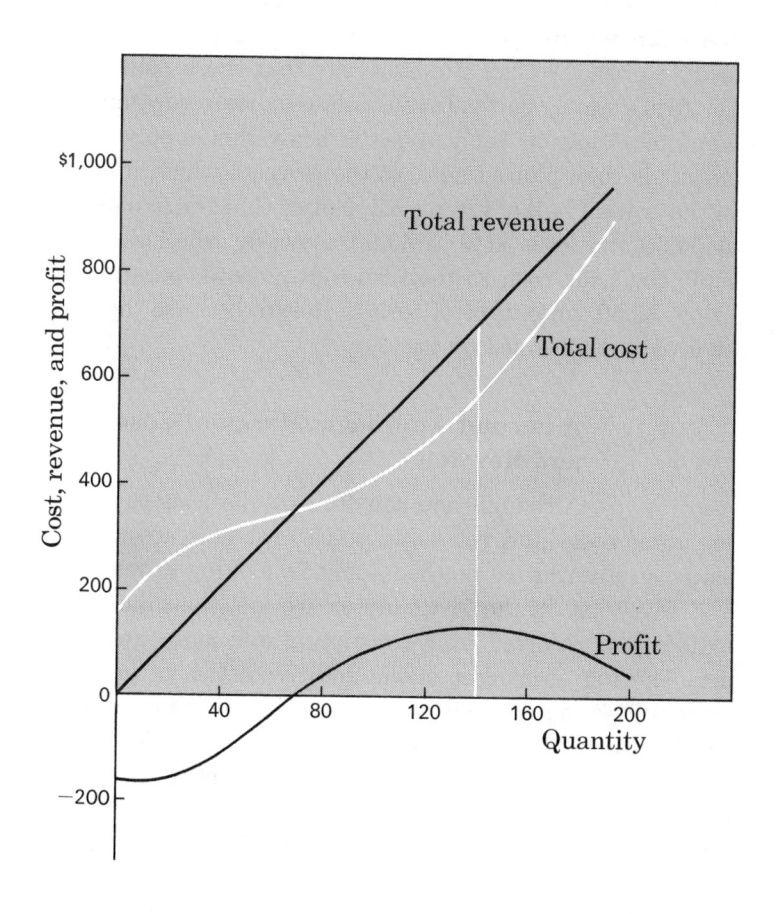

One can use the techniques of Figure 5.2 to derive the supply curve of the firm. For each possible price, a different revenue curve is drawn and a different best output is determined. This process is shown in Figure 5.3. Each of these outputs indicates the point where the firm would make the most profit at a particular price. We can therefore say that these points constitute the firm's supply curve, because they indicate how much it would want to supply at each price. To draw this supply curve, each output is then plotted against the price to which it corresponds in the bottom half of Figure 5.3. Notice that the firm breaks even at $4.00 and loses $110 at $3.00. However, the loss is less than $160, the fixed cost, so the firm continues to operate. For prices below $2.50, an output of zero is shown, because the loss would be greater than fixed cost.

A Second Approach: Marginal Cost and Revenue

Although one can find the best output by comparing total costs and revenues, some problems are simplified by using an alternative method—that is, looking at marginal costs and revenues. In the last chapter, we met marginal utility, the satisfaction received from consuming one more unit of a product. The marginal cost is the additional cost of producing one more unit, and marginal revenue is the additional revenue which would be received from selling one more unit. In the present case, where the price is set in the market and is independent of the action of the seller, the marginal revenue is equal to the price; if the firm sells one more unit, it will increase its receipts by the price of that unit.

Marginal cost is not quite so simple, but we can calculate it by subtracting the cost of producing n units from the cost of producing $n + 1$. The difference is, then, the marginal cost of producing the last unit, the $n + 1$st. If the data on total cost were given in wider intervals, say every twenty units of output, we would take the difference between successive points and divide by the number of units in the interval, in this case by twenty. An example is shown in Table 5.1. For example, between 100 units of

**Figure 5.3
Derivation of Supply Curve**

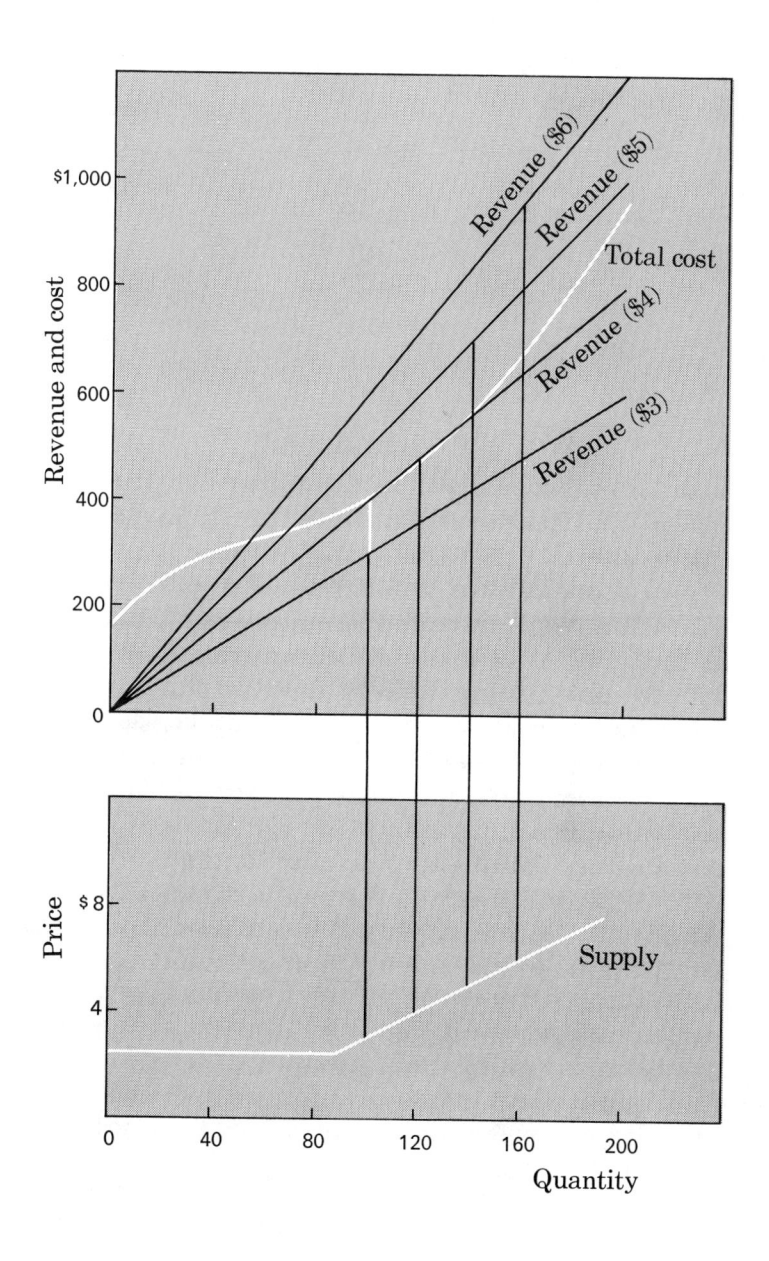

Firms and Supply

117

Table 5.1
Output and Costs

Monthly output	Total cost	Marginal cost
0	$160	
20	260	$5.00
40	310	2.50
60	330	1.00
80	360	1.50
100	410	2.50
120	480	3.50
140	570	4.50
160	680	5.50
180	810	6.50
200	960	7.50

output and 120 units, total cost rises from $410 to $480, or $70. Dividing this amount by 20, we find the marginal cost for these units is $3.50 per unit.

One can calculate the best output quite directly. As long as the marginal revenue (price) is above the marginal cost, it pays to produce those units; if price is below marginal cost, it does not. This conclusion follows directly from the firm's goal of profit maximization: it can increase its profit as long as its revenues from extra output exceed its costs for producing that output. If the price were $5.00, it would pay to produce 140 units. Notice that the marginal cost for the last 20 units is $4.50, less than the price, but that the marginal cost for the next 20 would be $5.50. This same procedure is shown in Figure 5.4. (The marginal costs for each interval have been plotted in the middle of each interval, in order to draw a smooth curve.)

The supply curve can be calculated directly from the marginal cost curve, as shown in Figure 5.5. For each price a horizontal line is drawn. Where that line crosses the marginal cost curve is the output which the firm will choose. Thus the marginal cost curve is the supply curve, as can be seen by comparing Figure 5.5 with 5.3.

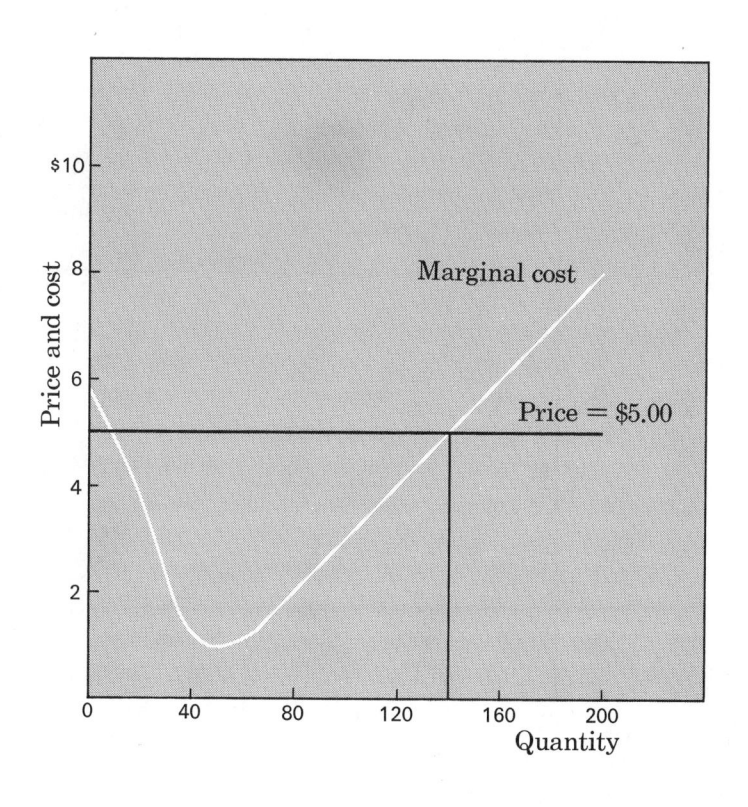

**Figure 5.4
Marginal Cost and Best Output**

**Figure 5.5
Marginal Cost and Supply**

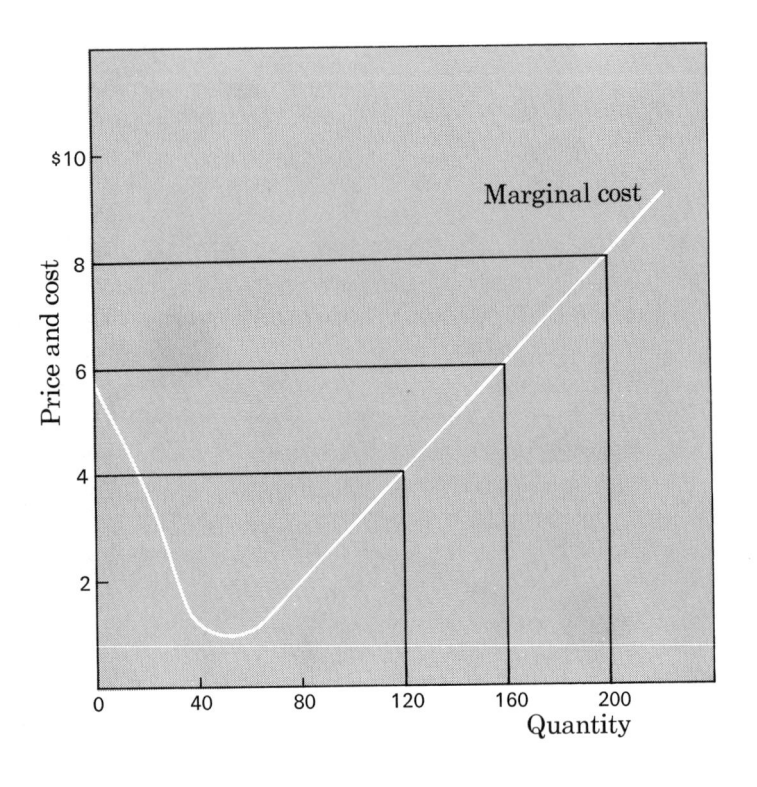

A Third Approach: Average Cost and Revenue

When examining the question of whether the firm will operate or shut down, a third approach is preferred. This approach involves the use of *average cost*, which is obtained by dividing the total cost by the output. One can also obtain the *average variable cost* by dividing variable cost by output. These curves are shown in Figure 5.6. (We could also calculate average fixed cost by dividing the fixed cost by output. In Figure 5.6, we can see the amount of the average fixed cost as the difference between average cost and average variable cost.)

We have already seen that the firm will shut down if variable cost is greater than total revenue at every output. If both these are then divided by the output, it develops that the average variable cost is greater than the price. Since the lowest possible average variable cost is $2.50, the firm will produce only if the price is above that level. Accordingly, it is often convenient to include the marginal cost curve on the same graph with the average curves, and then to say that the supply curve is that portion of the marginal cost curve which is above the average variable cost curve. This has been done in Figure 5.7. The supply curve is the specially shaded portion of the marginal cost curve.

An interesting relationship between the marginal cost curve and the average curves is also shown in Figure 5.7: the marginal cost curve always crosses the average curves at their lowest point. If the marginal cost (the extra cost of one more unit) is below the average cost, then the average cost must decline. (If the average height of three people in a room is 6 feet and a fourth person enters who is only 5 feet, the average height will fall to 5 feet, 9 inches.) Similarly, if marginal cost is above average cost, average cost must rise. Therefore, the marginal cost curve must cross the average cost curve at the lowest point, and be below it on the left and above it on the right. This is true of both average cost and average variable cost.

In the long run, it is the average cost which is most important. If the price is below the average cost, it will not pay the firm to remain in business. When the time comes to renew its fixed commitments, either by purchasing new machines or replacing old contracts, it will do so only if the price covers average costs. Similarly, if the price is higher than average costs, new

**Figure 5.6
Average Cost Curves**

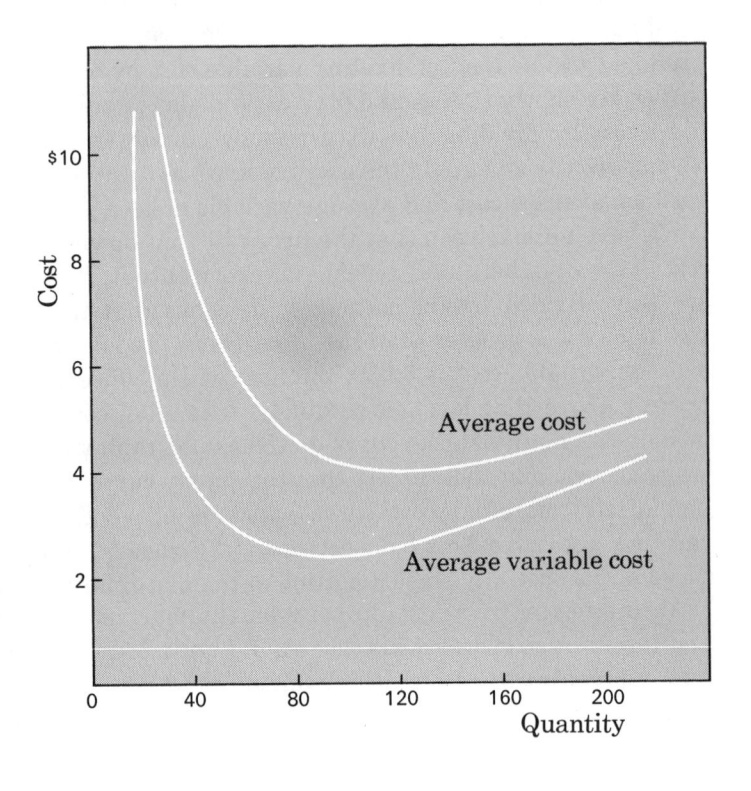

Figure 5.7
Marginal and Average Costs

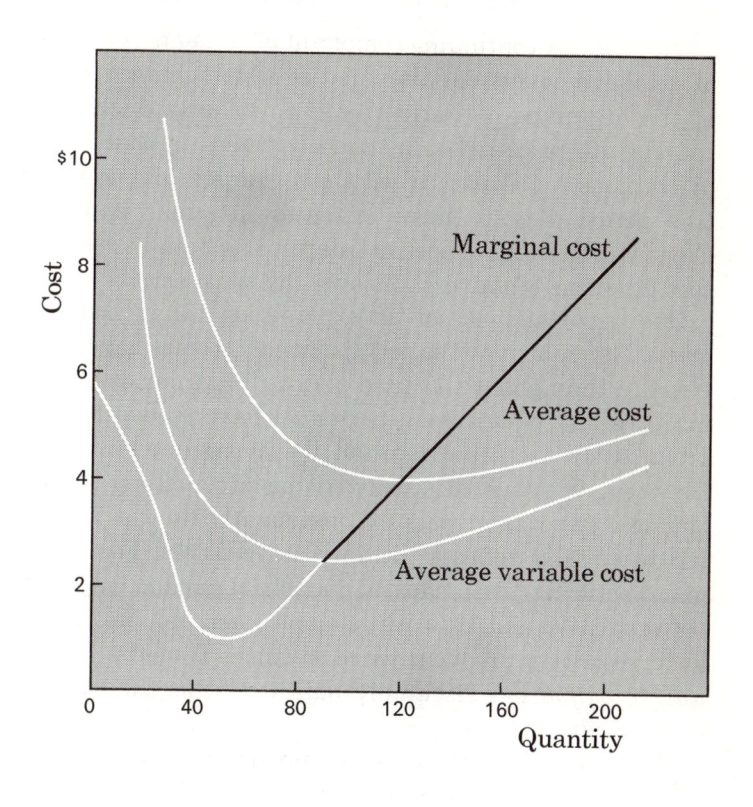

firms will enter the industry. We will return to this long-run problem in Chapter 7.

An Illustration: The Cost of Education

A continuing complaint of students is the rising cost of a college education. Universities which charged $400 a year at the beginning of World War II now charge $3,000, although the general price index has merely tripled in that time. Public institutions have also raised their charges comparably during this period, despite huge increases in public appropriations. Clearly something of special interest has been happening to the cost functions of universities over this time period.

One important part of the explanation lies in the role of salaries. Throughout our society, personal incomes have been rising steadily throughout the time period. The salaries of university faculties and nonteaching personnel have tended to rise at approximately the same rate, on the average, as other incomes. However, in much of society, rising productivity has counterbalanced the rise in wages. Consequently the rise in wages has not been fully reflected in increasing prices. For example: in manufacturing, the index of industrial production quadrupled between 1940 and 1970 while employment doubled, so that the average worker produced twice as much. Thus the wage cost *per unit of output* has risen only half as fast as the wage cost *per hour of input*.

The application of similar economies in education has been severely limited. If one were to use the student credit hour as the measure of output, it would be possible to increase productivity by increasing class size, giving lectures to larger and larger groups. However, this possibility is somewhat limited. Duplicate sections of introductory courses which are taken by many students can be combined into big lectures; but advanced courses have so few students that they are not duplicated, so no combination is possible. Furthermore, neither students nor teachers will agree that large classes are the equivalent of small ones, so that student credit hours are not a good measure of output. (Interestingly, most careful studies of class size show that students learn about the same in large classes, as measured by test scores, but develop much less enthusiasm for the subject.)

A second change has also contributed to rising costs in universities. Increasingly, more students in our society go on to graduate work. This has increased costs for two reasons: graduate class sizes are smaller and faculty qualifications are higher, so that salaries are higher. (Undergraduates may feel that it is unfair that they should have to pay the costs associated with graduate education, but they do receive some benefit from having better instructors.)

One problem which is unsettled is the question of the optimum size of an educational institution. In the next chapter, we will meet the concept of economies of scale—the tendency in many industries for costs to fall as firms get larger, at least to a certain point. In part, this tendency also applies to educational institutions, especially because larger classes may be possible. However, in universities the advantage of scale is apt to appear in diversity rather than lower cost. Instead of having all students take the same advanced courses, each department is apt to offer a wider variety, making better use of the specialties of the faculty and offering wider opportunities to the students.

Size is not an unmixed blessing. Larger institutions become more bureaucratized, so that students often feel they are mere numbers on a computer print-out. Personal rapport declines among students, between students and faculty, and among faculty members.

One attempt to compromise these tendencies has been for small colleges to become increasingly specialized. One college might, for example, aim principally at the education of elementary teachers, offering a selection of courses in that area which is comparable to a good-sized university, but only a limited group of courses in other areas—just enough to provide a rounded education. The principal problem with such a system is that a student who changes his major must often change colleges. A variant on this system utilizes the cooperation between several small colleges in an area to permit students to trade courses, thereby combining the diversity normally attained with size and the intimacy of the smaller institution. How well these arrangements can be made to work will be the subject of continued experiment and study.

Appendix to Chapter 5
The Nature of Firms

There are over 2½ million nonagricultural firms in the United States, and 3 million farms. These firms constitute the basic production units in the American economy. They are all alike in that they combine resources to produce products or services which can be sold; in most other respects, they show a great diversity. Some of them produce only a single product; others produce thousands. Some are very small, using only the labor of the owner and having no employees; others employ nearly half a million. Some have annual sales of a few thousand dollars; others range up to 20 billion. Some are owned by one man; others may have as many as 3 million stockholders.

In dealing with business in the American economy, it is customary to classify firms and their products according to their similarities. Depending upon the fineness of the classification, these categories may be as broad as "all manufacturing" or as narrow as a single product. Products can be grouped more finely than firms, because many firms produce different products which may be considerably different in classification. (For example, United States

Steel is one of the country's largest producers of cement.) Official statistics usually attempt to give as much detail as possible, so that particular users may make whatever groupings are best for their purposes.

In many aspects of economics, the concept of an industry, in which all firms sell the same product, is very important. For example, Part II of this book looks at different kinds of markets, depending upon the number of firms selling a product. In practice, the actual definition of an industry is quite difficult. In modern America, we seldom buy products merely by general category; we buy particular brands and models. In most cases, there is an entire spectrum to choose from. We speak of an automobile industry, but there is very little competition between a Volkswagen and a Continental. There are also important geographic differences; we are not apt to buy automobiles from dealers who are not near us. In each individual case, we must examine the particular circumstance to determine the appropriate market. The best criterion to use is the cross elasticity of demand, defined in Chapter 4 as the percentage change in quantity of one product sold compared to the percentage change in another price. Where the cross elasticities are high, the products can be said to be in the same market. Nevertheless, there are substantial practical difficulties: How can we measure cross elasticity? How high is high? Most of the testimony and argument in antitrust cases is devoted to defining markets in order to determine whether competition is affected by particular actions.

Within a given industry, there are more similarities between firms than in the economy at large, but there are still substantial differences. In most cases, giant firms exist side by side with very small, specialized ones. Usually the larger firms produce comparatively standardized products for mass markets, while the smaller ones concentrate on specialized products for particular markets. Because they serve different needs, large and small firms are often no threat to each other. This is simply an example of the fact that the statistical classification of an industry is not the same as the economic classification of markets; the cross elasticity may be very low.

Legal Organization

Three main forms of legal organization of a firm are possible: proprietorship, partnership, and corporation. Each of these has its advantages and disadvantages.

The simplest firm is the proprietorship. In this case, there is a single owner and, as far as the law is concerned, no distinction is made between the firm and its owner. No legal arrangements are required to start such a firm, and the owner is responsible to no one but himself. He merely announces to potential customers that he is in business. This freedom and independence provides the strength of the proprietorship, but also its weakness. The firm is limited to the capital which the owner can provide, or which he can personally borrow. If the business should fail, the creditors can take not only the business property but also the owner's personal property, such as his house or car. If it succeeds, all its gains are taxed at the personal rate, even if they are reinvested. As we might expect, most new businesses are formed as proprietorships, but most proprietorships are quite small. Growth usually requires the firm to go beyond the limits of the single owner.

The simplest way to expand is by a partnership, in which one or more other people join the firm. Often the new partners will share equally in putting up capital, in the work of the firm, and in its profits; but they might also arrange a different division of responsibility and benefits. No legal arrangements are required to form a partnership, but the partners usually wish to draw up a contract to spell out their relationship. The principal advantage of the partnership over the proprietorship is that it can command more resources; it can draw upon the talents and capital of all its partners. However, the partnership is a more fragile arrangement; all major actions are apt to require the agreement of all the partners, and the partnership can be dissolved by any of them at any time. The death of one partner automatically breaks the partnership, and the surviving partners might not wish to continue with their late partner's wife as a new partner.

The worst feature of the partnership is that it has the same liability provisions as the proprietorship; if the business fails, each of the partners stands to lose his personal assets. If the partners have enough funds, each of them pays the debts of the partnership in proportion to his share in the business. However, if only one partner has any assets, he must pay all the debts and may then try to recover from his partners. Thus the risk of loss is much greater in a partnership. (At one time, all brokerage firms were required to be partnerships. This fact advertised to prospective clients that they were protected not only by the reputation of the firm but by the personal fortunes of the partners as well. Although this requirement no longer exists, many brokerage firms retain the partnership form as a symbol of integrity.)

The corporation is a device to permit firms to grow beyond the proprietorship without the disadvantages of the partnership. The corporation is legally chartered by the state, and is a legal person apart from its owners. The owners of the corporation own differing numbers of shares of stock, each share indicating an equal proportionate ownership. All the affairs of the corporation are managed by its officers, who need not be stockholders. The only right of the shareholders over the management is the right to vote for members of the board of directors, who have the right to hire and fire the officers.

If a corporation fails, the most that the shareholders can lose is the amount which they have already invested in the firm. Their liability is limited to that amount. (British corporations are designated by the abbreviation "Ltd.," meaning limited, but the American "Inc." has the same implication.) With limited liability, it is easier to persuade potential investors to make investments in the firm, for they have no fear of losing all their possessions if it fails.

Because stock ownership does not involve management, shares of stock are freely transferable, and may be bought or sold without approval of other owners. (In contrast, a share in a partnership may only be sold if the remaining members are willing to accept the new partner.) The only requirement is notification of a secretary or agent so that dividends and official notices can be sent to the new owner.

Many corporations are quite small, and their stock, although legally transferable, is held by only a few people. As corporations get larger, it is desirable that arrangements be made to sell stocks to a wider group of potential buyers. Accordingly, stock exchanges, which are basically cooperative arrangements among brokers, are established to facilitate these sales. These exchanges, and any stocks listed on them, are regulated by a government agency — the Securities Exchange Commission. The commission's regulations mainly describe the information which firms must make available, so that potential investors know what they are buying.

These disclosure rules do not apply to unlisted companies, whose shares are not bought and sold through regular dealers. Most of these unlisted companies are small, but a few are quite large. (Perhaps the most famous of the unlisted companies is Hughes Tool Corporation, probably owned mostly by Howard Hughes. Because it is unlisted, no detailed information about it is available.)

It would seem that the corporation is a good setup, but it does have some disadvantages. Special taxes are levied on corporate earnings, in addition to the personal taxes paid by the stockholders on the dividends they receive. These taxes are a severe drawback to incorporating small firms if alternative arrangements can be made. The importance of the corporate firm in America is an indication of the great benefit which limited liability confers, in view of the substantial tax cost of incorporation.

Size of Firms

We have already mentioned that firms come in a wide variety of sizes, with sales ranging from a few thousand dollars a year to 20 billion. We should not be misled, however, into believing that firms are evenly distributed through this entire range. Most firms are comparatively small, and a relatively small number of them are very large. For example, the top two hundred firms in manufacturing account for half the total production, although they comprise only a tiny fraction of 1 percent of the existing manufacturing firms. The same phenomenon is observable in banking, insurance, and to some extent in retail trade. It is only in the service industries that business is not dominated by these large firms. We saw in the Appendix to Chapter 4 that there is a significant inequality in the distribution of income; the distribution of business among firms is far more unequal. When we remember that most of the largest firms are corporations, and that only about 15 percent of Americans own any stock, we begin to understand one reason for the unequal distribution of income.

We will look further at the largest firms in the Appendix to Chapter 9.

Chapter 6
Resources and Costs

The campus environmental action committee at Megalopolis University has held several meetings recently about "The Throw-Away Society." Although much of the publicity has been given to bottles and cans, the group itself is much more concerned with the problems of appliance repair. Even when a service man can be persuaded to come, all he seems to be able to do is remove and throw away an old part and put in a new one. The committee complains that this drives up costs and wastes materials. "Why should a washing machine have a new timer when it merely needed one wire resoldered in the old timer?"

The Committee arranged for an official of General House, an appliance manufacturer, to speak on this subject. Instead of being defensive, as expected, he proceeded to attack the group. "You people are so intent on not wasting materials that you don't seem to care about wasting human beings. Why must your love for the earth be accompanied by contempt for its inhabitants?"

He explained that replacement parts are made by an assembly line process, with individual components assembled into final units by specialized workers who are not highly skilled but are trained to perform their particular function efficiently and swiftly. If service men actually made repairs, they would have to be skilled general-purpose men with a substantial knowledge of mechanical and electrical engineering. It would be necessary for them to be able to identify the proper shape and function of every minor part in the mechanism in order to be able to repair it efficiently. It would be necessary to pay these men high wages, in accordance with the level of competence which they would have. In contrast, present service men are much less highly skilled. Their qualifications consist primarily of an ability to recognize what portion of the mechanism is responsible for the particular trouble. They can then replace that part by making a few connections.

"You may consider this system wasteful, but such a designation is myopic. We are saving the enormous amount of labor which would be required by a full replacement system, where skilled workers would search for and repair appliances on the spot. Our own tests indicate that repairs would cost fifty percent more, indicating a loss of other desirable goods and services."

Members of the committee were not quite convinced, but they were too taken aback to challenge the speaker.

The campaign against disposable containers has run into similar problems; the attempt to save on materials has begun to use up enormous amounts of manpower and other materials. At the current prices of containers, it is cheaper to give bottles (or cans) to the consumer and let him dispose of them. Returnable bottles require elaborate procedures for handling at the retail, wholesale, and manufacturing levels. When labor was cheaper and bottles were expensive, this handling was worthwhile; now the no deposit, no return system is cheaper. It is significant that only national brands of soft drinks, which sell at higher prices, have been willing to go back to returnables. The smaller companies which produce private label brands for supermarkets have been unwilling to do so.

One alternative is to collect bottles and cans for recycling. This too requires large amounts of labor, mostly volunteer. It also raises other problems. One undergraduate, a mathematics major, has been doing some calculations about the recycling project.

In view of the limited number of collection stations available, he has decided that all of the driving required to turn in bottles for recycling is adding significantly to the air pollution problem.

One Variable Input

In Chapter 5, we assumed that cost of production is simply a known fact. Actually, this view is highly simplified, for cost is partly the result of the firm's own actions. There are usually many different ways to produce any given output by using varying amounts and types of machinery, labor, and materials. For each of these methods there is a cost, and the firm must choose the lowest one. The cost curves we have been examining represent only the lowest of a wide range of possible costs for each output. Underlying these cost calculations are two facts that are largely beyond the control of the firm: the technological production relationships and the conditions of supply of inputs. Let us look at these production relationships.

As a firm changes its output, it will normally change the quantity of some factors which it uses, but not others. We call those which are changed *variable factors of production*. Those which are not changed are called *fixed factors*. (Remember that in Chapter 5 we used the same distinction for fixed and variable costs, depending upon their relation to output.) Suppose that a farm of 100 acres with one man working on it produces 5,000 bushels of output a year. If these are the only factors of production, one would naturally expect 10,000 bushels from a similar farm of 200 acres worked by two men, 15,000 bushels from a 300-acre farm worked by three men, and so on. Naturally one would not expect such proportionate increases if only one factor, say labor, were increased. We would therefore not be surprised if the 100-acre farm produced only 7,000 bushels with two men, or 8,000 bushels with three.

In economics, this relationship is commonly called *the law of diminishing returns*. This law states that as more of a variable factor is applied to a fixed factor, the output increases less than proportionately. In some cases, it was found that the law of diminishing returns did not hold exactly, especially for small outputs.

In some circumstances, an increase in variable factors increases the output more than proportionately. This unexpected result occurs because the fixed factor may be excessively large. Imagine the results if one man were trying to farm several thousand acres. He might actually increase his output by concentrating on less of the acreage. In agriculture he would do so. But in some forms of manufacturing, certain fixed factors are not divisible; one must use all of them, even if they are too big for the labor force. (Imagine trying to produce modest amounts of steel with a blast furnace or a few automobiles on an assembly line.) Because of these observations that there might be an initial period of increasing returns, the rule becomes a *law of eventually diminishing returns*.

The cost curves of Chapter 5 reflect this law of diminishing returns. This law explains why variable cost rises more and more sharply with increasing output. If production is subject to diminishing returns, the graph of output against input will rise steeply at first, then flatten out as diminishing returns become more important. Such a curve is shown in Figure 6.1. Since there is only one variable factor of production, all the elements of variable cost are implied in this graph. We can change this purely technical relationship into a variable cost curve by multiplying the input by its price.

In this example, we have assumed that labor costs $2.50 per hour, so the top scale of Figure 6.1 represents the variable cost of producing each output. For example, it takes 128 labor hours to produce 120 units of output per month. At $2.50, this labor will cost $320. The variable cost of producing 120 units is therefore $320.

Because we are mainly interested in the total cost rather than just the variable cost, we add the fixed cost to the variable cost. If we assume that the fixed cost is $160 per month, the total cost of production of 120 units is $480 — $160 of fixed cost and $320 of variable cost. This addition is shown in Figure 6.2. We have reversed the axes, putting cost on the vertical scale and output on the horizontal scale, because this is the customary usage among economists. This total cost curve is the same as the one shown in Figure 5.1.

**Figure 6.1
Production Function**

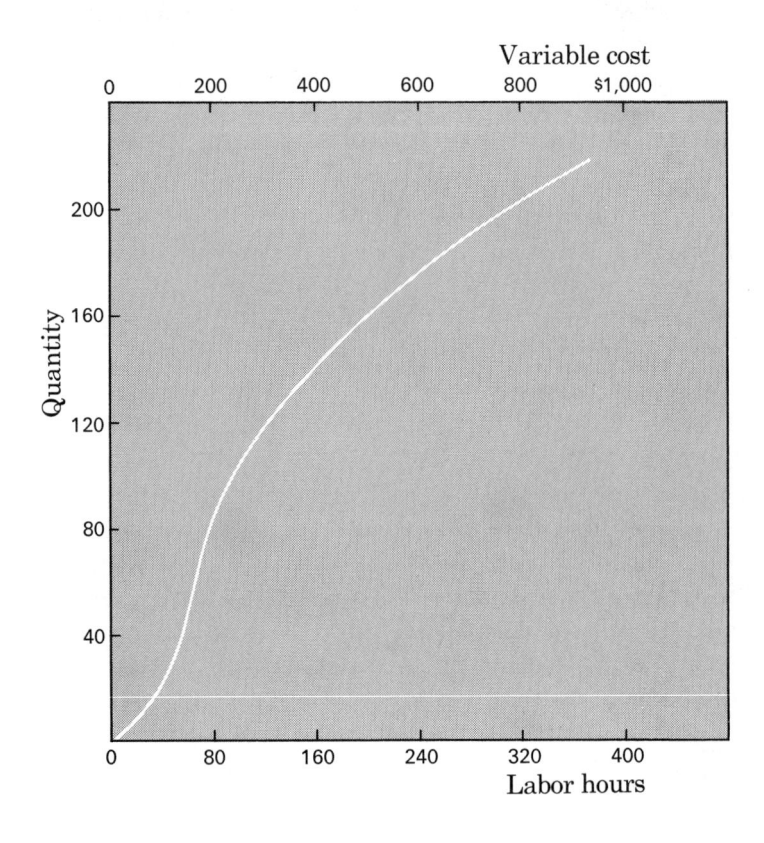

**Figure 6.2
Total Cost Curve**

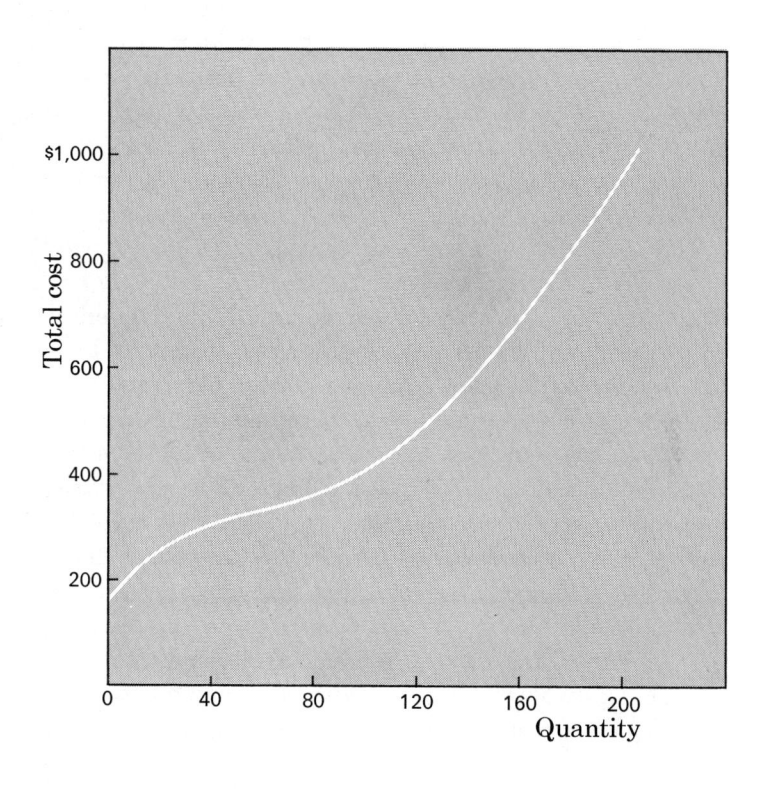

Two Variable Factors

This explanation of cost is sufficient if there is only one variable input, which may be the case with short-run decisions in many firms. In most small retail operations, even labor may be a fixed factor; the size of the inventory may be the only variable factor. For most firms, however, both labor and material are variable, so we must use a more complex form of analysis. If we allow a comparatively long period for adjustment, no firm fits the simple, one-variable model; with enough time, any firm will be apt to vary the size of its plant, machinery, and labor force.

The possibility of altering fixed factors is the criterion economists use to distinguish between *short run* and *long run*. In the short run, the firm may adjust its scale of production, but only within the confines of its present plant structure. In the long run, firms may buy new equipment or sell old; new firms may be started, and old ones may leave the industry. There are no fixed factors in the long run, and adjustments of all kinds may take place. You will remember that in Chapter 2 we observed that the long-run supply curve may be very elastic, while the short-run supply curve is less elastic. (In Chapter 2, we also discussed an immediate supply curve, but that depends upon a quantity of goods already in existence and involves no production at all.)

In order to analyze the production decision and consequent cost structure when there is more than one variable input, we use a technique similar to that which we used for analyzing consumer behavior in Chapter 4. In Figure 6.3, we have represented the relationship between the two variable inputs—machine hours and labor hours—on the axes. The output is shown by various levels of output curves. Each of these curves is drawn through all combinations of the two inputs which can be used to produce a given output, such as 80 units. (The similarity of these curves to the indifference curves of Chapter 4 is obvious.) Since each of these curves represents a particular level of output, they are called *equal-product curves*, or *isoquants*.

If there were only these two factors of production, the isoquants might show complete proportionality. In that case, every point on the 160 curve would use exactly twice as much labor and machinery as the corresponding point on the 80 curve. A line

**Figure 6.3
Production Isoquants**

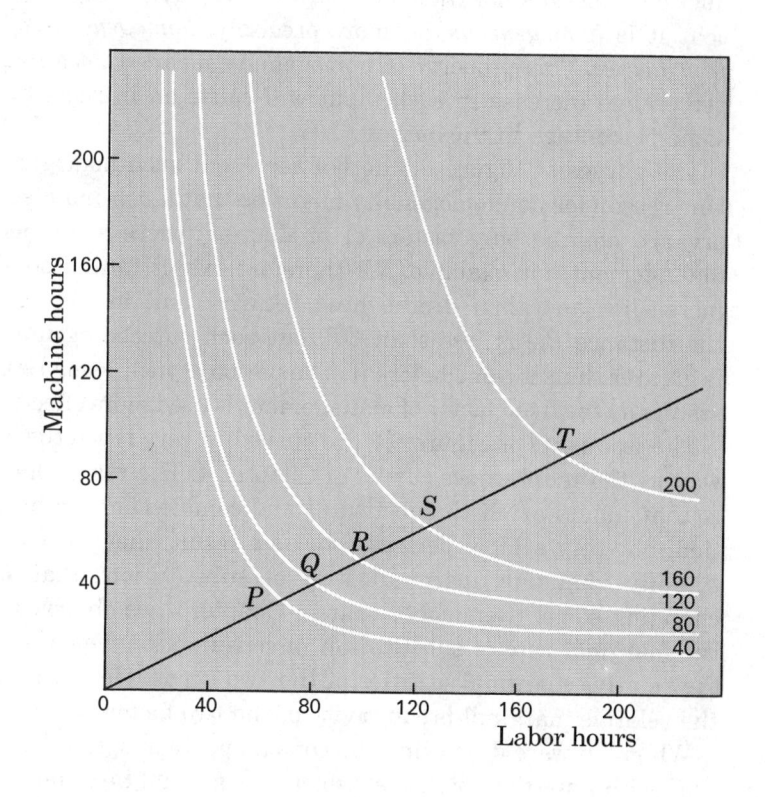

drawn from the origin outward would intersect successive isoquants at exactly equal distances. In Figure 6.3, the distances *OP, PQ, QR, RS* and *ST* would be exactly equal. When the production function has this property of proportionality, we say that it is *homogeneous,* or, more precisely, *homogeneous of the first degree.* This property of homogeneity means that an equal percentage increase in each input will cause an increase of the same percentage in the output.

The curves of Figure 6.3 do not represent such homogeneity. One reason for nonhomogeneity might be that labor and machinery are not the only factors of production; there are others—management, for example. We therefore expect to find possible increasing and then diminishing returns; and in Figure 6.3, the distance *PQ* is less than *OP,* but each succeeding interval is greater than the one before it. The period of increasing returns results as the fixed factor of management is used more effectively.

The isoquants of Figure 6.3 are curved in very much the same way as the indifference curves of Chapter 4. The reason for this is that inputs are both substitutes and complements in production, but very seldom perfectly so. As a result, they show a continually changing marginal rate of substitution—that is, a changing slope. (Remember that in Chapter 4 we observed that the marginal rate of substitution in consumption depends upon the relative marginal utilities of the two goods. Here it reflects the relative marginal productivity of the two factors.)

When we were discussing the consumer, we saw that he operated with a particular budget which was all that he could spend. The situation of firms is different. A firm would be willing to spend more or less for production, depending on the output which it could obtain. Consequently, we are not concerned with finding the best single combination of inputs as we were with the consumer; rather we are trying to find the lowest cost combination of inputs for producing at every different level of output. Nevertheless, there is a similarity between the decision process of the firm and of the household.

For the moment let us consider only a single output, say 80 units, and find the best possible way to produce it. In Figure 6.4, the single isoquant representing that output has been reproduced along with a set of *equal-cost lines,* each similar to the

**Figure 6.4
Production Costs**

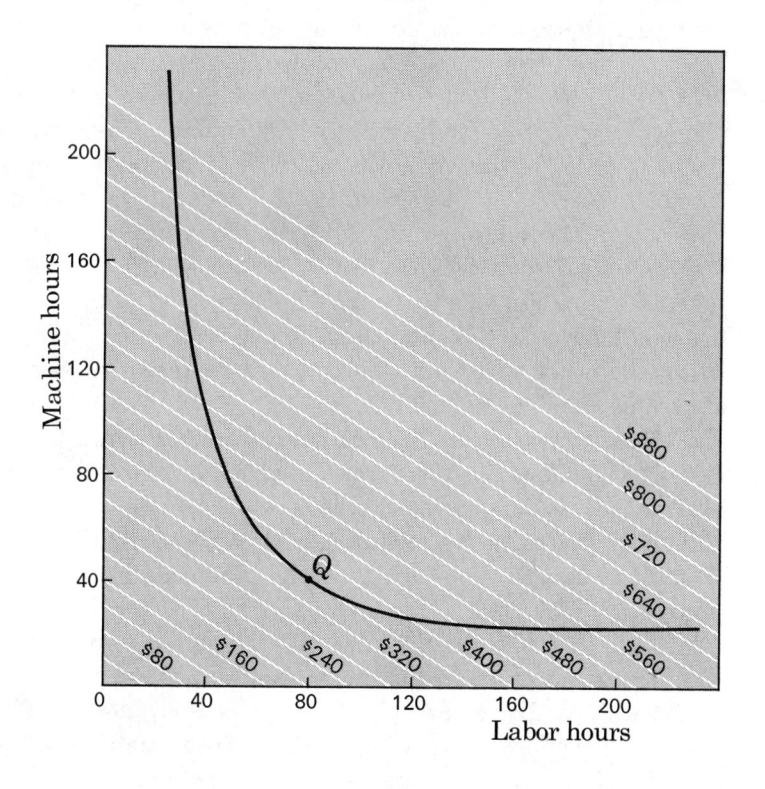

Resources and Costs

141

budget lines of Chapter 4. Each of these lines has been drawn on the assumption of fixed prices for each of the factors of production; in this case, they are $2.50 per hour for labor and $4.00 for machinery. Each of these straight lines represents all possible combinations of the two factors of production which can be hired for the given sum. For example, for the sum of $400 the firm could hire 160 hours of labor and no machinery, 100 hours of machinery and no labor, or any of the combinations in between them. In order to find the lowest cost for producing this output, we must search for that point along the isoquant which is on the lowest possible equal-cost line. Clearly, that point is at Q where the isoquant is just tangent to the $360 cost line. We see that the minimum cost of production is achieved at Q by using 80 hours of labor and 40 hours of machinery for a total cost of $360. All of the other points on this isoquant represent higher costs of perhaps $400, $440, or $480.

If the price ratios had been different, the best position would have been somewhere other than at Q, just as a consumer's equilibrium position changes in response to changing prices. The section on ecology at the beginning of this chapter gives examples of shifting combinations of labor and materials in response to changing wage costs.

In order to find an entire cost curve, it would be necessary to repeat this process for other outputs as well as the one we have just examined. The end result of this process is shown in Figure 6.5, where each isoquant of Figure 6.3 has been matched with the corresponding equal-cost line. In order to simplify the diagram, the intermediate equal-cost lines which do not correspond to optimum combinations for any of these isoquants have been omitted. The total cost curve which would result from this calculation is shown in Figure 6.6. This cost curve has been drawn by plotting each output against its corresponding cost.

In the process which we have just used, we have assumed that there are two variable factors of production, labor and machinery. In the calculations which led to the cost curve of Figure 6.2, we assumed that only labor was variable. Using the information we now have, we can see that the cost curve of Figure 6.2 is based upon a constant quantity of 40 hours of machinery at $4.00 an hour for a fixed cost of $160. We could reconstruct the cost curve

**Figure 6.5
Best Combinations**

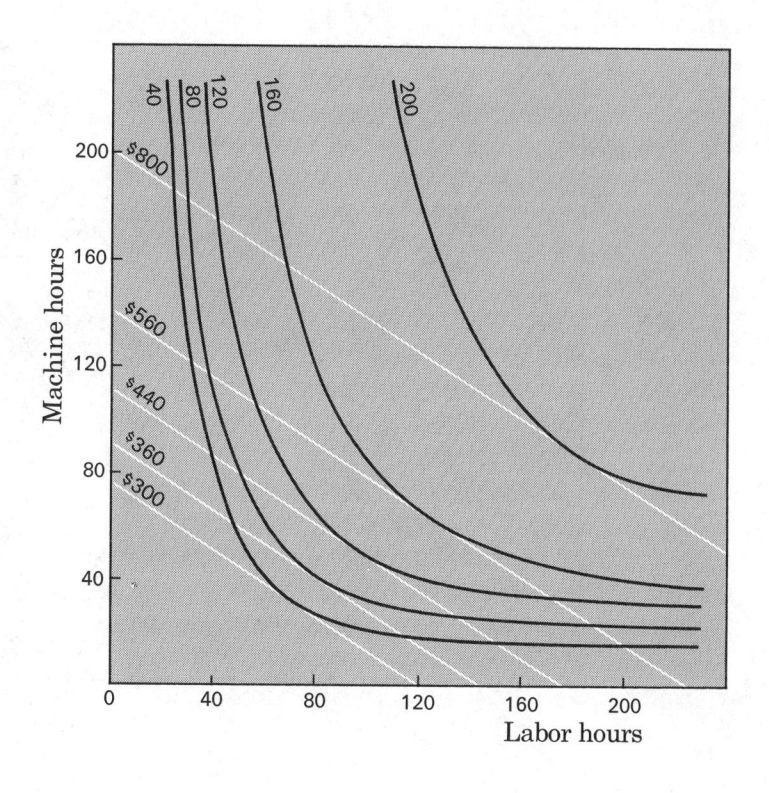

**Figure 6.6
Total Cost Curve (All Variable)**

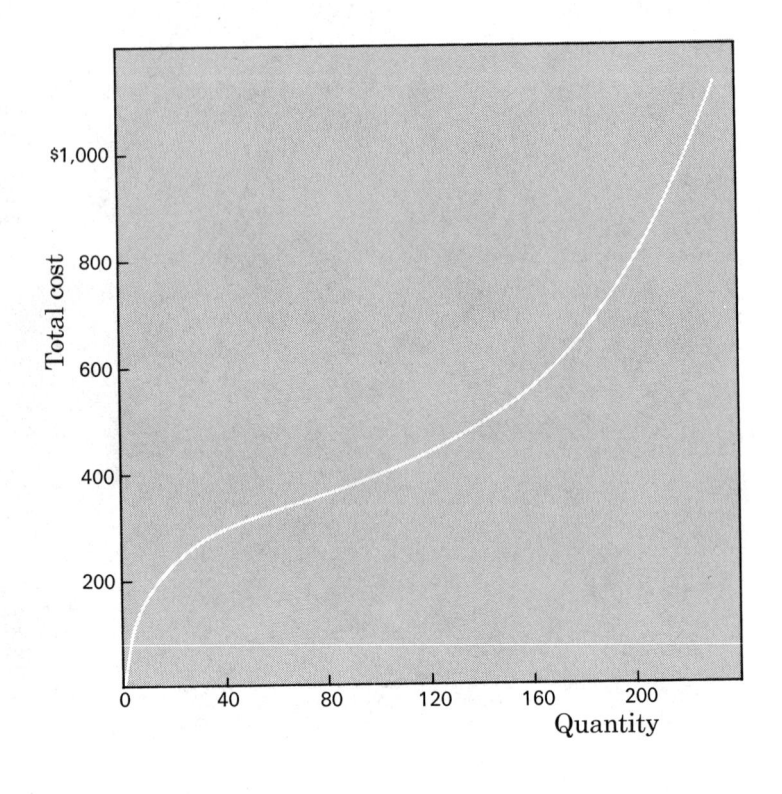

of Figure 6.2 from the isoquants of Figure 6.3 by observing the various quantities of labor which would be required to produce each output. We would draw a line across at a fixed level of 40 machine hours as in Figure 6.7, and observe where this line crossed each successive isoquant. We could then draw the cost lines through each of these points. It will be noticed that in Figure 6.7 the combination of goods used to produce each output except 80 is not the best point, as derived in Figure 6.5, but is instead some different and more expensive point. This is because the fixed level of machinery does not permit full adjustment in order to find the best point. We can now see that for all outputs less than 80, 40 hours of machinery is more than the optimum; and for outputs above that, 40 hours is less than the optimum. In other words, the plant is too large for small outputs and too small for large ones. In general, a firm will often discover that the plant which it has at any moment of time is not the ideal one for producing the output which it finds appropriate. In the long run, it would adjust its plant; but in the short run, it is often confined to adjustment of its labor force.

We can compare the long-run cost curve (which we have derived by means of the isoquants) with the short-run cost curve (which assumes fixed machinery) by putting the two together, as in Figure 6.8. In this case, we have used the total cost curve of Figure 6.6 along with three short-run cost curves; the one based upon 40 machinery hours, a larger one upon 50 machinery hours, and a still larger one upon 65 machinery hours. It can be seen that each of these short-run cost curves is identical with the long-run cost curve at one point, but is above it elsewhere. In other words, each level of capital equipment is optimal at only one output.

Economies and Diseconomies of Scale

If the production relationships represented by the isoquants were homogeneous, the long-run total cost curve would be a straight line. In the more usual case, however, this is not so; the long-run cost curve bends upward like the short-run curve, although it has a much flatter bend. The explanation for this is not found solely in the law of diminishing returns, which refers

Figure 6.7
Derivation of Short-run Cost

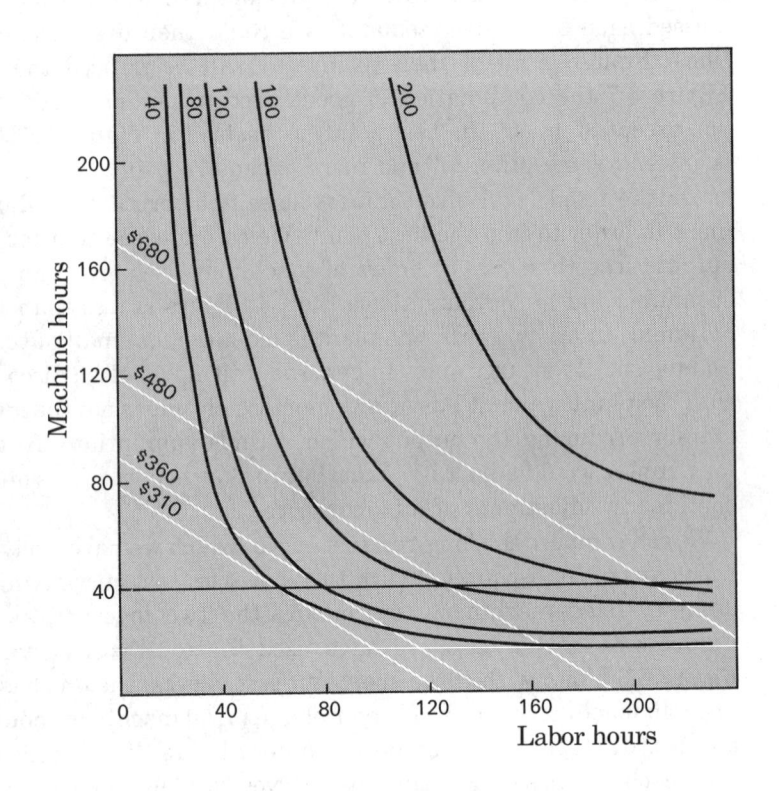

Figure 6.8
Short and Long-run Costs

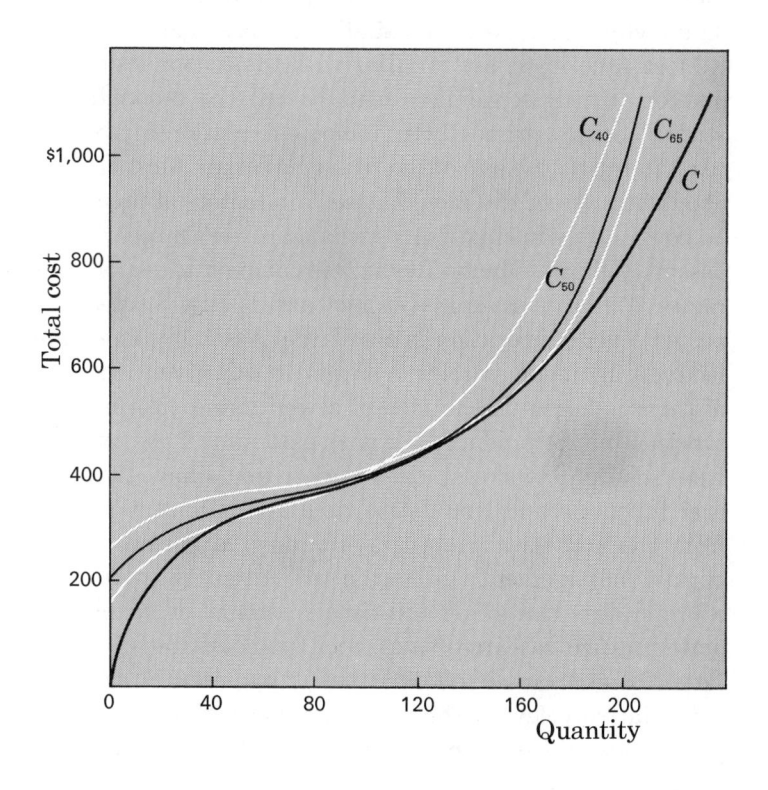

to applying extra variable factors to a fixed factor. In the long run, firms will feel free to change any factor, as old machines wear out and old contracts expire, and new machines can be provided and new contracts made. We must look elsewhere to understand why cost curves are usually of this shape.

Most Americans are familiar with the economies of mass production, which economists usually call the *economies of large scale*. These are primarily technological relationships which cause costs to fall as the size of the firm gets larger. Most of these come about because of the fact that certain factors of production may be bought only in single units which are very large. For example, assembly line production, which is common in many industries, requires a large scale investment and is only feasible if the expected level of operation is also large. Assembly lines cannot effectively be made smaller or larger in any given industry. Each of them is based on the idea of a workman performing a single function on the product as it goes past him. If the assembly line were smaller and slower, each worker would have to perform several functions and would lose time and efficiency as he shifted from one activity to another. Similarly, larger operations often permit management's full-scale utilization of specialists. Only a larger firm can afford full-time personnel departments or the optimum-size research, sales, and financial staffs. Often only a large firm can make efficient use of by-products, because there are relatively few of them and the most efficient scale for by-products would require a very large-scale operation of the main product.

Americans are so accustomed to speaking of the economies of mass production that they often forget that there are *diseconomies of scale* which force costs up as a firm becomes larger. One reason for economies of scale is that management is fixed and an optimum use of the manager can take place only if the scale of the firm is large; as the firm becomes still larger, however, it is often difficult to handle the managerial problems which result. Clearly, two plant managers are not twice as good as one in twice as big a plant; they may be worse if they issue conflicting orders. As operations become large and varied, the strain on the indivisible factor of management is often severe. It is significant that much of the study of business administration is devoted to methods of communication and decision-making that will make it possible for managers to supervise vast firms. The attempt to overcome the diseconomies of scale is responsible for operations research, the use of computing equipment to handle masses of data, and the elaborate study of the decentralization of decision-making.

We will want to give special attention to the problem of economies and diseconomies of scale when we examine the structure of certain partially competitive industries. In many of these, much of the discussion of economic reform focuses on the effect which any reorganization would have on the economies of scale. (See Chapter 9.)

An Illustration: Technological Change and Employment

Since the beginning of the Industrial Revolution, there have been many instances of opposition by workers to the introduction of new machinery, on the ground that their jobs were threatened. In the Luddite riots of the early nineteenth century, workers expressed their discontent with their conditions by destroying machinery. Our word *sabotage* dates to the late nineteenth century, when French workers threw their wooden shoes (*sabots*) into the machines. Karl Marx argued that technological progress created a reserve army of the unemployed, which exerted a continually depressing effect upon wages, even though the workers ultimately found re-employment.

By using the analysis of this chapter, we can see that the effect of technological change is not as simple as these arguments would indicate. New techniques which make certain machinery more effective have the same effect as if the price of that machinery had declined. Such a decline in price will cause firms to use more machinery, so that the amount of labor used for producing *any given output* will be less and the effective quantity of machinery will increase. However, the key phrase is "any given output," for the other result of this change will be to lower the level of costs. As a result of the decline in costs, there will also be an expansion of output, which increases the use of both labor and machinery. Whether the effect upon the quantity of labor used will be an increase or a decrease will depend upon the relative size of the two effects. Every case must be examined in order to determine which is true in the particular circumstance.

Many unions have decided that their best opportunities lie in exploiting the benefits from technological change. For example, before the development of Linotype, all printing was done with hand-set type. When the Linotype was invented, the Typographical Union chose not to oppose its introduction, but did provide training programs so that printers would be able to use these new tools. In many cases, the union encouraged the changeover. As a result, the cost of printing declined and the quantity of printed goods demanded increased tremendously. The estimates of the union proved quite correct: the demand for printed material was so elastic that there was a substantial increase in the employment of printers as a result of the new machinery.

The International Ladies Garment Workers' Union maintains a staff of industrial engineers, whose job it is to help any employers who have contracts with the union. These engineers offer suggestions to lower operating costs. As a result, employers are kept efficient and functioning, and able to provide jobs for union members. In some cases, the union engineers have recommended decreasing the employment in a particular establishment. They have done so because the garment industry is very competitive, and high costs are apt to mean bankruptcy within a relatively short time. In such cases, the union has usually felt that preserving the jobs of three-fourths of the workers was better than maintaining the jobs of all of them temporarily.

In many other cases, however, unions have not been convinced that this kind of possibility is open to them. There are many examples of cases where unions have opposed new techniques which they believed would decrease employment. For example, in the late 1960s, many of the construction trades opposed the building of houses under Federal Operation Breakthrough, which was designed to experiment with factory-built housing that could be erected with little labor on the actual construction site. The fact that many of these unions represented only the workers at the site explained their opposition. Proponents of the program argued that the unions would have been better off had they agreed, because a modest amount of labor would have been employed in building houses which otherwise would not have been built at all. However, the unions, making their own estimates of the total demand for such housing, held that it was not in their best interest to make such an adjustment. Their opposition was often reflected in political pressure upon local governments not to permit variance of zoning laws which would have allowed the construction of such housing.

Thus in almost every case of technological change in the last two hundred years, the specter has been raised that if machines do all the work, nothing will be left for men to do; meanwhile some groups have welcomed change as a way to find new employment. On the whole, technological change has been beneficial to workers, both in their capacity as workers and in their capacity as consumers of the cheaper products. However, the fact that this has been the result in general should not blind us to the fact that it has not always been so. There have been many instances in which workers have been seriously hurt by change. One should not be surprised that workers and their unions have not rushed to embrace every possible technological change; but one can hope that decisions about future changes will be made on the basis of the most complete information possible, after taking into account both the substitution of capital for labor and the increased demand for labor as output expands.

Appendix to Chapter 6
The Nature of Resources

Economists use the term *resources* to refer to the inputs into the economic process. When considering the entire economy, the name is usually reserved for the basic resources of land and labor; but in referring to a single firm, the concept is broadened to include machinery and other products which are used as inputs by the particular firm.

The income statistics in the Appendix to Chapter 4 show that the most important basic resource in the American economy is labor, accounting for about three-fourths of national income. Far below it in importance are returns for land and other basic natural resources. However, these statistics must be used with great caution, because much of the expenditure for natural resources flows through the government, and is therefore not specifically recorded as income. Furthermore, some of our uses of natural resources — such as our use of water and air as sewers to dispose of household and industrial waste — are not included in the national income at all. Nevertheless, it remains true that, even with all the appropriate adjustments of the statistics which one might adopt, labor is still the most important.

At one time, the most important form of labor was physical labor. The great change that has occurred in the twentieth century, however, is the continuing substitution of mechanical horsepower for manpower; most jobs today emphasize the control and decision functions which can be exercised by humans. Even low-skilled jobs like cleaning involve humans guiding mechanical scrubbing equipment, rather than the physical use of mops and brooms. Even the most sophisticated automated equipment emphasizes repetition of a job in a particular way, not the adjustment to varying circumstances. We will see in a later section that education has become an increasingly important factor in the labor supply, emphasizing the shift away from physical labor.

Other than labor, our economic system depends upon its natural resources, usually grouped under the general heading of land. Originally, economists thought of land as agricultural land, owing its productivity to natural fertility. However, in an urban society, land is often most important for its location and its proximity to other locations. The physical characteristics of the land are important mainly for their ability to support buildings and structures, not for their fertility.

The concept of land also includes the minerals which are so important to modern society. These include coal and oil, basic metals, and such prosaic elements as sand, gravel, and clay. In evaluating these minerals, however, we must be careful not to measure them at their market value above the ground. Such a value reflects not only their basic worth but also the cost of the labor and machinery used in making them usable.

We should also include the value of water and air resources in our concept of land. Water is important for its direct use, for the fish and other animals that grow in it, as a means of transportation, for the power which it can generate, and as a carrier for waste. Air is important in the economic process primarily for the waste it carries. This last use has been a subject of special concern in recent years, as we have become increasingly concerned with pollution. One of the principal problems has been that no charge has been made for use of our air and water for these purposes, and they have been overused. However, their capacity to perform these functions is limited, and methods to ration this limited capacity are being devised.

From the standpoint of the individual firm, other resources are important, even though they are not basic resources of the economy. Most of these resources are themselves products, which are supplied by some firms and used by others. (In economic terms, this means that the profit-seeking process determines both the supply and the demand for these goods and services.) The next section is devoted to these intermediate goods.

From the standpoint of the firm, money is also an important resource. Every firm needs funds in order to obtain the other resources which it will need, to buy raw materials, and to pay wages until the product is sold. Such funds are often called capital; but economists usually reserve the term to refer to the intermediate goods which are bought or produced with the money, not the money itself. Despite this different usage, it would be a major mistake to underestimate the importance of this financial resource. Indeed, our economic system is usually called capitalism to emphasize the key role of these investment funds and those who control their use. (Socialist societies have the same need for intermediate goods, but they are provided by government decision, not by the private decisions of "capitalists.")

Finally, the key resource of any firm lies in the process by which it makes its basic decisions. In the days when most firms were proprietorships, the owners were referred to as *entrepreneurs*, emphasizing their decision to undertake certain economic activity. (The French word, *entrepreneur*, means "one who undertakes," as does its German counterpart, *Unternehmer*. Since undertaker has another meaning in English, we use the French word.)

In the modern firm, and especially in the corporation, the basic decision process is apt to be more diffused; it is difficult to identify *the* entrepreneur, but the function is just as important as ever. Entrepreneurship is not simply another form of labor, nor is it merely the management of a process; rather it consists of the basic decision to produce new products, or old ones in new ways. Such decisions are so important that they are often separated from other activities and have been given the special name. Profit is the economy's basic reward for successfully exercising this function, and loss the punishment for failure to do so.

Intermediate Resources

In our society, goods often change hands many times before they reach the consumer. Coal and iron ore are sold to the steel mill; steel is sold to the automobile manufacturer; and finished cars are sold to dealers. In each case, these products become resources to the purchasing company. However, the principal intermediate resources are capital goods, especially since they often involve substantial time periods between purchase and use.

In 1971, the U.S. Gross National Product was $1,046.8 billion. Of this amount, $150.8 billion, or about one-seventh, was for capital investment. Of this amount, $108.1 billion went for plant and equipment, $40.6 billion for houses and apartment buildings, and $2.1 billion for increased inventories. The same year the allowance for using up existing capital equipment was $95.2 billion. We can therefore conclude that the capital stock of the country increased over $50 billion. (We cannot be too precise, because the allowances for capital consumption are only estimates.)

The most important form of capital equipment is the fixed plant and equipment of firms. Almost any firm needs some such capital, even if it is only a small shed in which to operate; but most modern business requires a very large investment in facilities and equipment. The typical large manufacturing firm has invested nearly $30,000 per employee, and their accounting procedures are such that this value is probably too low. Not all of this investment is in fixed assets, but a large proportion of it is. These investments often have an economic life of ten, twenty, or more years, so that the decision to buy or build such a plant and equipment always involves very difficult forecasting problems.

In forecasting, the firm must estimate the future demand for the product and must also guess at the future course of technology, so as not to build a plant which will soon become obsolete. It must also allow for the fact that it is spending money now for returns which will be realized only in the future. It therefore discounts the return, using the current rate of interest to determine the value of money to be received in the future. For example, at 6 percent, the present value of $100 a year from now is $\frac{\$100.00}{1.06}$ or $94.34; the present value of a return two years away is $\frac{\$100.00}{(1.06)^2}$ or $89.00; and so on. The mechanics of this discounting process can be learned from any textbook in commercial arithmetic, or looked up in readily available tables; but the process of forecasting which must be the basis of the process is among the most difficult business decisions. No short summary can possibly do it justice.

Investment in residential properties by commercial firms is very similar to the process outlined above; but it is complicated by the fact that residential structures usually have a longer life than business equipment, and sometimes even longer than plant buildings. However, many single family homes are bought by the people who intend to occupy them. Such owner-occupants are not immune from investment considerations, but they are buying the houses for their own use. Investment in such housing therefore represents an area between the typical business investment and the typical consumer purchase.

Inventories are a smaller, but no less important, part of the capital of a firm. In order to operate, firms keep on hand a supply of their raw materials, a certain amount of goods in process, and some of their finished product, holding it between the time it is produced and the time it is sold. Calculating the best level of inventories involves balancing several factors: the marketing desire to have all products available for sale at any time; the production desire for longer runs to minimize the ratio of setup time to running time; and the financial desire to keep the amount of money invested in inventories as low as possible. In addition, if prices are expected to rise, firms may want to accumulate stocks of raw materials or of finished goods in anticipation of the increase. In general, the higher the level of operations, the larger the inventories which a firm will need. Therefore, when consumer sales rise, raw materials orders usually rise even faster as firms accumulate inventories to service those sales. Finally, there is often an unintentional inventory accumulation which occurs when firms produce goods which they are unable to sell. It is therefore not surprising that inventory change is one of the most volatile elements in the economy.

In one sense, all fixed capital and most consumer durable goods can be thought of as inventories. When a firm buys a machine, it is not interested in owning the machine so much as having the service of that machine available. In that sense, the machine is really an inventory of services which will be used over a period of time. Thinking of the machine as an inventory often makes it easier to face decisions of buying or renting, or of purchasing the services directly. For example, a firm considering whether to install a computer facility or hire the work done by an outside firm is really considering whether to accumulate a stock of services for use over time. The only place where durables are more than a stock of services is in the case of consumer goods, where the owner gets pleasure from the actual ownership rather than merely from the services rendered.

Knowledge as a Resource

We seldom think of knowledge as a resource, because it is usually purchased in the form of educated labor or built into new machinery. Nevertheless, it is quite clear that most of our production would be impossible without the accumulation of new ideas and new techniques. In addition, even the more elementary forms of knowledge are an important resource. For example, consider the disadvantages of trying to run modern factories if the workers were unable to read signs, instructions, and work orders.

Because we do not think of knowledge as a resource, we often treat it incorrectly in our national accounts and in our legal system. For example, an education is an investment in higher earning capacity, as we saw in the Appendix to Chapter 4. Nevertheless our tax laws do not permit depreciation of this investment over the working life of the graduate. It is also usually easier to borrow money to buy equipment or fixtures than to obtain an education. Government loan programs are treated as welfare programs, not as investments (as indicated by the family income restrictions imposed). Indeed, why are federal education programs grouped in a department with health and welfare, rather than in the Department of Commerce?

Similarly, our national accounting understates the size of the education industry. Governments spent $56 billion on education in the fiscal year 1969-70; and, according to the national accounts, individuals spent another $10 billion (listed as consumption, not investment.) These figures include the cost of buildings and the salaries of teachers, secretaries, janitors, and deans. However, no allowance is made for the greatest input, that of the students. Even at rather modest wages, college and university students contribute at least $25 billion of labor to their education; and some amount should also be included for the nearly 20 million high school students and 30 million elementary students. If all these adjustments were included, we would see that the knowledge industry is one of the largest in the United States. We should not be surprised. It is an important resource which has profoundly increased our national productivity.

THE LOGIC OF PRICE

PART TWO

Markets

In Part I, we discussed the behavior of firms and households, which react to price but have no control over it. In Chapter 7, we consider the special conditions which produce such behavior. Chapter 8 discusses monopoly, where the firm has control over its price, subject only to the demand curve for the industry. Chapter 9 deals with industries which are only imperfectly competitive, either because there are only a few firms or because each firm sells a slightly differentiated product. Chapter 10 deals with the role of government in the functioning of markets. Chapter 11 considers the special characteristics of markets for resources, especially labor. Three appendixes discuss certain aspects of the modern scene: Big Business, Big Government, and Big Labor.

Chapter 12 is a summary of the way in which markets interact, and of the conditions for producing economic welfare.

Chapter 7
Competitive Markets

Washington, D.C., has always been a traveler's paradise, as far as taxis are concerned. One can step onto the curb, raise his hand, and have a cab within a few minutes. Even on rainy days, cab service is almost adequate. The fare is also a pleasant surprise. One can ride almost anywhere in downtown Washington and still pay a fare of less than $1.00.

Arthur Robinson is typical of Washington cab drivers. He is a GS-5 clerk in a government office. Some years ago, when his first child was born, he sought a source of extra income. He found that he could become a cab driver quite simply. He painted a sign on the side of his car and took out special liability insurance. He then applied at the District of Columbia Building (Washington's equivalent of a town hall), paid a small fee, and received a taxi license as soon as the records were checked to show that he had no police record. He was now in business.

Washington taxis are not metered, but operate on a zone system. The city is divided into zones and the fare is charged according to the zones which are crossed in the trip. Most of the major government offices and hotels are in Zone 1, the lowest fare area.

Mr. Robinson drove the streets looking for passengers. He soon discovered which hours are the most profitable and which are not. (His government job requires him to work odd hours, so he can often be on the streets during the day.) When it rains, he knows that many people will be looking for cabs, so he tries to work in the rain. Sundays are usually dull days, so he spends these with his family.

One of the other cab drivers advised Robinson to get professional help in preparing his income tax. He did so, and was very interested in the accountant's report. After subtracting for his automobile costs, license, insurance, and other expenses, he found that he earned a net hourly salary about 50 percent higher than he made on his regular job. He will certainly continue driving the cab, and is considering quitting government service entirely.

The Competitive Firm

The firm in pure competition is characterized by the fact that price is outside its control. Such a situation occurs when a large number of independent buyers and sellers deal in standardized products. There is also free entry and exit—that is, firms may leave or enter the competition at any time without great difficulty. In such an industry, every firm must sell at a market price which it is unable to alter. No firm in the industry could charge more, because the standardized product of the other firms would be just as valuable to the consumer, and no consumer would pay more. For the same reasons, no firm would ever find it necessary to sell for less than others.

Not only must the firm meet the market price, but it is also unable to affect that market price, for there are too many firms in the market. If each firm is producing only a fraction of one percent of the total output, it is clear that the price of the product would not change if he cut his output in half or withdrew it from the market entirely—even if the demand for the final product was very inelastic. If, for example, the market elasticity were one-half, that would mean that a one percent change in the output of the industry would be accompanied by a two percent change in the price. However, if there were, say, 10,000 firms in the industry, a single firm could change the output of the industry only by .01 percent and therefore could change the price of the final product by only .02 percent, or, in effect, not at all. Therefore the seller in pure competition views the market as an impersonal force determining the price, and reacts to that price by determining the quantity which he wishes to sell.

Because the market is impersonal, the individual seller does not feel a sense of competitiveness with other sellers even though they are in the same industry. For example, one wheat farmer has no qualms about helping a neighbor harvest his crop, because the neighbor is only one of a huge number of sellers of wheat and cannot alter the conditions which face them both. (We will see in later chapters that competition in other industry models is very much more personal.)

Even though no single seller can affect the price, it is true that all sellers can affect the price if all of them change their output in the same fashion. We have already seen an example of this in Chapter 3 where price control on housing caused a housing shortage.

Table 7.1
Output and Costs

Monthly output	Total cost	Average cost	Average variable cost	Marginal cost
0	$160	—	—	$5.00
20	260	$13.00	$5.00	2.50
40	310	7.75	3.75	1.00
60	330	5.50	2.83	1.50
80	360	4.50	2.50	2.50
100	410	4.10	2.50	3.50
120	480	4.00	2.67	4.50
140	570	4.07	2.93	5.50
160	680	4.25	3.25	6.50
180	810	4.50	3.61	7.50
200	960	4.80	4.00	

We have already examined a firm which reacts to price in Chapter 5. The cost curves of such a firm are shown in Table 7.1. Using the principles given in Chapter 5, we can calculate the supply curve of such a firm. It is the portion of the marginal cost curve which is above $2.50, which is the lowest point on the average variable cost curve. Below that price, the firm would shut down.

The average and marginal cost curves of this firm have been redrawn in Figure 7.1. We can see from this diagram that the firm would make a profit if the price were above $4.00, the lowest average cost. Between $2.50 and $4.00, the firm would be losing money, but not so much that it would immediately shut down. In the long run, of course, the firm would drop out of business if the price were below $4.00.

Industry Supply

In Chapter 2, we have already seen that the supply curve for an industry is the horizontal sum of all of the individual supply curves of the firms in that industry. As a result of the discussion we have just completed, we can now combine the supply conditions of the individual firm with the supply and demand conditions of the industry. This has been done in Figure 7.2. In the left side of the diagram, we have given the supply curve of an individual firm in the industry, along with its average cost curve. In the right side of the diagram, we see the conditions for the entire industry. For simplicity, we assume that the industry consists of 1,000 firms, all of which have exactly the same cost structure as the firm on the left. (It would be more realistic to assume several different kinds of supply curves, in which case the supply curve for the industry would be a weighted sum of the individual supply curves. Unfortunately, the diagram would be more complicated.) We now see that the industry price as determined by the intersection of the supply and demand curve would be $5.00 and that each individual firm will produce 140 units at this price. The entire industry will be producing 140,000 units.

The result which we have just seen represents a short-run equilibrium for the industry. No firm will wish to change its output as long as the price remains at $5.00; every firm will be content to produce 140 units. And as long as every firm produces 140 units, the price will remain at $5.00. Therefore this is an equilibrium point, because there are no tendencies to move away from it.

If we imagine a longer period of time, however, we can see that this condition cannot remain. Every firm in the industry is mak-

**Figure 7.1
Competitive Supply**

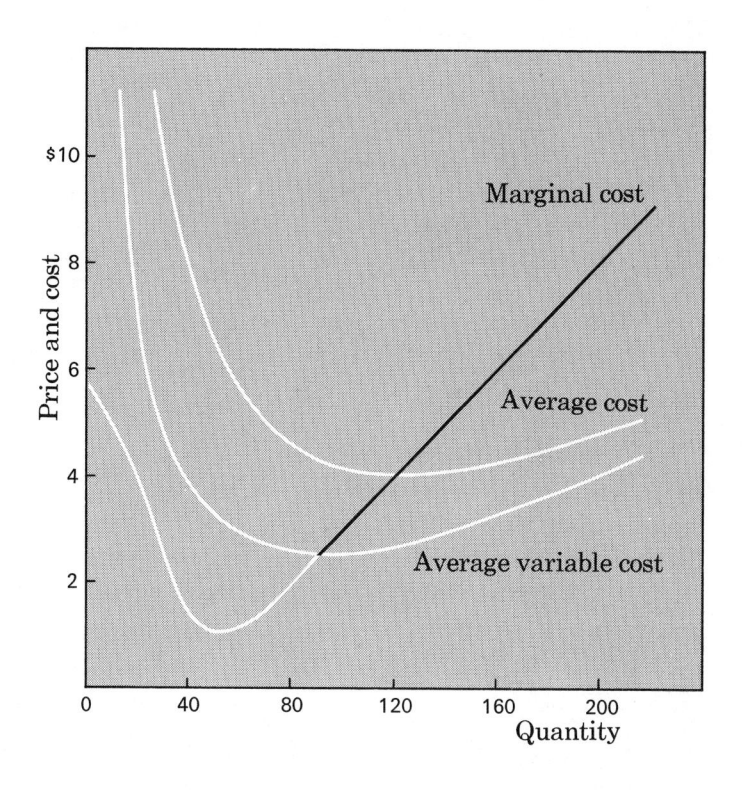

**Figure 7.2
Equilibrium with Entry**

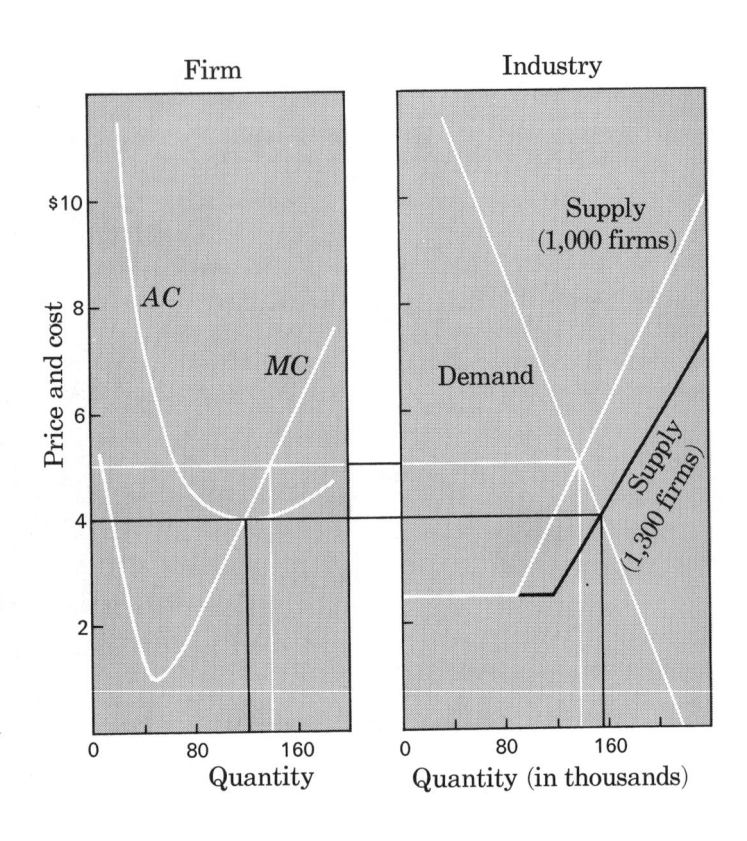

166   Markets

ing a profit of $130. Since, in pure competition, there is no barrier to the entry of new firms into the industry, we would expect that other firms will wish to enter in order to obtain some share of these profits. As new firms enter the industry, the industry supply curve will move to the right because it will no longer represent the sum of the supply of only 1,000 firms, but of a larger number. As the new firms enter the industry, the price will decline, which is the result we usually expect from an increase in supply. The result will finally be as shown in Figure 7.2. The right hand supply curve of this figure shows a new position where 1,300 firms are in the market and price has fallen to $4.00. We see that at the price of $4.00, the firms are making no profit at all. (Remember that we have defined costs to include a fair return to the owner for his services and investment. He will still be making an accounting net income, but no extra profit.) At this stage, the incentive for new firms to enter the industry ceases, because there are no longer excess returns to be obtained. Firms entering the industry would now expect to make only reasonable and normal returns on their money and for their efforts. Consequently, there is no longer any advantage in entering this industry.

We have now reached a long-run equilibrium position. There is no incentive for any firm to produce more than 120 units as long as the price remains at $4.00, and no tendency for the price to move from $4.00 as long as every firm produces 120 units. Beyond that, however, there is no tendency for new firms to enter or leave the industry. Consequently, we can say that the industry is in full long-run equilibrium, not only with respect to the firms which are actually in the industry, but with respect to all firms which might conceivably enter the industry.

If the initial price had been below $4.00, a somewhat similar process of long-run adjustment would have taken place to bring it back up. Such an example is shown in Figure 7.3. In the initial circumstances, due to a lower demand than in Figure 7.2, the price is $3.00. Because this price is above the minimum average variable cost, the firms in the industry would continue to operate, producing 100 units each, although they would all be losing money. Nevertheless, they would be losing less than if they shut down. However, in the long run, changes do come about. As

**Figure 7.3
Equilibrium with Exit**

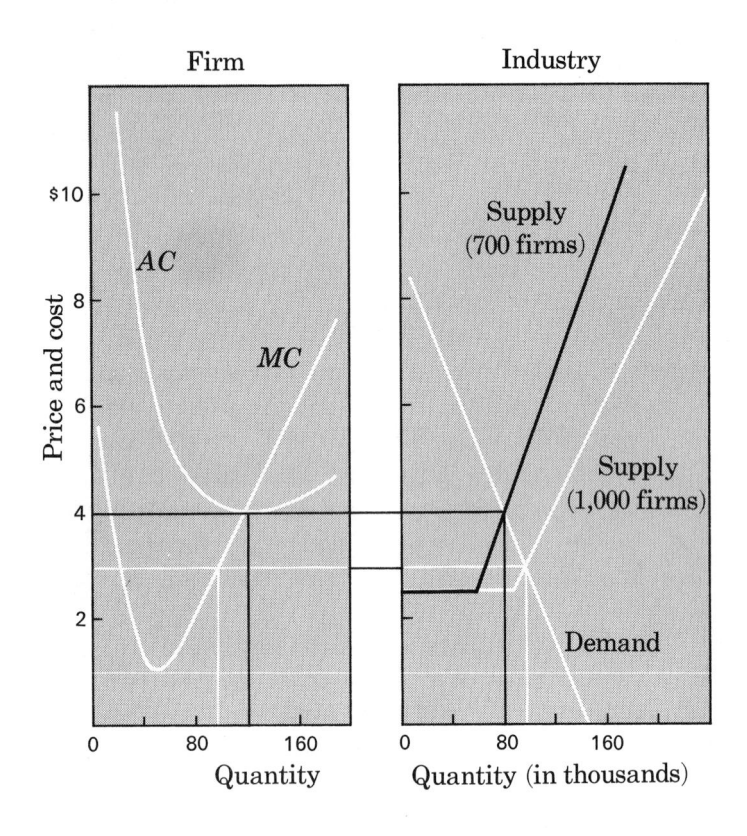

168　　　Markets

equipment wears out and fixed costs come up for possible renewal, some firms may decide not to continue operation in an industry where they are losing money. They will therefore choose not to replace worn-out equipment and not to renew expired contracts. (Remember that a firm will operate only if it can recover its variable costs. In the long run, all costs are variable.) In such a case, the number of firms in the industry will eventually decline. As the number of firms declines, there will be a decrease in supply. The final equilibrium position is shown with only 700 firms still operating in the industry and the price back to the $4.00 level. At this stage, there is no longer any incentive for firms to leave the industry, so the $4.00 price is a stable one and will continue. The remaining 700 firms presumably will replace their equipment as it wears out.

In summary, we may say that the short-run price will be determined where the supply curve meets the demand curve, and each individual firm will be supplying a quantity determined by its own cost curve. In the long-run, however, the price will always gravitate to the lowest average cost at which it is possible to produce the product, for any higher price will induce additional firms to enter the industry, and any lower price will induce existing firms to leave. Thus, the long-run price depends exclusively upon average cost.

External Economies of Scale

We have seen in the previous section that, in the long run, whatever quantity is demanded will be supplied at a price which is equal to the lowest possible average cost of the firms in the industry. We now see why the long-run supply curve in Chapter 2 was shown as horizontal. There are, however, certain questions which must be answered before we can accept this conclusion.

Must all firms in an industry have the same minimum average cost? In the short run, we can imagine that it would be quite possible for different firms with totally different cost structures to exist side by side. In the long run, however, this would not be possible. Let us suppose that there were merely two kinds of cost structure, one higher than the other. In the long run, new firms would come into existence, using the lower cost methods, because they would find it profitable to enter the industry at prices which would be unprofitable to the higher cost firms. Eventually, all the firms with higher costs would minimize their losses by leaving the industry and would be replaced by firms with the lower costs.

Sometimes the firms with lower costs are in that favorable position because of particular advantages—for example, a certain location or a particularly well qualified manager. It would be more appropriate to say that their costs are not truly lower, but, for some reason, they are getting a particular bargain on their resources. In the long run, they should expect the costs of these resources to go up, as other firms bid for them. Consequently, this kind of low cost cannot be permanent.

Will new firms entering the industry have the same costs as the old ones? In general, we would expect that there would be no difference between old firms and new ones; if there were, this would constitute a barrier to entry into the industry. In manufacturing, it is typically true that new firms can enter and produce in exactly the same way and at exactly the same costs as the old firms. In agriculture, however, there are apt to be some differences. Suppose new firms were entering the wheat-producing industry. Presumably, the old firms have already used the land which is best adapted to producing wheat; therefore, new wheat farmers would be forced to use land which is either less well adapted to wheat, or is more expensive because it has other valuable uses. In this case, their costs would be higher than the costs of the old firms. However, the costs of the old firms will also rise, because new firms entering the industry will certainly try to buy old wheat land rather than the more expensive new wheat land. They would thus drive up the price of the old wheat land and the costs of the entire industry would rise to match the costs of the new firms on the less suitable land.

In a case where the entry of new firms into the industry drives up the costs of all firms, we would expect that the industry price would not fall to the old level when there was an increase in demand, but would decline only so far as the new minimum cost. In such a case, the industry is said to be an *increasing cost industry;* and the long-run supply curve has an upward slope, although it is still much flatter than the short-run supply curve. We call such cases examples of *external diseconomies of scale* because costs are rising, not because the individual firms have gotten bigger, but because the industry of which they are a part is larger. (The economies and diseconomies which we spoke of in Chapter 6 are *internal economies* of scale because they depend on the size of the firm.)

External diseconomies of scale occur whenever an industry uses a particular resource which is limited, compared to the demand for it by the industry. We now see why external diseconomies are more likely to occur in agriculture, where any particular crop is apt to use a large portion of the land which is especially well suited to producing that crop. They appear less often in manufacturing, where few industries are apt to use a large portion of the total supply of any resource. External diseconomies of scale do occur, however, in manufacturing industries which use certain mineral inputs. For example, the expansion of the steel industry may require the use of lower grade iron ores in order to supply the increased demand by the entire industry.

Are there *external economies of scale* as well as diseconomies? The answer is that sometimes there are. Occasionally the expansion of an industry may make it possible for the individual firms within that industry to produce at a lower cost. Usually these external economies come about because certain auxiliary services make it possible to lower costs. For example, Holland has traditionally been the supplier of tulip bulbs for the world. Her dominance exists not because tulips cannot be raised elsewhere; if that were true, Holland would have no market. Rather, it exists because various kinds of specialized services can be found in Holland, but not in other places. (Does the land-grant university in your state have a specialist on the agriculture of tulips?) External economies of scale may result because of the growth of specialized knowledge and facilities in banking, transportation, education, or consulting services. Sometimes we observe that there are definite economies of scale in certain industries, but are unable to identify the exact reasons for these economies. They are nonetheless real.

The argument for using protective tariffs for infant industries in a country is based upon the idea of external economies of scale. When an industry is just beginning, it has not reached the stage where the associated facilities have developed to lower its costs of production, so that it can compete with the same industries in other countries where they have already reached the required size. Therefore, it is argued, one should use tariffs to protect the industry until such time as it becomes big enough to make the tariffs no longer necessary. There is a great deal of truth in this argument. There is also a major difficulty. How can one be sure that the particular industry asking for protection is one that will benefit from increased size?

When an industry is the beneficiary of external economies of scale, the long-run supply curve of the industry will be downward sloping. As new firms enter the industry, the costs of existing firms fall; therefore, new firms will keep entering until the price has fallen to the new minimum cost, which will be below the previous equilibrium price. If the industry were to contract, many of its advantages would disappear and the average costs of all firms would rise. Firms would keep leaving the industry until the price had gone above the previous long-run equilibrium level.

Pure Competition As An Ideal

Pure competition occupies a special position in economists' thinking, not because it is typical of many industries in America, but because it is an ideal form which can be used as a standard to measure others. These ideal aspects have been implied in the discussion above.

Technical efficiency.

We have already seen that, in the long run, a purely competitive industry will produce goods at the lowest possible average cost. Firms in pure competition are driven by the market to produce goods at maximum efficiency. Any firms which do not use the most efficient methods will, in the long run, be driven out of the industry and replaced by those who can do the job better. From the standpoint of the seller, pure competition is a ruthless master; but from the standpoint of the consumer, it is very benevolent.

Technological change.

A corollary of the argument above is that new production techniques will always be adopted rapidly, because firms which do not adopt new and lower cost methods will find themselves at a disadvantage in competing with firms which have done so. Thus, pure competition is ideally designed to foster the spread and adoption of new technology.

Consumer satisfaction.

Even in the short run, pure competition will provide the goods that consumers want most. We have seen that firms adjust their production and costs to price. It therefore follows that between any two goods produced under purely competitive conditions, the ratio of marginal costs will be the ratio of prices. The ratio of prices of competitively produced goods is a measure of the resources required to produce an additional unit of each. We saw in Chapter 3 that every consumer will adjust his purchases until his marginal utilities for any two goods are proportional to their prices. Putting these two conclusions together, we see that relative prices equate the relative costs of production with the relative desirability of goods. It follows that the economic system is producing the goods which consumers want most. Any departure from this combination would make consumers worse off, because it would involve withdrawing resources from the production of one good in order to produce another which would not have as much utility for consumers.

Adaptability.

We have already seen that the competitive system adapts readily to every change in technology in order to produce in the most efficient manner possible. It is also true that the competitive system adapts readily to every other change. If there are changes in consumer tastes, shifts in the demand curve will produce an immediate response in the production of goods. If costs of certain resources rise, firms will immediately shift their production to rely less on those resources, and therefore adjust to that change as well.

Many years ago, Adam Smith observed that every person in a competitive system, by seeking his own best interest, was led as if by an invisible hand to produce the maximum welfare of the entire society. We now see that Adam Smith's vision was a simple way of observing the efficiency of a purely competitive system.

Unfortunately, the results of pure competition are not entirely desirable. We must therefore look at certain of the disadvantages of a competitive system before we accept it too hastily as an ideal pattern.

Social costs.

Firms in pure competition react very effectively to the costs which they incur. Typically, however, they do not react to costs which they may create, but which they themselves do not have to bear. For example, there is little incentive for a firm in pure competition to worry about the smoke from its chimneys, even if that smoke is a nuisance to those in the neighborhood of the factory. Similarly, factories are apt to dump their wastes into rivers if that is a cheap method, even though it may greatly increase costs for users of the river further downstream. This failure to recognize social costs is not unique to pure competition, but is a characteristic of separated decision-making. It happens in all of private industry. It also happens with respect to local governments, which often pollute rivers without regard to communities downstream. We will see in Chapter 11 that an overall government can sometimes convert social costs into private costs, so that the economy will reflect them.

Social benefits.

Just as the private system recognizes only private costs and not social ones, so it recognizes only private benefits — not social ones. For example, a particular household might feel that is worth $50 to treat its trees against a certain disease. However, if it should cost $100 to do so, the household will not have the trees sprayed. If we were to examine the problem more generally, however, we might discover that there are at least ten neighbors who would contribute $5 each to the cost of spraying to protect their own trees from infection. Consequently, if we were to examine the benefits of the householder and of the neighbors, we would discover that it would have been worthwhile to have the trees sprayed. We call these benefits which are received by other than the primary recipient *social benefits*. The best way to handle the problem of social benefits is by means of joint purchasing arrangements, whereby groups of consumers can get together to buy those things which, in total, are worthwhile to the group, but which would not be desirable enough to any one person for him to bear the cost. The most common form of joint purchasing agency is a governmental unit, which imposes taxes upon everyone to provide for these social benefits. In order to recognize social benefits, we find it necessary to add a visible hand to the invisible hand of the market. One can even use the idea of social benefits to define the best size of governmental units: A government should be just large enough to contain all the people who receive the benefits of that government's activities. The taxes which it levies would then be an appropriate fee for those benefits. We now see why there should be various levels of government, each of which concentrates its efforts on certain activities.

Governments are not the only ways to provide social benefits. Various clubs, labor unions, and other voluntary organizations may be devices for providing services which are desirable from the total standpoint of a group, but which are not likely to be undertaken by a single individual. However, there are severe limitations on the ability of voluntary groups to perform this function. Sometimes the social benefits may be spread so widely that it is not feasible to form the corresponding group. In addition, all voluntary groups are plagued with the "free-rider" problem—those individuals who cheerfully accept the benefits of the group but do not pay their share to support them. As a result, the organization is almost always threatened with financial disaster.

Distribution of income.

Pure competition is a special form of democracy which responds to the dollar votes of consumers in providing them with what they want. However, unlike political democracies, the votes are not equally distributed in the economic system; obviously, they are distributed quite unequally. Each of us is apt to have his own moral views on how income ought to be distributed. But there is no reason to expect that income in a society will actually be distributed in that fashion, and therefore votes will often not go as we feel they should. (Most of us are apt to feel that we and those like us are morally deserving of more than the society actually gives us.)

Technological development.

We have seen that pure competition readily adopts new techniques as soon as they become available. However, the small firms in pure competition are not apt to undertake research to develop new techniques, because none of them is big enough either to afford the research or to make proper use of it. Agriculture, a competitive industry, has readily adopted new methods, but these new techniques originated outside the agricultural industry.

Stability of pure competition.

In some cases, a purely competitive industry might be self-destroying. If the industry was characterized by substantial internal economies of scale, each firm would start growing and seeking lower cost production techniques, until it occupied a substantial portion of the industry. The firms which expanded enough to take advantage of these economies of scale would have a substantial edge on those which had not, and the smaller firms would drop out. As a result, the fewer large firms would themselves destroy the process of pure competition. Examples of this are rarer than most people believe, but they do exist.

In still another sense, pure competition may also be self-defeating. If a firm should decide that it could make more profit by differentiating its product, rather than by producing the standardized product which is characteristic of pure competition, the process of differentiation would thereby change the conditions of pure competition. Thus we see that the search for profit by firms in pure competition might lead either to monopolistic competition or to oligopoly, market forms which we will discuss in Chapter 9.

Consumer incompetence.

It is often argued that pure competition is unsatisfactory because it responds to the demand of consumers, who often do not know what is best for them. There is undoubtedly a certain truth to this argument, but it is not clear what alternatives are available. One could, of course, imagine an all-powerful, all-good, and all-wise supervisor who might provide everyone with what he ought to want instead of what he really does want.

However, such a system could only be an authoritarian one. It is impossible to imagine a democratic government protecting consumers from their own incompetence. The consumers are the same voters who choose the government, and there is no reason to believe that they will be more competent in their choice of elected representatives than they are in their choice of goods.

An Illustration: Business Taxes

Governments often impose taxes upon businesses, both for purposes of revenue and for purposes of control. In order to see the effects of these taxes, we must examine their impact upon the cost structures of the firm and, subsequently, upon the industry supply and demand curves. Business taxes can be generally divided into three main categories: (1) taxes which vary with the total revenue of the firm, such as sales and excise taxes; (2) taxes which are levied upon the assets of the firm, such as property taxes; and (3) taxes which are based upon the income of the firm, such as income taxes. Each of these has a different effect and must be examined separately.

Sales taxes.

Where a tax is levied on the basis of sale, the revenue received by the firm differs from the price paid by the consumer by the amount of the tax. Accordingly, one could reflect the tax either by drawing a demand curve decreased by the amount of the tax or by drawing a supply curve raised by the amount of the tax.

In Figure 7.4, the effect of a 20 percent sales tax is shown by drawing a second demand curve 20 percent below the original. The immediate result is a decrease in the total quantity sold in the industry. The revenue received by sellers declines to $3.60, and the price paid by buyers increases to $4.50. The difference between these two prices is equal to the total amount of the tax. Exactly how the burden of the tax will be divided between the buyer and the seller depends upon the relative elasticities of supply and demand. In the example shown, about 55 percent of the tax is reflected in higher prices and about 45 percent in lower revenues to the sellers. The amount of the quantity change is

Figure 7.4
Sales Tax and Demand

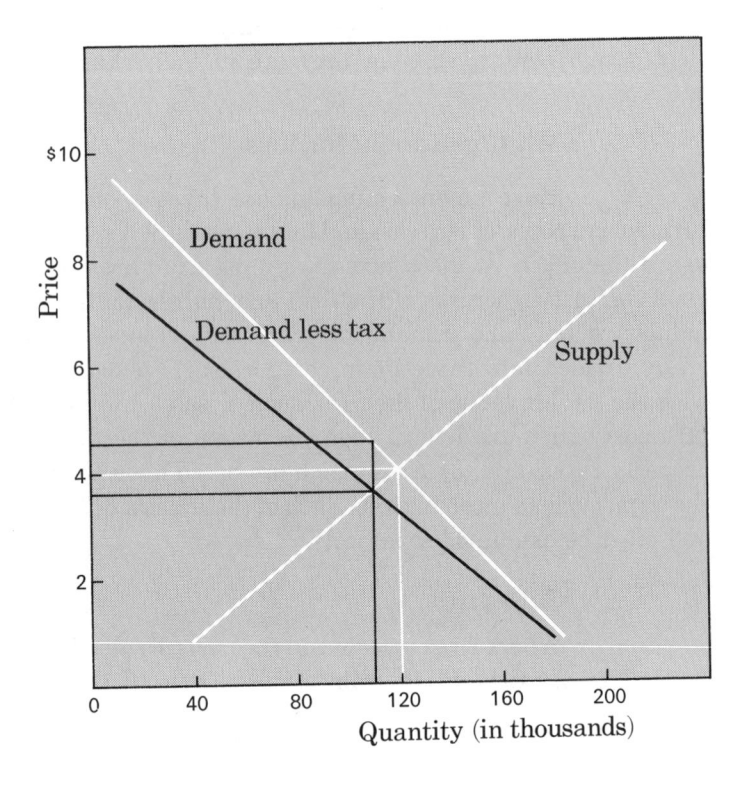

a function of the total elasticities of the supply and demand curves. If both are relatively inelastic, the quantity change will be small; if both are relatively elastic, the quantity change will be quite large.

In Figure 7.5, the same impact has been shown by increasing the supply curve by 25 percent. (Note that a 20 percent tax on the buyer's price is 25 percent of the seller's price.) The same result occurs as in the previous diagram: the buyer's price rises to $4.50, and the seller's price falls to $3.60.

The long-run effect of the sales tax is shown in Figure 7.6. In this case, the entire cost of the tax is borne by the consumer, because the long-run supply curve is horizontal; in the long run, firms will drop out of the industry until the price has risen enough to cover the entire tax. Exactly how much the quantity will decline depends upon the elasticity of demand for the products of the industry.

In examining the effects of taxes—especially the extent to which they will be passed forward (borne by the consumer) or backward (borne by the supplier)—the result depends upon the the exact details of the particular tax. If a general sales tax was imposed in one municipality, but a nearby area had no such sales tax, a number of consumers would do their buying where they could avoid the tax. In such a case, the only way that sellers in the first community could stay in business would be to bear most of the tax themselves. Many discussions of local sales taxes hinge upon the problem of consumers buying in other jurisdictions in order to escape the tax.

If the tax is uniformly on all products, the consumer will feel an income effect of the tax; but there will be no substitution effect, because the impact of the tax will be identical on all goods. On the other hand, if the tax is imposed only on a single product, the effect will be to create both an income and a substitution effect, and to encourage consumers to buy less of the product on which the tax is imposed. Sometimes, a tax is imposed deliberately to produce this distortion. Many people argue in favor of taxes on alcohol in order to discourage drinking. Tariffs are usually imposed with the intention of discouraging the purchase of imported goods and encouraging the purchase of domestically produced competing goods.

Figure 7.5
Sales Tax and Supply

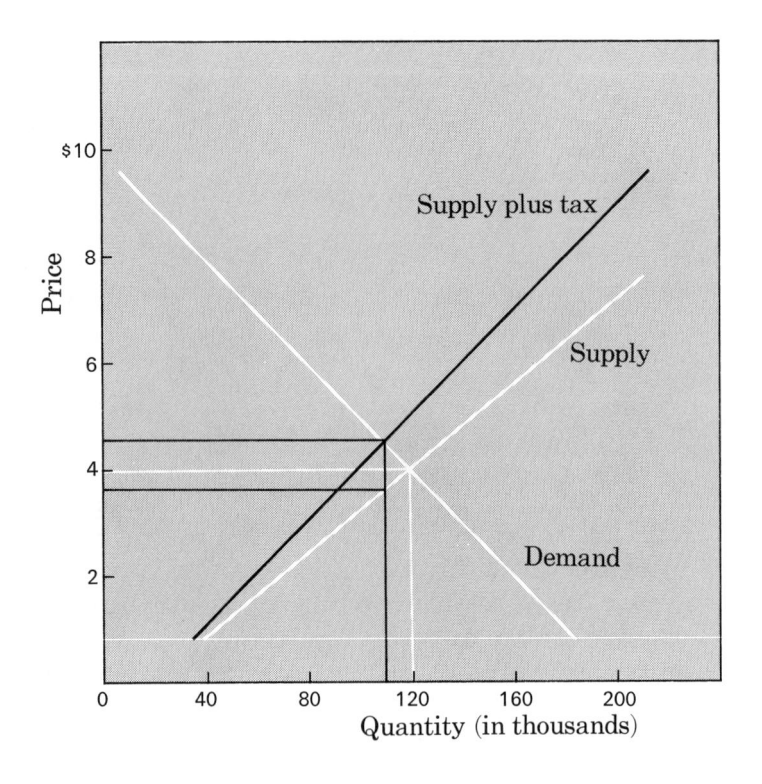

Figure 7.6
Sales Tax – Long Run

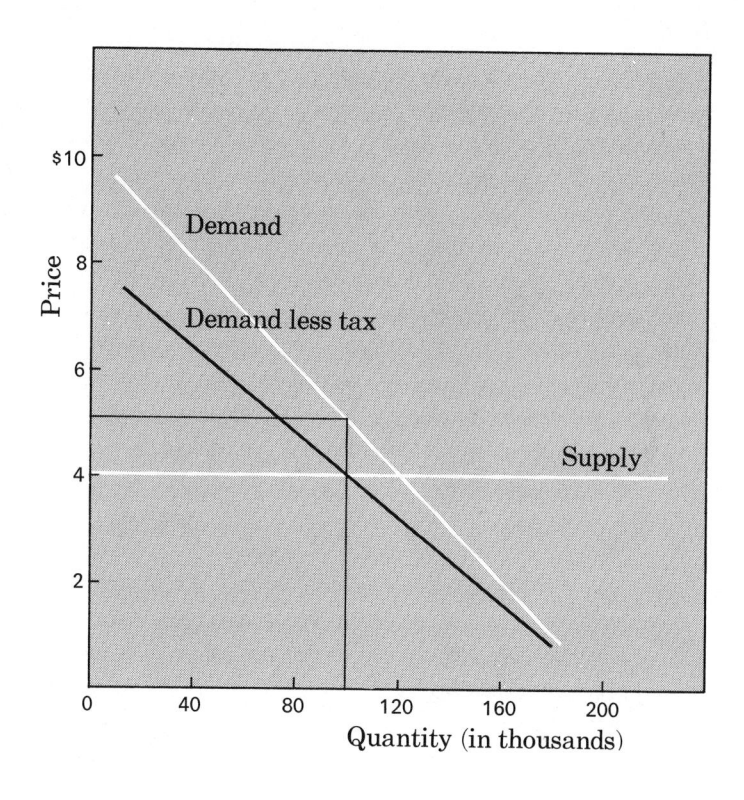

Competitive Markets

181

Property taxes.

If taxes are imposed upon property used in production, the effect will be an increase in the fixed cost of the firm. Although the increase will raise the total cost of production, the shape of the cost curve will not be altered and therefore the short-run supply curve will be unchanged. (The marginal cost curve is unaffected by changes in fixed costs.) Since there will be no effect upon market price or quantity in the short run, all property taxes are borne by the seller. The long-run supply curve rises by an amount which includes the tax because the cost of production has risen. Therefore, in the long run, the effect of a property tax is exactly the same as that of a sales tax of equivalent yield, because it raises the average cost by an amount which covers the tax. We must remember that, in the long run, firms in pure competition make no profit, but merely cover their cost, including compensation of the owner. Consequently, any increase in cost, such as that created by a tax, must ultimately be included in the price at which the product is sold.

Business income taxes.

If it were possible to design a tax which applied only to economic profit—the return after all costs have been deducted—there would be no impact upon output or prices. The tax would be a percentage of the profit, and the maximum level of profit would come at exactly the same output as before. Only the level of profit after taxes would have changed. In most cases, however, the taxes which are actually imposed are based not on economic profit but on accounting net income, which includes many elements which are properly considered cost. The usual method of measuring net income for tax purposes includes not only the pure profit, but also many implicit costs—the wages of the owner, the return on his capital, and the like. For this reason, most actual income taxes have the effect of raising the cost curves and therefore should be treated like one of the previous taxes. Since most implicit costs are fixed costs to the firm, the impact of most income taxes is similar to that of a property tax—they have no effect in the short run on output or prices, but in the long run lead to an increase in prices high enough to cover the tax and to a decrease in quantity according to the elasticity of demand. We must also remember that a tax imposed upon the pure profit of competitive firms would yield no permanent revenue, because, in the long run, competitive forces drive prices down to the level where firms make no pure profit but only enough to cover their total costs.

Chapter 8
Monopolistic Markets

The New York city taxicab situation provides an extreme contrast to that in Washington, D.C. The city has issued medallions which must be affixed to the taxicab. The principal difference between New York and Washington is that the number of medallions is limited; one cannot simply walk into city hall and obtain a new medallion to drive a cab.

Because of the restricted number of cabs, those drivers who are on the street at any time are usually quite busy. Drivers spend very little time cruising; they can pull into a taxi stand, a hotel, or a transportation terminal and obtain a fare immediately. When passengers are discharged, it is quite common for new passengers to appear and get in the cab before the old occupants have paid their fare. The only way a driver can stop long enough to eat or have a cup of coffee is to post an "Off Duty" sign in his window. Even so, he is apt to be hailed, and passengers may try to enter the cab when he stops at a traffic light. The combination of a full cab most of the time and relatively high fares produces a high gross income per cab.

Under these circumstances, many people want to

become cab drivers but are unable to do so. The only way to become a cab owner is to purchase a medallion from an existing owner. (The city will transfer medallions for a nominal fee.) Those who wish to be owner-operators usually find themselves outbid by cab companies which will use two or three shifts of hired drivers to keep their cabs on the street most hours of the day. It is ironic that medallions which were issued by the city practically free are sold for about $22,000. The price was higher, but owners find it increasingly difficult to keep their cabs on the street after dark. Drivers are not willing to risk being beaten and robbed. As revenues per cab have fallen, so have the prices of medallions.

Who are the beneficiaries of this system? Not the customers, who pay high fares and have difficulty finding cabs. Not the cab drivers, who are merely hired employees and are paid just enough to induce them to drive rather than take other jobs. And somewhat surprisingly, not the cab owners; most of them paid large sums for their medallions, and barely manage a reasonable return on their investment, after subtracting the salaries of drivers and the costs of operating the cabs. The beneficiaries are the people who owned the medallions at the time the demand increased beyond the number of medallions available. (In many cases, the gain was distributed over a number of owners, each of whom sold his medallion for a few thousand more than he paid.)

Because this system seems to benefit no one, it would have been better if the city had permitted free licensing of cabs as Washington did. Unfortunately, it is easier to see that a system should not have started than to find a way to end it. If New York permitted free licensing of taxis now, the present cab owners could find themselves holding medallions for which they paid over $20,000 and which had become worthless. In this sense, the owners are the victims of the system as much as their customers.

One proposal has been made that the city should buy back all medallions at $22,000, and issue new ones without limit. The city could recover its cost in a few years by a special tax on hotels and expensive restaurants. This tax would probably be passed on to the patrons, but they are the principal users of taxis and would be the main beneficiaries of the increased supply. City officials are reluctant to adopt the proposal, on the ground that New York has enough financial problems without spending millions to buy up taxi medallions. As a result, New York remains one of the worst places in the world to try to get a taxi.

The Monopolistic Firm

Monopoly occurs when a single seller provides a product for which there are no reasonably good substitutes. The firm and the industry are identical, and there is no competition. In this case, the individual producer faces a downward sloping demand curve. From it he chooses a price-quantity combination which will maximize his profit.

Monopolists are more likely to engage in promotional activities and advertising, which the firm in pure competition finds unnecessary. However, the kind of advertising they will choose is of the form "Use *more* of product X," rather than "Product X is *better* than Product Y." The latter kind of advertising and promotion is reserved for the two market types which follow. The monopolist uses advertising and promotion only for the sake of shifting his entire demand curve directly or indirectly through improving the general company image.

We saw in Chapter 7 that one of the characteristics of pure competition is free entry into the industry. In contrast, monopolies exist only because there are significant barriers to entry into the industry. Sometimes a monopolist may obtain his position because he has complete control over a basic raw material. Many monopolists exist only because the government has given them exclusive rights to provide a certain service in a given area, such as the case of public utilities providing gas, electricity, and telephone service. However, such legal monopolies often come with government regulations and therefore are not completely unrestricted. Firms are sometimes monopolies because they have new and unique products which other firms are kept from copying either by patent laws or some form of secrecy. However, since patent laws give absolute rights only in physical terms, not economic ones, it is often possible for competitors or would-be competitors to find ways to break patent monopolies without breaking the law. Often a firm can enjoy a monopoly only until such time as his competitors can find ways to match his product. Sometimes monopoly is the result of various kinds of technical limitations or control over raw materials; and, in rare cases, it results from economies of scale.

In every case where a monopoly occurs, however, a distortion results, leading to higher prices and lower outputs than would be the case if the industry were more competitive. Often monopoly is accompanied by high profits, but not always. Sometimes the profit which could have been obtained is capitalized by an early owner of the monopoly right and charged to later monopolists in higher costs. Thus, New York cab owners as a group are monopolists, but do not make high profits; they were appropriated by the original holders of the medallions.

Table 8.1
Monopolists' Profit Maximization

Output	Price	Total Revenue	Total Cost	Total Profit
0	$8.00	$ 0	$160	−$160
20	7.50	150	260	− 110
40	7.00	280	310	− 30
60	6.50	390	330	60
80	6.00	480	360	120
100	5.50	550	410	140
120	5.00	600	480	120
140	4.50	630	570	60
160	4.00	640	680	− 40
180	3.50	630	810	− 180
200	3.00	600	960	− 360

The behavior of the monopolist, like that of any firm, is based on maximization of profits. Unlike the firm in pure competition, the monopolist faces a sloping demand curve. This means that his price is not given; he must choose, from all the price-quantity combinations given by his demand curve, the one which produces maximum profits. The process is illustrated in Table 8.1. The first two columns show a hypothetical demand curve. In the third column, the two have been multiplied to obtain a total revenue curve. In the fourth column, the total cost curve of Chapter 5 is given. These costs can then be subtracted from total revenue to obtain profits.

It is clear from Table 8.1 that the maximum profit is obtained at an output of 100 units, sold at a price of $5.50. The monopolist would therefore choose that price and quantity.

We notice that below the price of $4.00, the revenue actually declines with increased sales. We can therefore see that the demand curve must be inelastic within this range, for revenue is falling as the quantity increases.

The process of choosing the best output can be performed graphically as well as numerically. Such a graphic solution is shown in Figure 8.1. This diagram is similar to Figure 5.2, except that the total revenue curve is a straight line for competitive firms and is bent downward for monopolistic firms.

In one sense, the analysis of monopoly is simpler than that of pure competition. There is no long-run analysis to be made. Remember that in the long run in pure competition, it was necessary for us to consider the way in which new firms entered the industry and what the effect of their entry would be. In a monopoly, where entry to the industry is blocked, we need not consider this possibility. It is possible, however, to consider one kind of long-run adjustment: the firm might find it better to expand or contract the scale of its plant to take full advantage of its long-run cost curve. This, however, would involve no new principles, but merely a substitution of long-run costs for the short-run costs of this example.

The Second Approach: Marginal Cost and Revenue

An alternative approach to finding the best output is shown in Table 8.2. In this table, the marginal revenue has been calculated from the total revenue of Table 8.1, by subtracting successive totals and dividing by the change in quantity. For example, the total revenue from selling 80 units is $480, and the total revenue from selling 100 units is $550. The marginal revenue for these last units is therefore $70 divided by 20 units, or $3.50 per unit. By the same process, marginal cost is calculated from total cost. (Notice that both marginal cost and marginal revenue are between the lines for the totals, indicating that the marginal calculations apply to the intervals between successive outputs.)

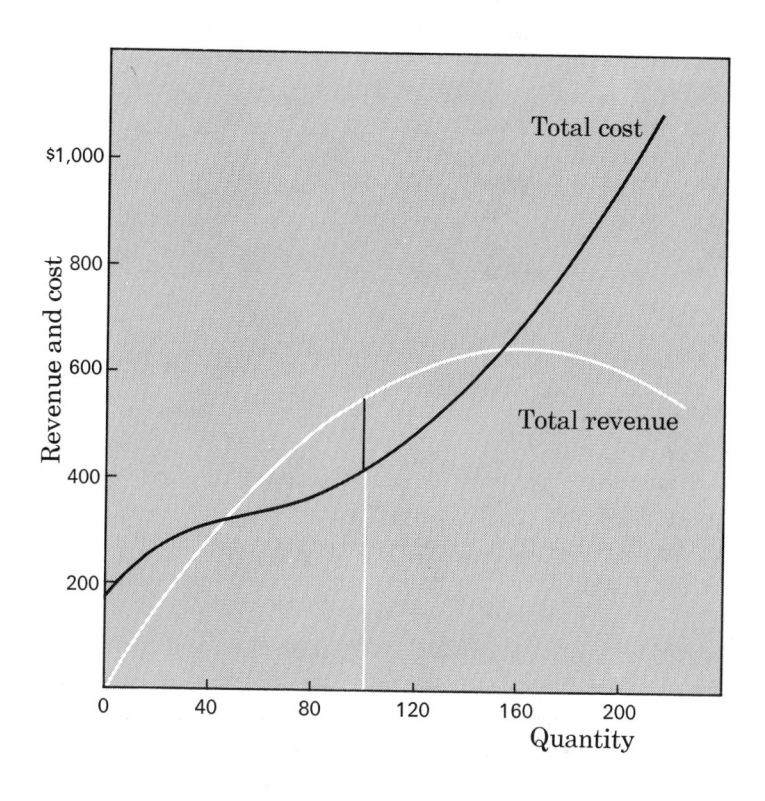

**Figure 8.1
Monopoly—Total Revenue and Cost**

Monopolistic Markets

Table 8.2
Monopolists' Marginal Revenue and Cost

Output	Total Revenue	Total Cost	Marginal Revenue	Marginal Cost
0	$ 0	$160		
			$7.50	$5.00
20	150	260		
			6.50	2.50
40	280	310		
			5.50	1.00
60	390	330		
			4.50	1.50
80	480	360		
			3.50	2.50
100	550	410		
			2.50	3.50
120	600	480		
			1.50	4.50
140	630	570		
			.50	5.50
160	640	680		
			−.50	6.50
180	630	810		
			−1.50	7.50
200	600	960		

From Table 8.2, it is clear that it pays the firm to produce 100 units. The last twenty units (from 80 to 100) increase revenues by $3.50 per unit, but increase costs by only $2.50 per unit. Thus profit increases over this interval by $1.00 per unit, or $20 total. For the next 20 units (from 100 to 120), the marginal cost is $3.50 and the marginal revenue is $2.50, so that profits would actually be *decreased* by $1.00 per unit. Remember that in Chapter 5 we saw that a firm increases its profits by producing more as long as marginal revenue is greater than marginal cost, but decreases its profits if marginal cost is larger.

The comparable graphic solution is shown in Figure 8.2. The demand curve and marginal revenue curve are shown, along with marginal and average cost. (The marginal curves have again been plotted in the middle of the interval.) The best place to produce is where the marginal revenue curve crosses the marginal cost curve, in this case at 100 units. Having found the best output, we can then read from the demand curve the price, $5.50, which corresponds to that output.

As we would expect, there is a close relationship between the elasticity of demand and marginal revenue. If demand is quite elastic, price and marginal revenue are quite close together; if demand is less elastic, price and marginal revenue diverge; and

Figure 8.2
Monopoly — Unit Revenue and Cost

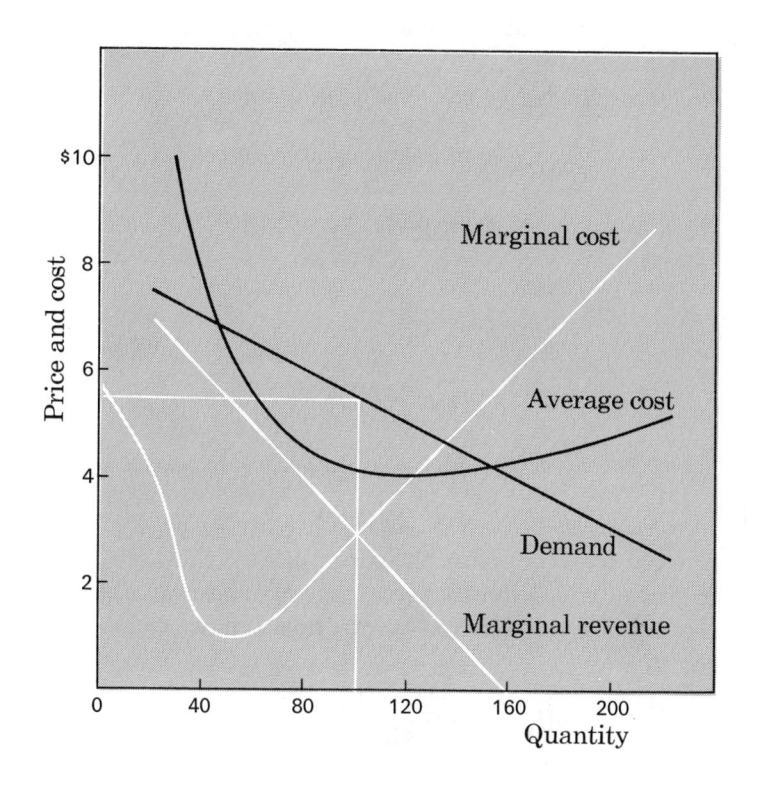

Monopolistic Markets

if demand is inelastic, marginal revenue becomes negative, as it does in Table 8.2 and Figure 8.2 at outputs above 160.

Let us examine this relationship somewhat further. As the monopolist increases his output from q to $q + \Delta q$, price falls from $p + \Delta p$ to p. Total revenue therefore changes from $q(p + \Delta p)$ to $p(q + \Delta q)$. Marginal revenue is the difference between these amounts, divided by the change in quantity; that is,

$$\begin{aligned} MR &= \frac{p(q + \Delta q) - q(p + \Delta p)}{\Delta q} \\ &= \frac{pq + p\Delta q - pq - q\Delta p}{\Delta q} \\ &= p - \frac{q\Delta p}{\Delta q} \\ &= p\left(1 - \frac{q\Delta p}{p\Delta q}\right) \\ &= p\left(1 - \frac{\Delta p}{p} \times \frac{q}{\Delta q}\right) \end{aligned} \qquad (8.1)$$

The second term within the parentheses is the percentage change in price divided by the percentage change in quantity—that is, the elasticity of demand turned upside down. We can therefore say that:

$$MR = p\left(1 - \frac{1}{\text{elasticity}}\right) \qquad (8.2)$$

We now see that if the demand curve is very elastic, the second term in parentheses will be close to zero and marginal revenue will be quite close to the price. This comes about because it is not necessary to cut price much to sell an additional unit, so that marginal revenue is not much lower than price. On the other hand, if there is less elasticity, the marginal revenue will be quite different from the price. For example, if the elasticity is 2, the marginal revenue will be one half of the price; and if the elasticity is 1.5, the marginal revenue will be only one third of the price. If the elasticity of demand is 1, the marginal revenue will be zero. This is consistent with our previous observation that a demand curve of unit elasticity has constant total revenue, and therefore zero marginal revenue. If the demand curve is inelastic, then marginal revenue will actually be negative. We can therefore conclude that no monopolist will ever operate on that portion of his demand curve where the demand is inelastic.

We could have derived Equation 8.2 by starting in a different manner. The marginal revenue from selling a few more items is equal to the price at which those items are sold, minus the loss on all previous items of the amount by which the price is cut. Thus, if output is increased by an amount Δq, the marginal revenue for those items will be:

$$MR = p\Delta q - q\Delta p \qquad (8.3)$$

The marginal revenue per unit is obtained by dividing by the increase in quantity, Δq:

$$MR = p - \frac{q\Delta p}{\Delta q} \qquad (8.4)$$

Equation 8.4 can then be used to derive the rest of Equation 8.1.

It is sometimes alleged that firms do not maximize profits, but simply use a percentage markup to set prices. We can use the relationship previously derived between elasticity, price, and marginal revenue to see that this practice might be equivalent to setting marginal cost equal to marginal revenue. In many retail businesses, it is reasonable to treat the marginal cost as a constant—that is, the cost of purchasing the goods themselves. Most of the costs of operating the store (even labor) are apt to be fixed costs, which are required if the store is even to open its doors. If demand is subject to fluctuations at various times, but it is believed that the elasticity of demand remains the same as it shifts, then an easy way to maximize profit is to use a simplified percentage markup. We have already seen that:

$$MR = p\left(1 - \frac{1}{\text{elasticity}}\right) \qquad (8.5)$$

If the elasticity is constant, then the term in parentheses may be treated as a constant. If price were set by using the inverse of that constant as a ratio to apply to marginal cost, then marginal cost would be equal to marginal revenue. For example, if the elasticity of demand were 3, the number in the parentheses would be $2/3$, and the price would then be $3/2$ of the marginal cost. In this case a 50 percent markup would be appropriate. If the demand were more elastic, say 5, the number in the parentheses would be ⁴/₅, and the markup would be 25 percent.

It is a common observation that firms which use such procedures for setting price often vary the markup from department to department. In cases where there is a relatively high degree of competition, the elasticity would be large and the markup percentage would be small. In cases where there is less competition, elasticity will be smaller and markups will be larger. For example, in department stores, it is customary that markups on high fashion dresses are higher than on casual clothes. And in the infants' department, many stores distinguish between "parent items" (the necessities bought by parents for their children) and "grandparent items" (frilly extras which are most likely to be bought by grandparents). Typically, the markup is much higher on grandparent items, indicating that the store believes that it faces a less elastic demand curve there than for parent items.

Regulated Monopoly

Some industries cannot be competitively organized. These include the so-called octopus public utilities, where the largest costs are the distribution systems, and where the actual costs of providing the service are apt to be quite low compared to those distribution costs. Among these are the water, electric, gas, and telephone systems. For this reason, it is customary in the United States to give a grant of monopoly to a firm which will serve a community with these utilities. In exchange for the grant of monopoly, the firm is subjected to regulation. It is not permitted to set the price that would maximize its profit, but instead must set a price which is socially acceptable. To examine such pricing, we use the third approach, with average costs and revenues.

Because of the character of these industries, most of them have the very high basic cost of getting the service to the customer but the relatively low cost of producing the service, with the result that the average cost is declining over the entire range of probable outputs. The marginal cost is always below that average cost. A typical example is shown in Figure 8.3, along with a demand curve and a marginal revenue curve. If the firm

**Figure 8.3
Regulated Monopoly**

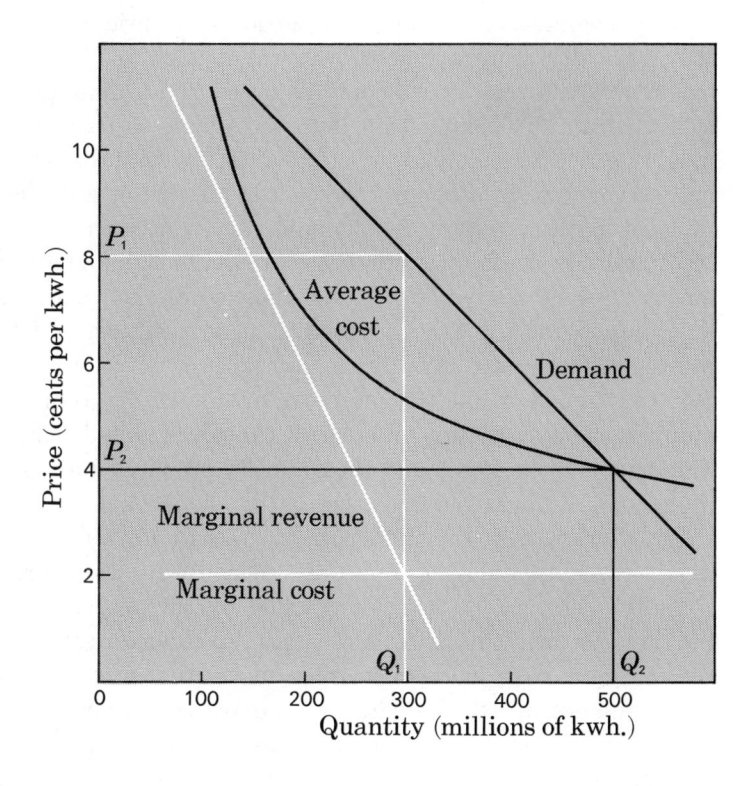

were an unrestricted monopolist, it would choose the output Q_1, at which marginal cost equals marginal revenue, and would set the price at P_1, which corresponds to that output. Such a position would be highly profitable. However, the public utilities regulatory commissions would not permit such pricing. Instead, they typically require much lower rates, such as P_2, at which the firm would sell Q_2. It should be noted that a main principle of the regulatory commission is to set a price so that all costs, including a fair return on the value of the assets of the company, will be covered. In other words, the commission usually tries to find the position where the demand curve crosses the average cost curve. (In actual practice, there are apt to be many disagreements between the accountants of the commission and those of the company on the exact method of measuring cost and determining a fair return and a fair valuation.)

It can be seen that the price set by the utility commission eliminates much of the problem of the unregulated monopoly. The price will be lower and the quantity produced significantly higher than would be the case of the monopolist were unrestrained. However, the monopolist will still not be operating under the most efficient conditions. Because his costs are continually declining, he has not reached his lowest possible cost. Further, because the price is set equal to the average cost, not the marginal cost, it is not possible to say that price is a measure of the extra cost of producing an extra unit. In other words, consumers are still paying more than the extra cost of the resources used. If the price were set lower so that it were equal to marginal cost, it would produce the same result as in pure competition. However, the total revenue would be less than the total cost, and the company would lose money. In the long run, it would be unable to provide the service required. Economists have often argued that it would be better if the price were set at marginal cost and the losses of the company were subsidized by general taxation, but they have never been able to convince public officials that this would be desirable.

In certain rural areas, a special form of pricing electrical service manages to come very close to approximating the economist's ideal. Because it is very expensive to provide the wires to serve a particular farm (especially if it is some distance from its neighbors), there is a high monthly charge for having electrical service at all. Since it costs the company relatively little to provide the electricity over those wires once they are in, the electricity charge per kilowatt-hour is quite low. In this fashion, the consumer pays a substantial portion of the overhead cost of the company by the monthly charge, and then pays a wattage rate which closely approximates marginal cost. The result is that farmers typically use more electricity per household than city dwellers because their marginal cost of electricity is much lower. Surprisingly, the *average* cost of electricity is also quite low, chiefly because the monthly charge is spread over a large number of kilowatt-hours. The final section of this chapter discusses a special problem in the pricing of electricity.

Monopsony

When a firm is the only buyer of a product in the market, it is called a monopsony. Monopsonies occur most frequently in labor markets when a single firm is the only important employer in a locality. The textile mill towns of New England and the coal mining towns of Pennsylvania were examples of labor monopsonies, although better transportation is widening labor markets and lessening monopsony power. A monopsonist normally faces an upward sloping supply curve of labor, since workers will offer different amounts of work at different prices. Just as a monopolist is often unwilling to sell additional goods because the lower price would have to be given to all buyers, so a monopsonist is often unwilling to hire additional labor because the increased wage would have to be paid to all workers. He will therefore prefer to keep employment low as a means of keeping wages down.

In looking at the monopsonist, we use the term *marginal factor cost*, which is the increase in factor cost from hiring one additional unit. When the factor is labor, we use the term *marginal labor cost*. For a monopsonist, the marginal labor cost is higher than the wage. The marginal labor cost is equal to the wage of the last worker plus the total increase in wages paid to the previously hired workers. Exactly how much higher the marginal labor cost is than the wage depends upon the elasticity of the supply of labor. In Figure 8.4, the marginal labor cost is shown, together with the supply curve of labor from which it is derived and the firm's own demand curve for labor. The monopsonist will hire additional workers only until the marginal cost per worker crosses his demand for labor. In the example shown, he will hire twenty-five men paying a weekly wage of $80.00. An additional man would be worth about $110.00 to the firm, which is far more than the wage. The extra cost of that man would be more, however, for the wage of each of the previous twenty-five workers would rise $1.60, making the marginal factor cost more than the $110 which the firm would be willing to pay.

If an employer could discriminate among employees, he could escape this problem. However, this would require complete secrecy about wages. With discrimination, an additional worker could be hired without affecting the wages of the previous workers. In such a case, the marginal labor cost would be only the wage of the additional worker; and the employer would hire the number of workers determined by the intersection of the demand and supply curves—in this example, thirty workers. There would be no such thing as *the* wage rate, since every worker would receive a different sum. Such hiring practices are rare for ordinary workers, since the secrecy required is impossible; but they still exist for professional and executive groups.

These cases can only occur if workers are unorganized. In Chapter 11, we will examine what happens when an employer monopsony faces a union monopoly.

An Illustration: Electricity Prices

In the early 1930s, the customary price for electricity was about 6 cents per kilowatt-hour. This price came about because the cost curve seemed to cross the demand curve at about that point. Electricity was typically used in most households only for electric lighting. A few utilities in various parts of the country had experimented with minor variations in the price and had discovered that the demand was quite inelastic. The results as known then were approximately those shown in Figure 8.5. The price P_1 and quantity Q_1 corresponded to the usual rules of regulatory agencies.

**Figure 8.4
Monopsony**

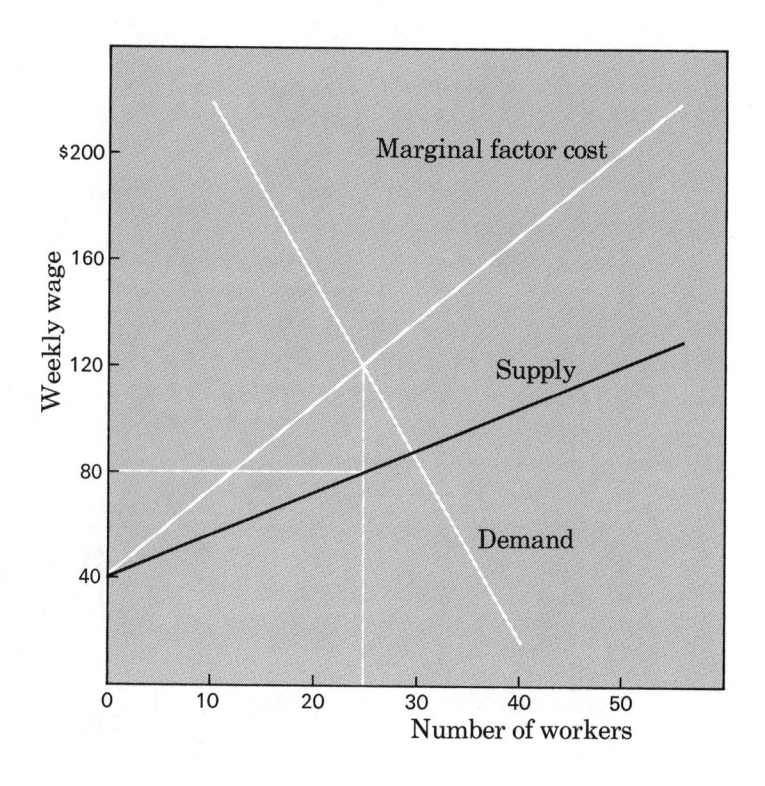

Monopolistic Markets

Figure 8.5
Electricity Prices Before TVA

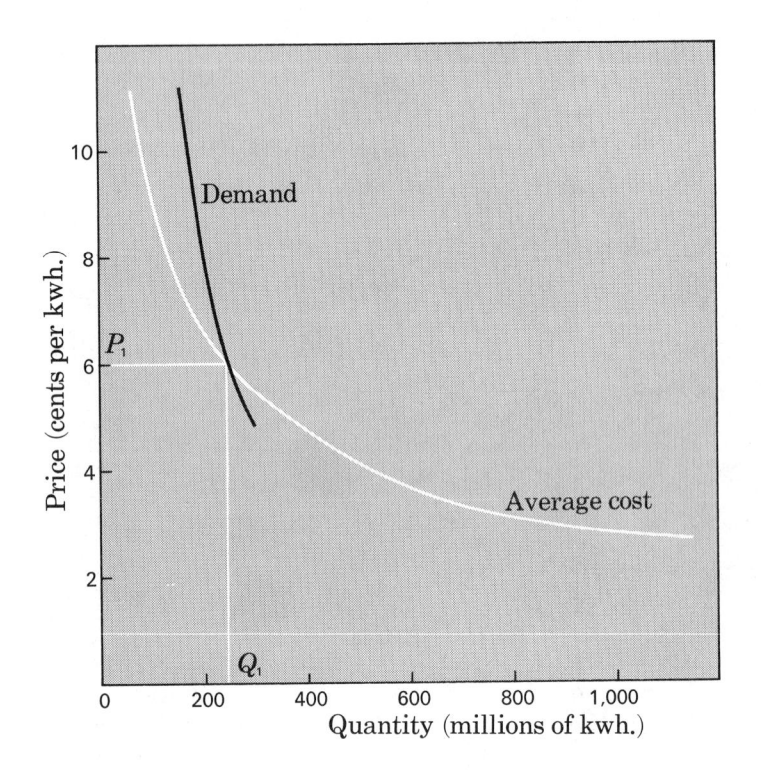

During the mid '30s, the Tennessee Valley Authority was established with a multipurpose goal of developing the Tennessee Valley by building dams and providing for navigation, flood control, recreational facilities, and, almost incidentally, electricity. Because TVA was a governmental agency primarily concerned with uplifting a depressed area of the country, it was not especially concerned with making a profit on its electricity sales. Furthermore, determining the cost of electricity when it is provided through a multipurpose project such as this is virtually impossible. As a result, TVA set a low price of less than 3 cents a kilowatt-hour, primarily as a means of helping the people in the valley. It came as something of a surprise to everyone that the quantity of electricity subsequently used was not that which would have been expected from a simple extension of the "known" demand curve, but instead was several times that amount. On the basis of the TVA experience, it became clear that the demand for electricity was like that shown in Figure 8.6. The demand curve becomes very elastic at lower prices for electricity, and many uses other than lighting come into existence. Home appliances, machinery, and the like become feasible at lower prices, although they are considered too expensive if prices are higher.

The interesting result of this episode was that most of the private utilities began applying for drastic rate reductions. In a few cases, some of the regulatory commissions (perhaps because they were accustomed to opposing whatever the utilities asked for) rejected the new lower rates, giving as their reason the fear that such rates would threaten the financial stabilities of the companies. Eventually, however, the new lower rates became common almost everywhere in the country. Another interesting result also occurred. Because the electric companies now perceived their demand as elastic, they felt it in their own interest to find ways to cut costs and prices in order to expand the total use of electricity. As a result, the relationship between electrical companies and regulatory commissions has become much less an adversary proceeding and much more a process of cooperation in order to find the best position. Despite years of generally rising prices and rising costs for the companies, the price of electricity today is still lower than it was in 1930.

Figure 8.6
Electricity Prices After TVA

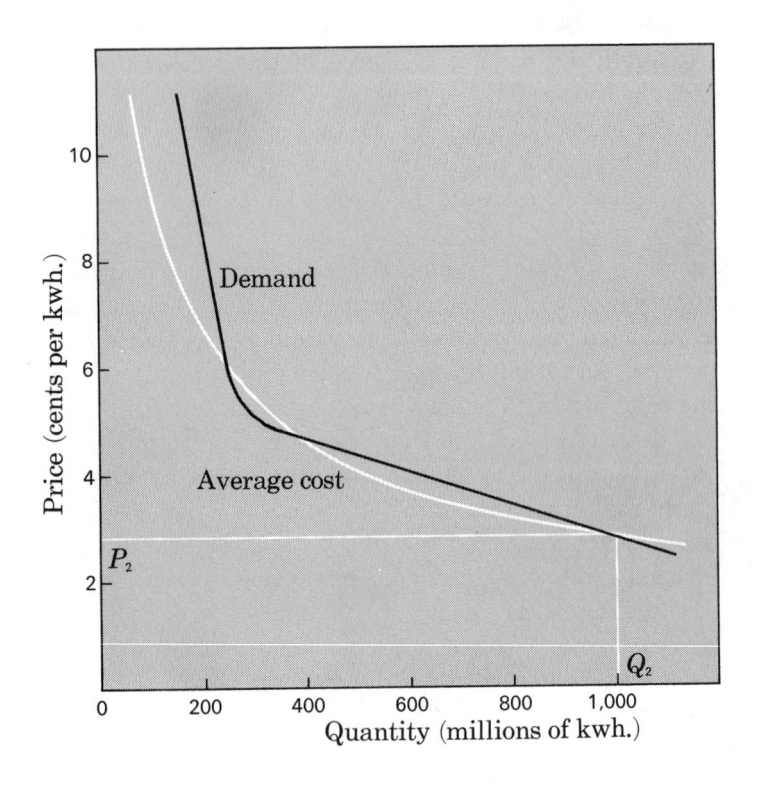

Chapter 9
Imperfectly Competitive Markets

When Joe Nettuno was discharged from the army, he decided to use his poker profits (the money he saved from not playing) plus a little money he had inherited to open a restaurant. He planned to specialize in north Italian cooking, using the recipes which he had learned from his mother. (Her *tacchino alla Bolognese* and *scampi alla marinara* were especially famous in the neighborhood.)

He considered opening the restaurant in the Italian neighborhood where he had always lived, but decided that there were too many similar restaurants there. He felt that there would be a better opportunity either in the downtown area or in one of the more affluent suburbs.

If he located in the suburbs, he would try to operate a moderately priced restaurant which could attract a family trade. (He had observed that the successful restaurants there had used this formula, but that more expensive places had usually failed.) In the downtown area, he would operate a more expensive restaurant, which would cater to business trade for luncheons and the visitors to the city who stay in the downtown hotels. Such a restaurant would require a well-stocked bar and an elaborate wine cellar, and would naturally accept all major credit cards. Many of its customers would be the "expense-account trade," who would expect, and be willing to pay for, first-class service.

After comparing the different costs of the two types of restaurants, Joe decided to open downtown. He hired his cousin, Ray Enzo, to serve as *Maitre d'hotel* and take general charge of the dining room, while Joe supervised the kitchen. Between them they checked every detail of operation, because they were convinced that the little things make or break a restaurant. Joe even initiated a special training program for bus boys, so that they could learn to clear a table and have it ready for new customers within two minutes.

Since the opening six months ago, the restaurant has been quite successful; but a cloud has recently appeared on the horizon. It is rumored that another luxury Italian restaurant plans to open nearby. If it does, Nettuno's will almost certainly be less profitable. Joe has made an appointment to discuss the matter with the other owner, in hopes that they can make an arrangement which will keep them from destroying each other's profits.

Forms of Imperfect Competition

In pure competition, there are a large number of firms selling identical products; competition can become imperfect if there are only a few firms or if the firms sell differentiated products, or both. If there are only a few firms, the situation is called *oligopoly;* if the products are differentiated, it is called *monopolistic competition.* When there are only a few firms selling differentiated products, the situation is usually referred to as *differentiated oligopoly.*

In monopolistic competition, every firm is selling a product which is in some ways similar to others and in some ways unique; hence the contradictory name monopolistic competition. Sometimes the differentiation is in the product itself, sometimes in the location of the firm or in the services provided, and sometimes only in the buyers' imaginations.

Monopolistic competition is the most common form of market in our society. Every retail store differentiates its products from every other by its location, the personality of its clerks, its terms of sale, and the selection of goods offered. Almost all consumer goods are differentiated by brands, style, and advertising. Just about the only undifferentiated products in our society are raw materials, such as grains and other agricultural products, and metals and simple metal products. Metal products often come in different qualities; but, since the qualities are standardized and can be provided by a number of different sellers, quality does not differentiate the products of one seller. The only differentiation which can be used by firms selling such products is in delivery dates, credit terms, and the like.

Once we admit the idea of differentiated products, it becomes rather difficult to define an industry. Normally, we say that an industry is composed of all the firms selling the same product; but in monopolistic competition, all of the products are different, although similar. It is customary to regard goods as being in the same industry if the cross elasticity of demand is fairly high. One can often rank different products according to their cross elasticity with respect to a particular product, and then define an industry as extending to a gap in the size of the cross elasticities.

When viewed from the standpoint of differentiated products, it is clear that there are relatively few monopolies in our society. For example, before World War II, Alcoa was the only manufacturer of ingot aluminum in the United States; but aluminum was used for making automobiles, transmission lines, and cooking materials, and had to compete with steel, copper, glass, and cast iron for these purposes. In that case, should one say that Alcoa was a monopolist in the aluminum industry or a monopolistic competitor in a broadly defined industry? The question is a confusing one. And for this reason, a large portion of the court record in antitrust cases is devoted to a precise definition of the industry, because it is impossible to decide whether a monopoly does or does not exist until the industry has been defined.

Geography may be a source of product differentiation. It is clear that a supermarket across town is not really in the same market and is not providing the same products as a grocery store a block away. In some cases, the gap may be so large that geography actually breaks one industry into several. In other cases, there may be a continuous range of substitution, and the geography may be an important part of product differentiation.

It is hard to decide whether entry into a monopolistically competitive market is easy or difficult. In one sense, it is easy: it is always possible for someone to produce a product which is similar to those already in the market. In another sense, it is difficult: it may prove extremely hard for a firm to match the characteristics which are the most appealing to consumers. The process of searching for new techniques, new products, and new approaches is a constant one in industries of this sort.

Oligopoly exists whenever there are only a few sellers in the market, or where a few dominate. For example, there are three major producers of aluminum in the United States, four of automobiles, and five of tires. In such industries, firms can no longer think of the market as impersonal, but must take account of the actions of each of their competitors. For this reason, the behavior in such industries is quite different and is based almost entirely on the reaction process.

Because each major firm supplies a large portion of the total output of the industry, it is clear that each can have an important effect upon the industry price. It is also clear that if one firm changes its price, other firms are apt to change theirs, because they will feel the repercussions of its actions.

Oligopolists may produce either standardized or differentiated products. If they are producing standardized products, they often feel they have little choice except conspiracy—that is, they must all get together and agree on a policy which is satisfactory to all. Otherwise, each would be in a position to destroy the others. If the products are differentiated, the oligopolists have an alternative. They can settle on a price, either by collusion or by a form of mutual understanding, and then concentrate their efforts on nonprice competition—attempts to increase their sales by means of advertising, product innovation, and the like. When the oligopolists sell differentiated products, the industry takes on the characteristics of both monopolistic competition and oligopoly. (Tobacco manufacturers do not compete in price, but use advertising instead.)

In oligopoly, there are typically substantial barriers to entry or the industry could not remain an oligopoly. Sometimes these barriers may be technical in nature—that is, the efficient size of the firm is very large compared to the size of the industry. In most cases, however, the barriers to entry are economic, in the sense that they result from the behavior of the firms. For example, industries which have built a strong acceptance of their trademarks by means of advertising over the years usually can not be easily challenged by newcomers. Sometimes the barriers to entry may come about because of the distribution system which the existing firms have established, or because of their knowledge of production techniques in the industry. In many cases, the domination of existing firms is the result of the continuous emphasis which they have placed upon their research divisions, and their ability to develop new products or variations more rapidly than they can be matched by competitors.

The Monopolistically Competitive Firm

Let us first discuss the case of monopolistic competition when there is free entry for new firms. In the short run, the firm will make its price and output decisions in a manner rather similar to that of a monopolist. In general, however, a firm in monopolistic competition will have a demand curve which is relatively elastic; as it lowers prices, customers will not only enter the industry attracted by the low price, but will also switch from other firms. Nevertheless, the firm does not have a perfectly elastic demand curve like a firm in pure competition, because there are always distinctions of the monopolistic competitive firm; therefore, some customers will not switch from competitors even as the price goes down, and sometimes will stick with a firm even if the price goes up. In the short run, a firm will produce up to the point where its marginal cost equals its marginal revenue. It will charge the price, shown in Figure 9.1 as P_1, which corresponds to that output. If the firm is lucky, that price will be greater than the average cost at that output and it will make a profit. The firm in Figure 9.1 has done so.

In the long run, however, the firm in Figure 9.1 cannot expect to remain safe in its profits. New firms will be likely to enter the industry, copying some of the characteristics of the firms already there, but adding special characteristics of their own. As these firms move in, the demand curve facing the original firm will shift to the left. It will also become more elastic if the new firms

Figure 9.1
Monopolistic Competition (Short Run)

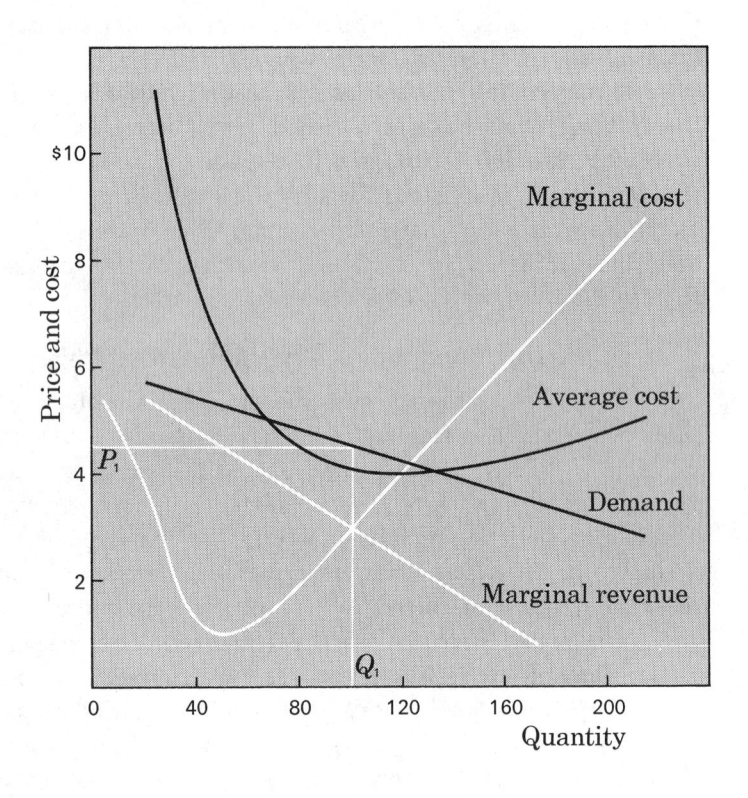

copy most of their characteristics from the present firm. The demand curve will probably become somewhat less elastic if the new firms find unique characteristics which will tend to satisfy a particular group of customers and take them away from the original firm entirely. In any case, entry would continue as long as the industry seems profitable. Therefore, in the long run, the firm will find itself in the position shown in Figure 9.2, where the demand curve has shifted to the left until it is just tangent to the average cost curve. At that stage, the firm will be breaking even and covering all of its costs, including a normal return. It will not be making any profit in the economic sense of the term.

If the firm had originally found itself incurring a loss instead of making a profit, one would have expected that some firms would leave the industry; therefore, the effect would still be approximately the same as shown in Figure 9.2.

In the present case, we can see that the industry is not as efficient as it could be. Even in the long run, the individual firm will not be operating at its lowest cost point; instead, it will be operating somewhere to the left of it. The reason, of course, is that, with differentiated products, the only way that the firm can increase its output is to cut prices. If it does so, it will find that it must cut its prices more than its costs fall. Naturally, it will choose to keep its prices high and its volume low.

Consumers pay higher prices in monopolistic competition than in pure competition, but they also receive an extra benefit. They are no longer confined to buying a single standardized product, but are able to choose from among a variety of products available. In some cases, the variety is clearly a benefit and probably adequate compensation for the higher costs. In other cases, the variety may be an illusion and consumers may be paying higher costs but receiving little benefit. For example, is a consumer really better off if he has the alternative of buying four different brands of gasoline from four different stations at the same intersection when each of those stations operates at low volume and high cost? Or would he be better off with a single brand sold by one optimum-sized station?

Figure 9.2
Monopolistic Competition (Long Run)

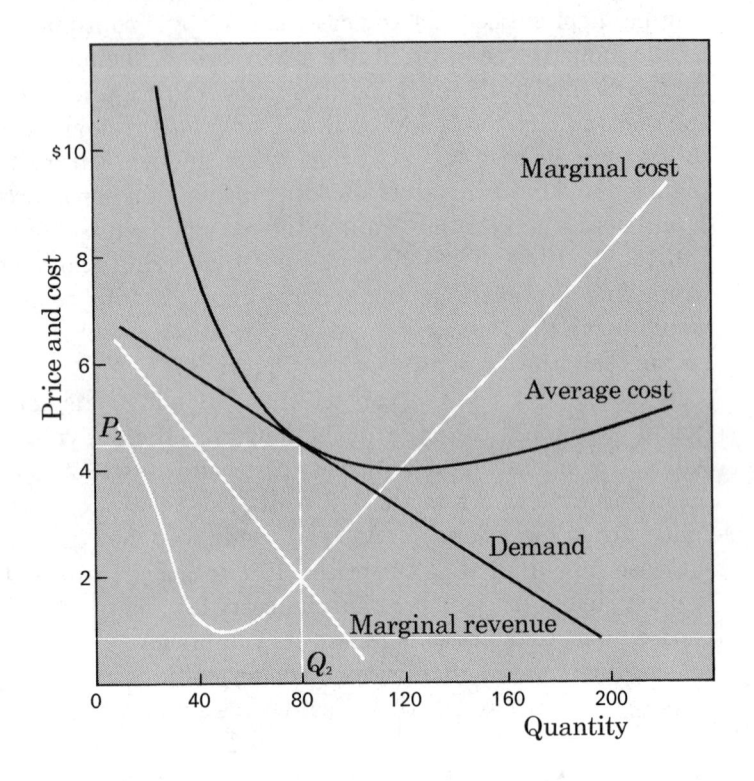

Nonprice Competition

The simplified result shown in Figure 9.2 describes exactly what would happen if, for example, the only form of competition between firms was in their location. In fact, this is seldom the case. Most firms compete in a large number of different dimensions: in terms of the design of the product, the services offered, the credit terms available, and so on. They also compete in advertising campaigns which may be both informative and persuasive. The long-run equilibrium of Figure 9.2 is less likely to be reached than the long-run equilibrium of pure competition. As new firms enter an industry, old firms are apt to be changing their behavior. They will engage in a large number of different activities, trying to maintain their position. These actions will have two effects. They will tend to shift the demand curve for the firm to the right, but they will also raise the costs of operation. Clearly, the firm will try to choose only those activities which will shift the demand curve more than they shift the cost curve. The firm in monopolistic competition must be continually striving to improve the bundle of satisfactions which it offers to the consumer with its product. Simply sitting and waiting for other firms to copy its past success will clearly not lead to success in the future. We should not evaluate monopolistic competition in terms of a static long-run equilibrium model as we have done with pure competition. We must think of it as part of a dynamic process whereby the goods and services which consumers receive are constantly changing, as producers seek new ways to please the consumer and increase their profits.

Nowhere is the phenomenon of dynamic change more evident than in the field of product design. In the automobile or refrigerator industry, there are only slight differences at any one time between the models put out by different firms. Over a decade or two, however, we see important changes in all brands. Today's low-priced car is superior in many ways even to the luxury cars of twenty years ago. As long as the firm continues to make such changes, it may avoid having its demand curve forced to the left and its profit eliminated by competition. We can say that the industry is always tending towards an equilibrium, as new firms try to copy successful designs. But before the equilibrium is reached, the better firms will have altered their conditions and the industry will have moved on, heading towards a different equilibrium which it probably will never reach.

The Behavior of the Oligopolistic Firm

Unlike any other market form, oligopolistic behavior cannot be described by a simple maximizing process. The reason is that the firm does not face any given set of conditions; its world depends upon the response of its competitors, who may, in turn, be reacting to its actions. Even such a basic concept as a demand curve is meaningless without making some assumptions about reactions. One common theory suggests that firms assume that competitors will match their price cuts, but not their increases. Under such conditions, the firm would be virtually paralyzed—afraid that a price increase would cost them their share of the market, and that a price cut would not help them. Prices would tend to remain wherever they happened to be.

Such an assumption makes it possible to describe a pattern of oligopolistic behavior, but it is doubtful that this pattern is typical. Usually, relationships among oligopolists are not nearly as distant as this. Competitors often get together in various ways, as, for example, at industry conventions or trade association meetings. It would be stretching the bounds of one's imagination to believe that they do not consider their mutual economic problems at that time. In *The Wealth of Nations* (1776), Adam Smith said that "People of the same trade seldom get together, even for merriment and diversion, but the conversation ends in a conspiracy against the public and a contrivance to raise prices." Although his language was perhaps harsh, the phenomenon which he described then is still quite common today. Even though conspiracy in restraint of trade is contrary to the antitrust laws, a great deal of such conversation still takes place. Under the antitrust laws, firms cannot sign contracts for such conspiracy or enforce the agreements at which they have arrived.

Many of the informal agreements which are reached by means of conspiracy are apt to be unstable. The reason is that although all firms realize that a high price is in their interest, it is profitable for any one of them to cut price as long as it expects the others to keep their prices up. Consequently, secret price concessions to large buyers are common occurences in oligopolies, even where there is an agreement among the firms. Most forms of discipline which could be imposed upon price cutters would involve overt action which might bring the industry to the attention of law enforcement officials. Furthermore, it is in the interest of the buyers of these products to encourage price concessions and often to claim offers of such concessions even if they have not received them. Perhaps the only thing which holds conspiracies together is a general belief that any price concession will become known very soon, so that no firm could obtain any advantage from price cutting, even for a moderate period of time.

Collusion can take many forms. The simplest form is obviously when all firms get together to arrive at a decision. Because different firms often have different cost structures, the price which is the most profitable for one firm may not be so for another. Their different interests can best be harmonized by discussion and compromise. Unfortunately for the participants, this kind of collusion is the easiest to observe and is the most likely to produce reaction on the part of customers and law-enforcement authorities.

Where meetings of competitors are not feasible, an alternative method is for one firm to become the price leader in the industry. It will set its price in the full knowledge that in so doing it is setting the price for the whole industry. It will therefore be operating as if it were the decision maker for a monopoly which consists of the entire industry. It will then convey its new price to other firms which will follow suit. Many years ago, the United States Steel Corporation sponsored the regular Gary dinners, at which Judge Gary, the head of U.S. Steel, made a speech which exhorted all firms not to become price cutters, and which announced U.S. Steel's price for the coming period. These dinners were abandoned shortly before an antitrust case was filed against the company. The usual method now is for firms which are price leaders to send a press release to the *New York Times* or the *Wall Street Journal* announcing the new price. Other firms in the industry then read this report and set their prices accordingly.

The extreme form of collusion is merger, whereby two firms, which were previously competitors, join together and become a single firm. In this case, the competition between the two ceases; and any form of price competition is eliminated, at least as far as these firms are concerned. Increasingly, however, the antitrust authorities are apt to take action against any merger between competing firms, if the firms are of any significant size. The general rule of thumb which has been adopted is that horizontal mergers are forbidden if the effect is to create a firm which will control more than 30 percent of the output of the industry. Mergers are discussed further in the appendix to this chapter.

Another way to eliminate price competition would be for a more powerful firm to undercut a weaker one to the extent that the weaker firm goes bankrupt. Although such aggressive behavior is not unknown in the American economy, it is not common; the process of driving a competitor out of business is apt to be very costly, and it is somewhat doubtful whether the firm could make enough profit from its later monopoly position to justify the costs of achieving that end.

These few examples do not exhaust the possibilities of behavior in oligopolistic industries, but they do indicate the kinds of relationships which are typical. Every oligopoly is unique and will produce certain results which are peculiar to it. These generalizations are no substitute for the study of specific cases.

In cases of differentiated oligopoly, individual firms are apt to recognize quite clearly their interdependence with respect to price; as a result, a system of quasi-agreements not to compete on a price basis develops. However, the individual firms are apt to continue to compete by nonprice means which are more difficult for other firms to match. Firms constantly use advertising, new product design, and development as a way to attract customers from their competitors and expand the market for their product. It is significant that almost all of the firms listed among the hundred largest advertisers in America are oligopolists producing consumer goods. In most cases, their advertising is matched with continual development of their products. The goal of any firm in a differentiated oligopoly is to differentiate its product enough so that the cross elasticity of demand with respect to its competitors will decline. In such a case, the firm will be able to behave almost like a monopolist, and will begin to acquire a certain freedom, even in setting prices; while other firms may be able to match the price, they will be unable to match the product. All forms of nonprice competition can be used for this purpose, including advertising, performance changes, design changes, changes in the repair facilities which may be available for service, and new manufacturing methods to lower the cost of production.

Advertising

Advertising is one of the most controversial aspects of the American economy. It is also one of the most important tools that a firm can use in differentiating its product. Even where there are important physical differences, it is advertising that makes the public aware of these differences and turns them into economic assets.

The arguments on advertising cover a wide range. At one extreme are the people who look upon advertising as utter waste, seeing it as 2 percent of the Gross National Product which contributes nothing to the economy whatever. At the other extreme are those who give advertising credit for the entire American way of life. The truth lies somewhere between these extremes.

One argument which is often given in favor of advertising is that it supports radio, television, magazines, newspapers, and other communications media. Although this is true, it is hardly a justification for advertising. Clearly, the total cost of providing the communications themselves is much less than the total cost of advertising. Furthermore, such an argument ignores the impact which advertising has on the structure of the economy, which is clearly far more important than simply the subsidy.

A second argument given in favor of advertising is that it conveys information. In large measure, this is true. Many people are so concerned with purely persuasive advertising—such as that used for cigarettes, beer, and, to some extent, automobiles —that they forget that many forms of advertising are primarily designed to convey information about what products are available and where. Typically, business advertising and much of the advertising which appears in photography, sporting goods, and home improvement magazines are of this sort. Similarly, much of the advertising which department stores and grocery stores place in daily newspapers is informative advertising, serving notice that certain goods are available at certain prices. Nevertheless, it remains true that a large portion of total advertising is not designed to convey information, but to be persuasive. In some cases, in fact, the advertising may be designed deliberately to confuse rather than to clarify. (For example, have television advertisements for headache remedies actually clarified the problem of how best to deal with headaches?)

It is probably true, however, that those who object to advertising most vociferously probably overrate its importance. Advertisers are often credited with the ability to persuade consumers to want goods for which they have no use. It is doubtful that they can actually do so. It is more likely that advertisers must start with a basic need that the consumer already has, and then try to persuade him that the commodity which they have to offer will help to satisfy this need. Thus manufacturers of luxury automobiles often emphasize the status which the owner of such an automobile could obtain, while the manufacturers of smaller sportier versions often concentrate on a particular image of the young, swinging sophisticate. It is a moral judgement, not an economic one, to say that these appeals are wrong, and that individuals should buy automobiles only for the transportation which they provide.

Ultimately, the argument for or against advertising must be based upon its effect on the process of product differentiation. If advertising merely serves as a method of dividing the market among a large number of firms, each too small to achieve efficiencies of scale, the impact of advertising is undoubtedly undesirable—especially since the consumer must pay not only the costs of small scale operation, but also the costs of the advertising which keeps the firms so small.

If advertising succeeds in increasing the scale of operation of some firms, which otherwise would be too small, then it may be possible that the gains from the efficiencies of large-scale operations may outweigh the costs of the advertising which made it possible. If this is the case, one can say that advertising has desirable effects. Unfortunately, there is no reason to believe that advertising will increase the size of the firms just far enough to take advantage of economies of scale. If the advertising is sufficiently successful, the size of the firms may increase beyond the most efficient point to a stage of diseconomies of scale. In such cases, advertising is triply undesirable: the advertising itself raises the cost; the firm is inefficient because it is too large; and the amount of competition in the industry is decreased.

The principal effect of advertising lies in its relation to changes in product design and style. If a firm utilizes advertising in combination with these changes, then the advertising can clearly increase (1) the speed with which new products are introduced on the market and (2) the extent to which these new developments will provide consumers with goods which they want. This does not mean that every new product which is introduced will be successful. The Edsel, which the Ford Motor Company launched with one of the biggest campaigns of all time, was a dismal failure. Many advertising men admit that the most they can do is produce an initial sale of a product; repeat sales depend upon the product itself. If this is true, it is clear that advertising and product design and development are not alternative strategies for a firm, but complementary ones which must be used together.

In conclusion, we may say that advertising is a very important facet of our economy, but that its importance should not be measured merely by the money spent on it. The importance of advertising is measured in what it does to the markets for which the goods are advertised. If the impact on those markets is desirable, advertising can take much of the credit. If the impact is undesirable, advertising must also accept the blame.

Efficiency and Imperfect Competition

In the simplest sense, imperfect competition is clearly inefficient. Monopolistically competitive firms are usually too small for lowest cost production. Oligopolistic firms which behave in a noncollusive manner are apt to settle into a rigid form of behavior, holding prices constant without response to cost or demand. On the other hand, if they do engage in collusion, the arrangements available to them are apt to produce almost as much rigidity as if there were no collusion at all. Furthermore, we sometimes find cases of aggression that destroy firms which could have made a significant contribution to the economy.

The difficulty with evaluating imperfect competition is that we are comparing it with a hypothetical pure competition in the same industries. In many circumstances, pure competition would not be conceivable in those industries. It is rather unlikely that it would be feasible to have one hundred or a thousand manufacturers of television sets in America, because differences between types of sets are inevitable, and product differentiation would almost certainly lead to the concentration of the industry within a few firms. Furthermore, there are cases in which economies of scale are such that firms can achieve lowest manufacturing costs only by being a large portion of the industry. It is true that there are probably fewer such industries than many people believe, but they do exist.

A further problem is that imperfect competition is being compared with pure competition in a static sense, although the major arguments to be made for it are dynamic—that is, they emphasize the new developments and new products which result as firms try to compete. We have already seen the emphasis which these firms place on nonprice competition. It is also true that oligopolists usually have both the means to engage in research on product development and the ability to profit from that development. Firms in pure competition are apt to have neither. Consequently, we find a number of circumstances in which development is more apt to take place in oligopolistic industries.

There has been some study in recent years about the origins of inventions. These studies have indicated that inventions may arise anywhere. Many of them are still made by small independent inventors, and many of them develop outside the industry in which the inventions are to be used. However, even where the *inventions* are originally made by outsiders, the *product development* usually takes place in large differentiated firms within the industry. Very often, getting a product from the laboratory design stage through pilot plant operation and actually into commercial production may involve years of work and the expenditure of millions of dollars. Such action is most unlikely to occur in purely competitive firms.

The foregoing argument does not prove that imperfect competition is uniformly progressive; only that it sometimes is. In any particular case, one must look very carefully at the specific facts.

Oligopolies often attract the attention of government antitrust agencies. In looking at these industries, both the Department of Justice and the Federal Trade Commission give particular attentions to the questions of economies of scale in manufacturing and the degree of progressiveness of the industry. Ordinarily, cases are prosecuted only where there have been serious inhibiting effects upon competition without substantial compensation in other dimensions. Where the firms have managed to lower costs substantially, or to provide genuinely progressive product development, there has been little tendency to prosecute or to attempt to break up these companies. It is typical that no major antitrust case has even been filed in the automobile industry, although there have been cases filed against automobile firms with respect to their role in certain other industries. For example, General Motors has been prosecuted with respect to its control of the bus industry. The only major case involving the automobile industry was an allegation of collusion with respect to delay on installing pollution control devices, but no attempt has been made to break up the very large firms in this industry.

An Illustration: Fair Trade Laws

Many firms in monopolistic competition are bothered by the problem of the lack of profit in the industry. Accordingly, they often want some kind of arrangements made within the industry to keep prices from going too low. Because there are so many firms in the industry, it is seldom possible to engage in any kind of conspiratorial agreement on prices. However, many state laws permit an arrangement whereby the *manufacturer* of a brand product may set a retail price below which no retailer in the state may sell his product. If the manufacturer takes advantage of this law, then the effect will be that all retailers in the state must raise their price to the fair trade price. Because the price goes up in all stores, not simply in one, the firm does not suffer from the high elasticity of demand for its individual sales, represented by demand D_1 in Figure 9.3. Instead, each firm receives its proportionate share of the total industry demand, shown as D_2. As all firms move up such a demand curve, they will all be making a profit. Unfortunately, the fair trade

**Figure 9.3
Fair Trade Laws**

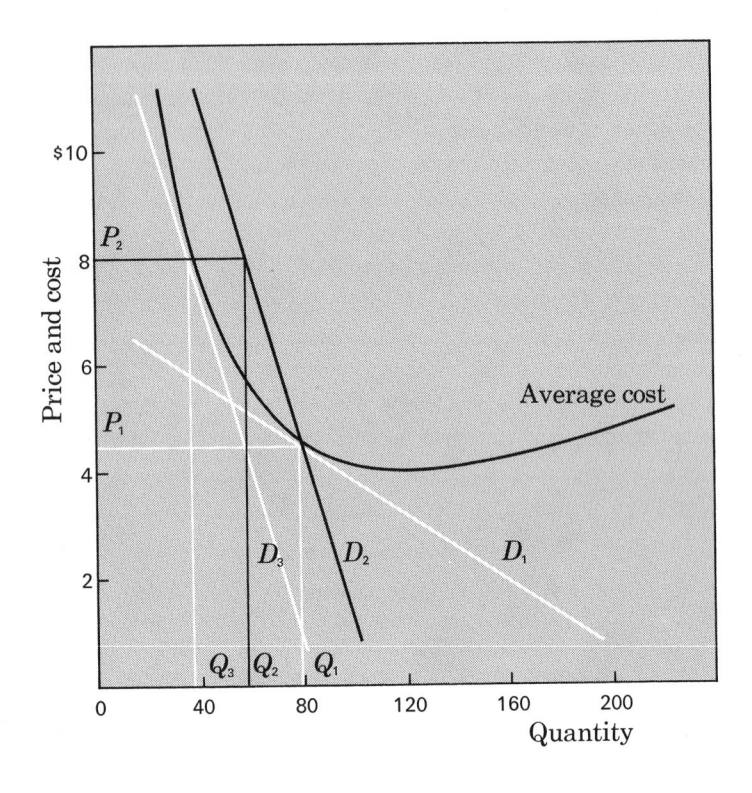

laws deal with only one of the two reasons why firms do not make profits. They solve the price-cutting problem, but not the problem of entry into the industry. Accordingly, one would expect new firms to enter the industry until the typical demand curve for individual firms is pushed backward to the level shown as D_3. At that point the firms are no longer making any profit, but consumers now suffer from higher prices. The effect of fair trade laws is to create a proliferation of dealers of the product, but it does not produce any long-run profits for the industry.

It is doubtful that manufacturers gain substantially from having fair-traded their products. Even without the law, the manufacturer can set the price at which he sells his product to the retailers. By the fair trade law, he sets a price that the retailer may in turn charge. Since the price he sets is usually higher than many retailers would normally charge, the manufacturer is guaranteeing a higher profit margin to the dealer; but he is probably also cutting the consumer demand for his product. Some manufacturers admit that they set fair-trade prices only because they are, in effect, blackmailed by retailers into doing so. In many cases, the customer may ask the retailer which brand is the better one. The retailer will certainly be more likely to advise the purchase of a fair-traded product. It is no coincidence that fair-trade pricing is especially common in drugs and liquors, two areas where consumers are quite apt to rely on the advice of retailers. It is almost nonexistent in groceries, where consumers make most choices unassisted.

There are, however, manufacturers who believe in fair trade as a matter of principle. These manufacturers believe that the image of their product is damaged by price-cutting. They set fair trade prices to convince consumers that theirs is a first-quality product. But it is questionable how many of the manufacturers who use fair trade really do so for this reason.

Many of the fair-trade laws were first established in the depression of the 1930s. At that time, the general decline in demand had led to a situation where many retailers were actually operating at a loss. Figure 9.4 shows such a case. In this circumstance, when the manufacturer set a higher fair-trade price, the retailers again moved up the demand curve D_2 to the price P_2. At this stage, they were still making no profit, but they were at least covering

**Figure 9.4
Fair Trade Laws
(Depression)**

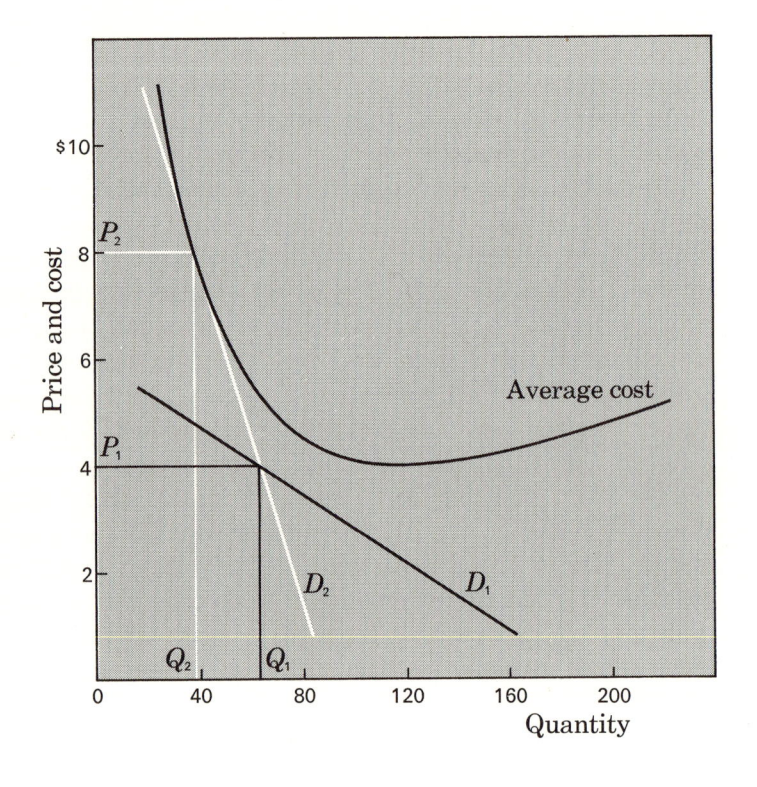

their costs. In cases like this, one could make an argument that fair-trade laws helped retailers who had a long-run future in the economy, but who were seriously threatened by the depression. The problem with utilizing fair trade at that time was that it should have been abandoned immediately as business improved—that is, as soon as the demand started a shift to the right of D_2. That would have prevented the wasteful entry of new retailers, which produced the results which we saw in Figure 9.3.

We have thus seen that fair-trade laws may be a useful device for temporarily maintaining firms during a depression, but they should not be used during prosperity. In prosperous times, they only create excessive entry and fragmentation of the industry. Unfortunately, it is easier not to apply fair-trade laws in the first place than to eliminate them. If fair-trade laws were repealed and prices fell, individual firms would find themselves suffering losses. It would be necessary for some retailers to leave so that the total demand of the remaining firms could rise high enough for them to break even. The firms now in the industry are naturally opposed to such a change for fear that they may be among those who are forced out or that they will lose money during the adjustment period. Consequently, it is not surprising that retailers in industries where fair trade is common are very strong in their support of continued use of this kind of pricing. The situation in this respect is somewhat similar to that which we observed in the New York taxi case. Even a policy which should not have been started at all is difficult to terminate.

Appendix to Chapter 9
Big Business

We saw in the Appendix to Chapter 5 that there are millions of firms in the United States, but that most of the business is accounted for by a small number of them. In this appendix, we wish to look at these large firms in somewhat more detail.

Every year, *Fortune* magazine publishes a list of the 500 largest industrial firms, along with the 50 largest banks, insurance companies, retailing companies, transportation companies, utilities, and diversified investment companies. The report on these 800 companies for 1971 is included in the May 1972 issue. This has become a regular feature of recent years, and "Fortune 500" has become an identifying description of large corporations. (Companies sometimes use the identification in help wanted ads.)

In determining the largest firms, one must first decide what is the basis of measurement. For example, are the largest firms those with the greatest sales, the largest assets, the most employees, or the greatest profits? *Fortune* uses sales for choosing the largest industrial companies, but a good argument can also be made for using assets or employees. The

Census uses "value added," the difference between sales and purchases, and therefore a good measure of the amount of production which takes place in a given firm. The Census definition is probably the best one; but it is almost impossible for anyone except the Census to use, because companies do not publish value added figures.

In 1971, the sales of the Fortune 500 totaled nearly half as much as the Gross National Product. This comparison overstates the importance of the 500 firms, because it does not account for the portion of their product which they purchase from other firms. (Their value added is certainly less than 50 percent). Nevertheless, there is no question that the largest firms account for a very large proportion of total production.

Another measure of the importance of these firms is employment. In 1971, all industrial firms (most of them manufacturers) employed about 24 percent of all civilian workers. The 500 employed about 18 percent of the total and about 75 percent of the industrial employment. Even within the 500 there was a substantial amount of concentration. The largest 50 employed about 8 percent of all workers, 35 percent of the industrial total, and 45 percent of the 500.

Causes of Growth

Although it is easier to look at the size of these few firms or their percentage of the total economy, it is far more interesting to inquire how they become so large. If they grew by producing better and cheaper products than their competitors, their size would be something to applaud—a sign that they had been performing well for the economy and their customers. On the other hand, if their growth resulted from forcing other firms out of business, their customers would be offered less choice and there would be no guarantee that consumers were receiving either the best products or the best prices. As is so often the case in economics, the facts are somewhere between the two extremes.

Some of the largest firms in our society have grown primarily through their own internal expansion. A prime example is International Business Machines. Starting with a patent monopoly on punch-card equipment, IBM continually expanded the kinds of equipment which it offered. In the early years, the company's equipment was largely confined to addition and subtraction; but gradually new units were added, until today IBM is the dominant firm in the computer field and one of the dozen largest industrial firms. The company did not, however, rely entirely upon the ingenuity of its research staff to achieve this position. It also adopted a policy of renting its equipment, not selling it, and refused to rent to firms which used equipment of other companies for any part of the installation. This policy made it almost impossible for other firms to enter the industry, because it was necessary for competitors to provide an entire line, not merely a better single-purpose machine. This policy was abandoned many years ago after an antitrust settlement, but it had persisted long enough to permit IBM to expand its initial headstart to domination of the field.

What, then, should be our attitude toward the growth of IBM? On the one hand, its growth resulted from a strong emphasis upon research and the development of equipment which was continually improved and expanded in capabilities. It grew because it was better than its competitors. On the other hand, its practices, at least in its earlier years, made the competition somewhat unequal by forcing other firms to compete on a broad range rather than the narrow scope they would have preferred. In part, IBM was better because its potential competitors were made worse. In the years since the antitrust settlement, IBM has shown continued growth against stiff competition; but it is hard to estimate how effective it might have been in open competition in earlier years.

Such expansion from internal sources is comparatively rare among large companies in the United States. Most of them achieved their initial size primarily through mergers, which economists usually classify into three major types: horizontal, vertical, and conglomerate.

Horizontal mergers occur when firms which were previously competitors combine into a single firm. (In the extreme case, a horizontal merger converts an oligopoly into a monopoly.) The greatest wave of horizontal mergers occurred in the last quarter of the nineteenth century, resulting in the formation of Standard Oil, U.S. Steel, and many other large firms. Many of these mergers were attacked under the Sherman antitrust law of 1890, and some legal loopholes were plugged by the Clayton Act of 1914. As a result, horizontal mergers between large national companies became quite rare after World War I. However, few of the companies formed before that time were broken up; so much of our big business legacy dates from that original group of mergers.

Vertical mergers occur when two firms which had a buyer-seller relationship combine into one. Sometimes the impetus for such mergers comes from purely managerial considerations—such as better scheduling or quality control—but they may also result from attempts to lessen competition. The control of an entire supply chain, from raw material to customer, by existing firms makes the entry of new firms into any particular stage of the market more difficult. Gradually the antitrust laws have been extended to apply to vertical mergers; so they too have become comparatively rare, at least among the largest firms. Again, however, many of the fruits of earlier mergers remain.

Conglomerate mergers are all mergers which are neither horizontal nor vertical. Such mergers may be of various types, and occur for many reasons. Very few of the mergers which we call conglomerate really consist of the union of two firms with no relationship whatever. One of the most common kinds of conglomerate merger is the territorial expansion; for example, two dairies in different areas might merge. Such mergers usually produce some net advantage to the merged firm. For example it might be possible to centralize some aspects of management or certain kinds of purchasing. (Sometimes mergers which seem to be territorial expansion when viewed from the product end are really horizontal mergers on the supply side—e.g., the two dairies might have been competing in purchasing milk from farmers. The merger of regional food chains into national chains has often fit into this category.) One common advantage of territorial expansion mergers is the ability to use certain kinds of advertising which would not otherwise be available. For example, national television advertising is only feasible for firms which sell nationally under the same name.

Just as a firm which operates in one region might expand its territory, so firms which concentrate in certain products may wish to expand their line. Such mergers are called product extension mergers. Thus a manufacturer of radios might wish to expand into other appliances, or a detergent firm might wish to acquire a producer of bleaches. Such mergers usually are designed to take advantage of marketing economies, such as use of the same sales force or the possibility of quantity discounts on television advertising. It is also believed that use of a common trade name permits each product sold to become an advertisement for other products of the line.

In addition to these two kinds of mergers, there are genuine conglomerate mergers. These occur for various reasons. For example, our tax laws encourage corporations to retain a portion of their earnings and reinvest them, thereby increasing the value of the stock. When investors sell the stock, the resulting capital gains are taxed at a lower rate than ordinary income. This preference for reinvestment over dividends is appropriate when the firm wants to expand its facilities. In many cases, however, no such opportunities for expansion exist, and the management must seek other uses for the retained funds. Thus an industrial company becomes an investment company, seeking profitable uses for its funds.

Even highly diversified mergers often have a competitive impact, since different firms might be each other's customers and apply reciprocal preference in purchasing. It is not clear how important reciprocity is in promoting conglomerate mergers, but it does have some influence.

Competition Among Large Firms

There can be little doubt that the rise of the giant firms has profoundly changed the character of American capitalism. Such firms are usually oligopolistic, rather than competitive, in their major markets. They are large enough to develop training programs for their managers, and to maintain full-time "representatives" in Washington to look after their interests. Their stock is usually held by so many people that the managers effectively control the company, not the owners. In a sense, such firms seem to be totally out of control, responsible neither to their owners, the market, nor the government.

Such firms indeed have great power, but it is not boundless.

We need only remember that General Motors, the largest industrial corporation, produced the Corvair, a commercial disaster exceeded only by Ford's Edsel. (Ford is number three.) In many cases, smaller firms have made a significant inroad into the markets of large ones by their ability to see opportunities which the big ones have missed. No matter how big the firm, it must deliver the goods. However, such firms do seem to stack the deck, so that the game is hardly a fair one.

Some economists have argued that the changing position of firms in the top 100, 200, or 500 demonstrates that there is still a substantial amount of mobility among such firms, which is "almost as good" as competition. A careful examination of the data shows that there may have been such mobility in the early part of the century, but there is little of it now. The mobility that does exist comes largely from the disappearance of firms through merger (with the resulting increase in size of the survivor) and the general change in the size of entire industries as new developments shift consumer and business purchases. In almost every industry, most of the firms which were the largest in 1929 are still the largest.

Other authors have argued that the management of these largest firms (the "technostructure") have become so independent that they can now be the disinterested guardians of the public good, free from the narrow profit-seeking that characterized a previous generation. Even if this were true, it is doubtful that it would be desirable. Remember that profit is society's reward and signal for the expansion of products which it desires. Those who do not seek profit often do not seek to serve the public either. (In general, are government-run agencies more oriented to the good of their clients than profit-seeking firms?)

But we need have little fear of the disinterestedness of corporate management. All the evidence available, whether derived from systematic studies or casual observation, indicates that the present generation of executives is as money-hungry as its predecessors, despite its claims to devotion to the public. We should be neither surprised nor dismayed that this is the case. The character of business is its profit orientation; without that, we would be at the mercy of a self-selected authoritarian elite, still without responsibility to voters, owners, or customers. It would probably be desirable for government to exert more control over large firms, but such control should be exercised by officials who must answer at the next election for how well they have done their job.

Chapter 10
Government and Markets

Like most of the other states, Jeffersonia has passed various laws in recent years to control air and water pollution. Principal enforcement of these laws is in the hands of the Air and Water Pollution Boards, which establish standards and hear appeals. Both boards are composed of dedicated individuals who have been concerned with the problem of pollution controls for years.

Four years ago, the state legislature established an interim investigating committee to study the workings of the program. The committee's report, published two years ago, was filled with praise for the members and staffs of the boards, but concluded that the program had been quite ineffective.

According to the report, the boards have usually set reasonable standards. In almost every case, the problem has been the date on which the standards were to go into effect. For example, standards for emission of sulfur dioxide in smoke were established, with a deadline of one year. Community Federal Electric Company, which serves most of the state, appealed from the standard. Lawyers for Comm-Fed said that the company would be unable to find supplies of low-sulfur fuel, that they could not convert their boilers in the required time, and that the cost to users of electricity would be exorbitant. The board successfully defended itself in court, but most of the year had gone by. When the court finally ordered Comm-Fed to comply with the standards, the company was genuinely unable to meet the deadline. The board was forced to authorize an extenson, because otherwise the state would have been without power. Similar delays and litigation have characterized most actions of either board.

The legislative committee proposed a new approach. It suggested that the attempt to legislate standards be abolished, and replaced with a pollution fee system. Under this system, which the legislature adopted, all firms and municipalities which dump liquids into rivers will now pay a tax to the state on a gallonage basis, with the rate set according to the amount of pollutants contained and the difficulties of removal. Similar fees are also charged for air pollution. Special taxes are imposed on automobiles, with the rate based upon the amount of exhaust pollutants, as measured in the twice yearly inspections, and the annual mileage. A new special tax on leaded gasoline was also adopted.

The results of the last two years have been phenomenal. Almost every industry now maintains standards on its own which are far above those previously set by the boards. All large firms now have full-time pollution-control engineers, and several firms of consultants have opened to help smaller firms. The potential cost savings to the firms have induced them to install control devices very rapidly.

The automobile remains a problem, but automobile-produced smog has been greatly lessened. Dealers in the state have complained that sales are down until they can provide lower pollution cars. Manufacturers have promised their dealers such cars by the beginning of the next model year.

The Functions of Government

In modern America, it sometimes seems that governments are everywhere. Local governments provide schools, police and fire protection, and many forms of local regulation.

County governments operate courts, record real estate transactions, and often build local roads. State governments provide highways, universities, and general commercial regulation. The federal government provides defense, postal service, and a collection of other services so varied that almost every listing is bound to be incomplete. The different levels cooperate to provide health and welfare services, pollution controls, and many other benefits.

The most important economic funtion of government is one we seldom think of at all: the maintenance of the basic framework which permits a private economy to exist. Governments enforce contracts and set general rules for commercial law and for the formation of corporations, partnerships, or other businesses. Without this kind of control, no private economy could exist at all; and yet, because it works almost automatically, we forget the role government plays. Nevertheless, the availability of courts to enforce contracts is important, even though we seldom have to rely on them. Governments also establish the monetary system, define weights and measures, and, in many cases, regulate the actual quality of goods through state and local health departments or the federal Food and Drug Administration. Other agencies of government often police the truth of advertising claims and labeling standards—for example, the fiber content of clothing.

We have already seen that competition is a major regulating force in our society. However, we have also seen that under some circumstances competition does not exist automatically, but requires particular action to promote it. Government agencies at both the federal and state levels act to maintain the process of competition. Certain kinds of anticompetitive practices are eliminated, and actions which would lessen competition—especially mergers between existing firms—are often prevented.

Unfortunately, government action to alter the processes of the market does not always increase competition; for example, many of the actions which have been taken to promote agriculture have lessened the effect of competition upon farmers. In another area, the government has decided that the purely competitive process of wage bargaining gives an unfair advantage to the employer, and has encouraged the growth of unions as bargaining agents for workers. In other cases, as we have seen earlier, governments have stepped in to regulate the actions of monopoly where it did not seem possible to promote competition.

The working of the market process distributes income to people in accordance with their contribution to the productive process. The result is a distribution of income which is often felt to be unfair. Many households possess few or even no resources which are highly productive and capable of producing goods and services which society values highly. The very old and the very young usually have little valuable labor resource to sell; the physically handicapped and lone women who must stay home with their children can often offer nothing; and farmers operating on marginal land are for the most part able to produce only a very tiny income for themselves. Consequently, government often interferes in the distribution of income by providing extra income to those in need. Less justifiably, government occasionally acts to increase the incomes of politically powerful groups, regardless of their need. Sometimes this extra income is provided by interference with the market price system, as in the case of agriculture and wage bargains. In other cases, government alters the distribution of income by making direct payments in cash or providing special services which the beneficiaries need. The general system of income redistribution to the poor, which has come to be known as the welfare system, has assumed an increasing importance in government action in recent years.

The main function of government has always been to provide for social benefits—that is, to provide those goods whose benefits are dispersed throughout society. Governments serve as purchasing agents for those goods which need to be purchased jointly. As far back as history goes, governments have always provided a system of courts to judge disputes and a system of police and military forces to assure internal and external security. These same functions are still important, but in the modern world many other needs can be met only by government action. Among these are the processes of providing highways for transportation, programs for general health and sanitation, and, most recently, programs for clean air and water.

Social goods are distinguished by the fact that they provide benefits simultaneously to a number of people. Since no one person would be willing to pay the entire cost, it is necessary to provide joint purchasing arrangements. Private goods can be provided easily through the market process, because the individual who benefits is the one who pays; therefore, he is in a position to judge whether the value of the goods justifies their cost. Social goods must be chosen by some kind of joint decision.

As our society becomes more urbanized and people live closer together, many goods which were once private goods become social goods because they have an effect upon many people rather than on only one. If an isolated farmer chooses to throw his garbage out the window, this is a matter of concern only to him and his family. If city dwellers throw their garbage out the window, they affect the neighborhood. Consequently, garbage disposal arrangements, which were private goods in a rural society, become public goods in an urban society. Increasingly, the same is true of many other activities.

Where the benefit from public goods is widespread, government purchases may be the most effective way to provide them. Many goods, however, provide a combination of identifiable private benefits to one or a few persons, plus a more widespread general benefit to the community at large. In such cases, it is often useful to provide a partial subsidy while leaving a substantial portion of the cost to be paid by the primary beneficiary. For example, the poor are often expected to pay for their medical service, but they pay less than the full cost and the difference is made up by taxation. In this way, the system reflects the fact that these medical services provide both private and public benefits simultaneously. For similar reasons, firms and individuals are often subsidized for improvements to their property which will benefit the community as well as themselves.

The other side of this same problem is the use of taxation to make individuals pay social costs which otherwise would be borne by the public at large. In the example at the beginning of this chapter, we saw the possibility of using taxation to change the social costs of pollution into private costs so that they can be reflected in the price system. The task of compensating for social costs and social benefits is clearly one of the most important which governments can undertake to make the market system function more efficiently.

The Tools of Government

Government can use its powers in a number of different ways, many of which we have already seen. One of its most important powers is its general regulatory power, whereby it orders citizens to act in certain ways. Although this is the basis of most *general* governmental power, it is also of substantial importance in the economic sphere. Among the specifically economic actions which are based upon such power are the regulations of the terms of contract, the system of weights and measures, the regulation of the quality of goods, the setting of the terms under which collective bargaining may take place, and most antitrust legislation.

A government also profoundly affects the economic system by means of its *purchases* of goods and services. We have already seen that a private market economy cannot reflect social desires nor provide for social goods. By its collective purchases, the government can perform these functions. In so doing, it hires judges, policemen, firemen, soldiers, nurses, and teachers, and provides facilities for them. In addition, governments can sometimes direct their purchasing into certain areas to help particular suppliers of goods. For example, many state governments have provisions which give special advantages to suppliers within that state.

Sometimes it is simpler for the government to give money to individuals, rather than to buy goods and services for them. We call such payments *transfers*. Pensions and welfare payments constitute the largest category of these transfers. We have already seen that one of the goals of government is often to alter the distribution of income; transfers are one way to do this.

In order to provide the funds which can be used for the purchase of social goods, governments use *taxation* of many kinds. We have seen that taxation will have certain effects upon firms and households. We have also seen that it is possible to use taxes to change social costs into private costs. The power of taxation and the choice of the type of taxes to be levied are important tools of government.

Sometimes governments choose to become *lenders*, thereby offering a form of government support to certain activities short of full financing. In such cases, governments often make loans, usually on rather favorable terms, which will enable other agencies and people to carry out these activities. College students, their universities, and private hospitals are among the beneficiaries of such loan programs.

We often speak of "the government;" but in a federal system such as ours, there are many governments. It is often desirable to adopt a national policy and finance it by means of federal taxation, but to carry out the detailed administration through local governments which are better able to adjust to the particular needs of local communities. Accordingly, we have many programs of *intergovernmental grants*, where the federal government gives grants to state and local governments, and state governments give grants to local governments. An increasing proportion of locally administered education and welfare programs is financed by state and federal grants.

Increasingly, national governments have tried to use their powers to affect the general level of economic activity. Such an influence takes place through *fiscal policy*, the variation of total spending and taxation, and through *monetary policy*, the general control of money and the banking system. Allied with the latter is the control of government borrowing and repayment of debt. These topics are of great interest, but their analysis requires a different set of tools from those developed in this book.

Criteria for Public Activity

It is not possible to give simple unambiguous rules to determine what things government should or should not do. It is possible, however, to outline certain criteria which should be applied in evaluating the activities of government. Unfortunately, when we look at any particular activity, there is apt to be some disagreement about the application of these criteria.

Expenditures.

When we were examining consumer purchases, we saw that a consumer would try to purchase one good rather than another if the ratio of marginal utilities exceeded the ratio of prices. Governments, however, do not have marginal utilities, and it would certainly be wrong to have a government whose activities were entirely dependent upon the utility functions of government administrators. We must also remember that the essential characteristic of government is providing public goods. Therefore, a different set of criteria must be used than those for individual consumer purchases. Let us look at a simplified example. Suppose that a small town is considering having a band concert in the park in the center of town. Because of the town's size, almost everyone will be able to hear the band concert even if he does not leave his house; and everyone will be able to hear it if he goes to the park. However, this concert will cost money. The question is whether it is appropriate for the town council to pay for it. Let us imagine that it is possible to ask every individual in town how much the concert means to him, and actually to get a truthful answer. One man might answer $1.00 by making a comparison with the prices at the local theater. Another, who happens to like band music, might answer $2.00. A third, who does not feel that the quality of the local band is adequate, might say minus $0.50, indicating that he would be willing to pay if the band concert is not held. If we polled all the citizens in this fashion, we could get a set of figures indicating how various members of the town value this activity. If we added up all of the valuations, we could then see whether the sum total was as high as the total cost of the concert. If the benefit exceeded the cost, it would be worth having the band play; if the benefit was less than the cost, it would not. This process is different from the one used for a single consumer because it is necessary to add together the benefits to all the citizens.

In any actual case, one could not use the above procedure. It would not be feasible to take a poll of every citizen in town on every single issue which might come up. Furthermore, it is unlikely that the answers would be very truthfully given, especially if those answering thought that there was some possibility that they might be charged in accordance with the stated benefit. In such a case, there would obviously be a premium on lying. Instead, we must rely upon elected representatives to make the decisions on what things are to be provided publicly, and what things are not. In so doing, they are essentially being asked to determine the dollar value of the individual goods which their constituents would be willing to give up in order to have a certain public expenditure, and then to compare the sum total of those valuations with the expenditure.

With respect to most public activities, some citizens will consider the activities desirable and some will not. Since all of them pay taxes, it is clear that some gain by getting more than they pay for, and some lose. This tendency is partially compensated by the desire of the elected representatives to be re-elected. They can more easily attract a large number of voters if they can provide something for everyone; even though a particular citizen might object to any one program, he is apt to find others he likes. Naturally, any citizen will find that his views will carry more weight if he is organized with others of similar persuasion, especially if the group keeps up an active campaign for its views. When we remember how many elections are won by margins of less than five percent, we understand why politicians try to cater to various minority views.

We therefore see that the principal criterion by which politicians are chosen is their ability to estimate the general shape of the utility functions of their constituents, and that this is far more important than any particular expert knowledge which any one of them might have. It is also clear that there is no particular training for a politician other than wide experience in his community.

It is significant that an important part of every legislature is the cloakroom, where politicians get together and trade support for different bills. This bargaining decreases the chance of any group being completely left out of the legislative process, but it also means that no group is apt to get everything it wants. We can see that a republican form of government, in which laws are made by elected representatives, has an advantage over a democracy, in which the people make laws directly. The democracy has no cloakrooms, so minority views are less well represented.

A somewhat different problem occurs when government expenditures are used to redistribute income. For example, in our society it is customary to provide public housing and many forms of health services as a way to help the poor. One simple alternative would be to send the poor cash in the form of a transfer payment, and permit them to buy their own housing and medical service. It is almost certainly true that most of them would not choose the form of housing which is customarily provided for them. In most instances, the poor would not move into large, high-rise building complexes, but would stay in simpler, lower buildings. One of the reasons for using public housing is a fear that if money were sent to the poor it might not be used "correctly." The values of middle-class voters are imposed as a condition for this transfer of income. Such limitations cannot be justified only on the basis of the benefits to the poor themselves. If the poor want such housing, they will buy it if they are given cash. If they spend the money on something else, then that something is more valuable to them. One should understand, however, that public housing is also planned to provide benefits to the middle classes in terms of a better looking city, and to give assistance to the construction industry.

The case for giving medical services to the poor is somewhat different. Here, the argument rests in large part upon the fact that medical service to the poor provides two separate kinds of benefits: the direct service to the poor themselves, and a secondary benefit to the rest of society through improved general health which lessens the risk of contagion and increases the supply of labor.

Taxation.

The rules for determining the best method of taxation are less clear cut, primarily because several criteria have been proposed. The first of these is *benefit taxation*. If a primary function of government is to provide services to its citizens, then it is appropriate that taxation to pay for these services should be divided among citizens in proportion to the benefit which they receive. In effect, this principle extends the rules of the market, where everyone pays for what he gets, to government activities. We have seen that consumers adjust their purchases so that the price ratios of different goods correspond to their relative marginal utilities; an ideal benefit tax system would do the same for public goods.

It is usually impossible to measure benefit precisely in order to calculate the proper tax, but it can often be approximated. For example, the support of highways is drawn largely from gasoline taxes, on the theory that the amount of benefit which one receives from the roads is approximately proportional to the amount of gasoline which one uses. (Separate extra taxation is provided for trucks.) Because different automobiles get different mileage per gallon, the gasoline tax is not a perfect application of the benefit principle; but it is fairly satisfactory. The use of property taxes to support fire departments is often defended on the ground that the major function of the fire department is to protect that property. It is clear, however, that property taxes to support public schools cannot be defended on the ground of benefit. Why? Because the schools are not of benefit only to property owners, nor is the amount of one's property proportional to the benefit which one receives from the public schools.

A second principle of taxation is the *ability to pay*. Two arguments have been given for this principle. Ths first is an extension of the benefit principle. It argues that everyone receives approximately equal benefit from general government service, and that those with higher incomes should pay more in dollars because each dollar is worth less to them. The second and more common argument in favor of ability-to-pay taxation relates this form of taxation to the basic role of the government in producing an optimum distribution of income. In effect, it argues that those with more money should pay more than their benefit, while those with less money should pay less than their benefit, thereby producing a net redistribution of income. Many justifications given for property taxes are based on this ability-to-pay principle, but they have now become somewhat obsolete. In earlier times, there was often a close relationship between the rate of income and the amount of property one owned. In modern society, this is less often the case; consequently, property taxation is a poor reflection of ability to pay.

In the last quarter century, a new principle of taxation, the *countercyclical* system, has been proposed at least for federal taxes. It is explained in macroeconomics that one method of keeping the economy running on an even keel is to collect more taxes during a period of prosperity and fewer taxes during a period of depression. In this way, total spending will be cut at a time when there is too much of it, and will be supported during times when there is too little. Although this is an important principle for deciding the total amount of taxes to be collected, it does not help to determine who should pay those taxes nor in what form.

We have already met *incentive* taxation, the use of taxes as a control device rather than primarily as a means of obtaining money. In many cases, in fact, the use of incentive taxation may actually conflict with revenue taxation. For example, high taxes are often placed on imported goods to discourage their purchase and to aid domestic industry. Such tariffs, if effective, do not produce any revenue at all. In general, most taxes designed for control will produce little revenue. A second way that taxes may be used for incentive purposes is by forgiving taxes or providing exemptions from them for people in certain categories. One such case is the use of percentage depletion allowances as an incentive to the producers of oil; and there are many other exemptions written into our tax laws for the purpose of providing incentives for a particular form of behavior. (Sometimes, of course, benefits to favored groups and political supporters masquerade as incentive devices. Even though we might want to abolish this favoritism, we should recognize that special incentives have a legitimate place in tax policy, especially as a substitute for direct government expenditure.)

After having recognized all these theoretical principles which have been proposed, we must also admit that most legislators tend to follow the plucked-goose system. ("Get the most feathers with the fewest squawks.") Only this last theory will explain the popularity of the cigarette tax. Smoking shows little relation to income, so the tax certainly does not reflect ability to pay. It would be hard to argue that smokers benefit more from government spending. A half-hearted argument can be made that the tax is designed to provide an incentive to stop smoking; but all evidence points to the fact that the demand for cigarettes is extremely inelastic, so that no incentive effect results. However, the inelasticity of demand explains why tobacco dealers do not oppose the tax; they merely add it to the price and sell about the same quantity. Smokers often feel guilty about their smoking, so they do not complain. Thus the "squawks" are few and the "feathers" plentiful.

The three budgets.

It has been suggested that we could organize our thinking about government activity by treating it as three separate budgets and then combining the net results. The first would be a *service budget,* consisting of all of the goods and services the government provides for its citizens; it would be financed by benefit taxation. This budget would always be balanced, because it only makes sense to provide these services if citizens receive a benefit at least equal to their cost. The government "price" should be charged to those who benefit, just as market prices fall on those who receive the goods.

The second budget would be a *redistribution budget,* whereby money would be taken from those who have more than they need and given to those who have less. Receipts for this budget would certainly depend upon taxes, but the expenditures might be either in the form of transfer payments or in the form of a remission of other taxes which had already have levied on the benefit principle. Because we are taking from one group in the society and giving to another, this budget too would always be balanced. The tax system would be based on an ability-to-pay principle.

The third budget would be the *stabilization budget.* In it taxes would be either increased or decreased in order to control the total level of the economy. In general, this budget would not be balanced, because in some years it would be appropriate to give the economy a boost, and in others to put on the brakes.

When the three budgets are combined, we see that individuals would be paying partly on the benefit principle and partly on the principle of ability to pay, while the total level of all taxes would be changing from year to year on the basis of the stabilization needs of the economy. Although this might be an ideal way to think of government activity, it is quite clear that this is not the way in which government budgets are calculated; nor is it the way in which the political process determines expenditures and taxation. It is significant that, in the U.S. Congress and in most state legislatures, appropriations measures and tax measures are seldom considered together and are even examined by separate committees. It is therefore quite clear that the basic principles of the three-part budget with carefully matched benefits, costs, gains, and losses are seldom closely applied in practice.

An Illustration: How the West Was Won

America is often portrayed as a land of free enterprise, especially until very recent times. In fact, however, the

United States has always used its own form of economic planning, which consists of certain *major* governmental decisions to determine the broad outline of the society; and it has encouraged individual activities to fill in the *details* of that outline. It is significant that the first action of the first U.S. Congress was to pass a tariff law which combined the revenue needs of the young country with protective tariffs to encourage the development of domestic industry.

Another example of the use of this kind of planning was the development of the American west after the Civil War. History books and cowboy movies often imply that the development of the American frontier was largely the work of a group of rugged individualists who went there for their own reasons. Although they form a part of the picture, it is also true that the development was the result of a major effort by the U.S. government. The government actions can be grouped under four categories: transportation, land, education, and law and order. The key year was 1862.

Transportation.

In 1862, a grant was given to the Union Pacific Railroad. This grant provided that, on condition that a railroad be built connecting the Missouri River with the Pacific coast, the railroad would be given a grant of ten square miles of land per mile of railroad built. The Union Pacific Railroad, which started building west from Omaha, used this land either as collateral for loans or sold it to prospective settlers to obtain cash. Meanwhile, the Central Pacific Railroad started building east from California, using much the same method of financing, until the two met in Utah in 1869. The effect of this grant was that a major transportation link was opened, making it possible for the settlers of the area to receive goods from the east at lower cost and to ship their produce to eastern markets. Similar grants later encouraged the building of other railroads north and south of the Union Pacific route. In this way, government policy toward transportation, followed by private action, made the settlement of the west economically feasible.

Land.

A second part of the policy for the development of the west was the Homestead Act, also passed in 1862. Under this provision, a settler could obtain one-fourth of a square mile of land, on condition that he occupied it and used it for a period of years. This policy of free land, conditional upon use of that land for agriculture, helped to build up the farming industry which had been made possible by the railroads; that industry, in turn, made the railroads profitable.

Education.

The third part of the policy for the development of the west came with the Morrill Act of 1862, which gave a grant of land to each state or territory on condition that it provide a college to teach agricultural and mechanical arts. These land grant universities provided the basis for modern scientitic agriculture; through their research stations and extension agencies, they made American farmers the most progressive in the world. Although this last policy was not a necessary accompaniment of the first two policies, it is clear that it made them more effective than they otherwise would have been.

Law and order.

The last requirement for the development of the west was a system of law under which settlers would be safe and their possessions protected. Such safety was especially critical for farmers who were tied to one place and whose property was the key to their livelihood. It had not been as necessary in the earlier stages of development, when the population had consisted primarily of trappers, traders, and scattered cattle ranchers. As a result, the federal government provided a dual system consisting of United States marshals, who served as local peace officers, and of the United States cavalry, whose function was to control major bands of outlaws and to keep the Indians from interfering with the preemption and agricultural development of their region. It is now clear that the action of the cavalry against the Indians amounted to genocide, but it was very effective in changing the entire character of the American plains.

Beyond these four major actions which set the character of development of the plains area, the government relied upon the actions of individuals. It was therefore no surprise that many kinds of commercial establishments appeared and elementary manufacturing began, especially that which was closely related to agricultural products. The net effect of this combination of major governmental policies and of individual private action was the development of western America into a pattern which formed the basis of what we see today.

Appendix to Chapter 10
The Nature of Governments

When we refer to government, most people automatically think of the national government. However, in our federal system there are also fifty states, thousands of cities and towns, and more thousands of special fire, sewage, conservation, and school districts. This collection of governmental units constitutes our governmental system.

When the United States was formed, the thirteen original states relinquished certain of their powers to the federal government through the Constitution. All remaining powers were kept by the states. There have been changes in emphasis over the years, but it is still true that there is a substantial division of labor between the levels. The federal government has the primary responsibility for national defense, international relations, interstate and foreign commerce, and control of the money supply. From these responsibilities, especially the control over interstate commerce, the federal government has also acquired the principal responsibility for maintaining general full employment and for controlling the conditions of labor.

The state governments retained the basic responsibilities for domestic governmental services, especially education, welfare, roads, and police and fire protection. In order to carry out many of these services as closely as possible to the people, the states established local governments, including counties, cities, towns, and special districts. Unlike the state and federal governments, however, which exist in their own right, local governments are the creatures of the states and have only such powers as the state authorizes. Because the rules are specific for each state, local governments in different states are apt to have different powers and structures. For example, in some states, schools are run by municipalities, in some by counties, and in others by special districts whose sole function is schools. Another important difference is the division of responsibility for certain functions between the state and its municipalities. For example, welfare is divided almost evenly between the states and local governments, if we take the nation as a whole. In individual states, the percentages vary from Alaska, where the state spends 100 percent of the welfare money, to Minnesota, where the state spends only four percent.

In recent years, we have had an increasing use of the intergovernmental grant-in-aid. With this device, one level of government may accept a substantial responsibility for financing a certain activity, while another level actually does the spending. For example, in the 1969–70 fiscal year, the various levels of government actually spent $56 billion for education. Of this amount, the local governments spent $39 billion, mostly for local schools; the states spent $14 billion, for higher education and auxiliary services; and the federal government spent $3 billion, for supporting services. However, the federal government granted $5 billion to the states and $1 billion to local governments for education, while the states transferred $17 billion to local governments. Thus the federal government provided $9 billion of the education total, the states $26 billion, and local governments only $21 billion. In terms of providing the money, the local schools accounted for only 40 cents of every education dollar, although they spent 70 cents. Similar transfers are very important for highways and welfare, but they are also used for almost every kind of governmental service.

Table A10.1 shows the pattern of revenues for all governments.

Table A10.1
Governmental Revenues, 1969-70
(Billions of dollars)

	Federal	State	Local
Total Revenue	205.6	88.9	89.1
Intergovernmental	–	20.2	29.5
From Federal	–	19.2	2.6
From State	–	–	26.9
From Local	–	1.0	–
Own Revenue	205.6	68.7	59.6
General Revenue	163.6	57.5	51.4
Property tax	–	1.1	33.0
Income tax	123.2	12.9	1.6
Customs duties	2.4	–	–
General sales tax	–	14.2	2.0
Motor fuel tax	3.8	6.3	–
Alcohol tax	4.7	1.4	0.1
Tobacco tax	2.1	2.3	0.1
Other sales taxes	5.3	3.1	0.9
Vehicle and operators licenses	–	2.7	0.2
Death and gift taxes	3.7	1.0	–
Other taxes	0.9	3.0	1.0
Charges and other general revenue	17.5	9.5	12.5
Utility Revenue	–	–	6.6
Liquor Stores Revenue	–	1.8	0.3
Insurance Trust Revenue	42.0	9.4	1.3

Source: *Governmental Finances in 1969-70,* U.S. Census, p. 20.

These show that in 1969–70, all governments received 333.9 billion dollars, over one-third of the total Gross National Product. (If this number seems large, remember that various levels of government perform many different functions. Whether it is too high depends upon how you value those functions compared to the private goods produced with the other two-thirds.) The federal government received $205 billion, most of it from the individual and corporate income tax. Significant revenue was also received from the payroll tax; it went into the special trust fund for payment of social security benefits. Various charges, including postal revenues and national park receipts, constituted another significant revenue source. The remainder came from special excise taxes on motor fuel, alcohol, tobacco, and various other products.

State governments received $89 billion, including $20 billion of transfers, mostly from the federal government. Their own revenue sources include income taxes and sales taxes, including specific excise taxes. In some states, liquor stores are operated by the state. Their gross revenues are included here, although most of this revenue is used for operations. Liquor stores are only a minor source of net revenue to the states which have them, probably accounting for little more than the alcohol taxes in other states.

Local governments received $89 billion, $30 billion of which came from state and local governments. The principal local revenue source is the property tax.

One special concern in taxation is the relation of taxes to income. If members of all income groups pay the same percentage of their income in taxes, the tax is called *proportional*. If the percentage rises as incomes rise, the tax is called *progressive*; if the percentage falls as incomes rise, the tax is considered *regressive*.

Of all our taxes, only the income tax shows a significant degree of progressivity. Because it is levied on the basis of income, it is possible to apply increasing rates to higher incomes. However, because there are many special rules for calculating income, the income tax is far less progressive than one would think merely by looking at the rates. Although the rates for the federal income tax go as high as 70 percent, no income group actually pays as much as half its income in federal taxes.

Most other taxes are actually regressive. For example, general sales taxes are levied at a standard rate on all sales of covered items. Since low income groups spend 100 percent or more of their income, but higher bracket groups spend less, the low income groups pay a larger percentage of their income in sales taxes. In addition, many states exempt services, which account for less spending by the poor than the rich. Accordingly, the tax is even more regressive.

Selective excise taxes are usually even more regressive. For example, low income smokers usually pay the same tobacco tax as high income smokers, and therefore a much larger percentage of their incomes. In general, any excise tax on a product with an income elasticity less than one will be regressive, for the percentage of income paid in tax will decline as incomes rise. Liquor taxes are about as regressive as general sales taxes; motor fuel taxes are even more so.

The impact of property taxes is less certain. There is some modest evidence that ownership of property does not increase quite proportionately with income; so the tax would be slightly regressive. However, the property tax is usually included in the rent paid by low income families, so it becomes even more regressive. The regressivity of the property tax falls especially heavily upon the elderly, who may own a house but have little income.

The various other taxes and charges are even more difficult to analyze, partly because of their diversity and partly because it is hard to trace their ultimate effect. For example, economists are uncertain whether corporate income taxes are reflected in higher prices to customers or lower earnings to stockholders. If the first is correct, the corporate income tax is like a sales tax; if the latter, it is a rather progressive income tax. (Opinion leans toward the higher prices, but the view is not unanimous.) Social security taxes are proportional up to the maximum, but slightly regressive beyond, since no tax is collected on incomes above that level.

On balance, the general view is that our total tax system is regressive up to about $8,000, proportional from there to about $15,000, and progressive beyond that.

Governmental Expenditures

The various levels of direct expenditures by governments are shown in Table A10.2. These figures give only the level of direct spending by each level of government, whether the funds come from intergovernmental grants or from its own sources. In addition, these figures refer only to general revenues, and exclude expenditures from insurance trust funds or for public liquor stores or utilities.

We see that over half the spending by the federal government goes for defense and international relations. Other large cate-

Table A10.2
Direct General Governmental Expenditures, 1969-70
(Billions of dollars)

	Federal	State	Local
Total	143.7	48.8	82.6
National defense and international relations	84.3	—	—
Education	3.1	13.8	38.9
Welfare	2.8	8.2	6.5
Highways	0.3	11.0	5.4
Health and hospitals	3.9	4.8	4.9
Police and fire	0.4	0.7	5.8
Sanitation	—	—	3.4
Parks and natural resources	8.7	2.2	2.5
Postal service	7.7	—	—
Interest on debt	14.1	1.5	2.9
Other	18.4	6.6	12.3

Source: *Governmental Finances in 1969-70,* U.S. Census, p. 20.

gories of expenditure include parks and natural resources, interest on the debt, and operation of the postal service. (This last is almost entirely financed by postal fees, so it is more like a business than a governmental activity.)

State governments spend most of their money on education, highways, and welfare. The principal activity of local governments is provision of schools, but their activities are important in all areas of government service.

Ideally, it would be desirable to examine the distribution of government services among various income classes in order to find the net burden of government. If every income group received services in proportion to the taxes paid, we could say that there is no net redistribution caused by government.

Although such allocations have been attempted various times, they have been unsatisfactory and none are reproduced in this book. An examination of two forms of government spending will indicate some of the problems. Let us first consider education. One might argue that a suitable way to measure benefit from education is to take the number of children from each income group in public school, and divide the total expenditures proportionately. This procedure has two drawbacks. First, it assumes that all the benefits of public education flow to the children being educated. However, the reason we make education a public good and not a private one is because we believe that all of us share in the benefits. In other words, the allocation of benefits assumes away the reason for public education. Second, this allocation assumes that each child receives the same benefits from education. But one common complaint against public schools is that they are totally middle class in values and orientation, which is not surprising in view of the fact that most teachers and administrators are middle class. It can therefore be argued that these schools do little for children of low-income families. (If the children are black and the school staff white, the problem is even worse.) Again, school enrollment is a poor measure of benefit.

Comparatively, however, education is an easy function to analyze. How can we begin to allocate benefits from military expenditure? No criterion seems to provide a useful allocation. One possibility is simply to divide the benefit equally among the population, but this is more a confession of failure than a method of analysis. The same problem applies to many of the general functions of government. Accordingly, it is impossible to allocate benefits to different income groups and, therefore, to determine the net redistribution which takes place through government.

Chapter 11
Resource Markets

Jim Anderson quit high school last year and took a job in a filling station, so that he could support his car in the style it seemed to demand. Last month the station was sold and the new owner told Jim he would no longer be able to use him. When Jim started looking for a new job, he discovered that most of the stories about the employment problems of dropouts are true.

Jim was discouraged and surprised at the total lack of interest in hiring him. He was neat and personable, and his last employer gave him a good recommendation. Finally, one of his high school teachers arranged an interview with Mr. Allen, who was personnel manager for one of the largest firms in town.

Although Mr. Allen was sympathetic, he offered Jim little encouragement. "You see," he said, "our firm is engaged in rather competitive business. In order to make it, we have to produce everything just as cheaply as we know how. In many cases, this means using machinery with semiskilled operators. Wherever possible, we have eliminated skilled, general purpose workers and replaced them with workers who know only one skill.

"We have also eliminated a large percentage of unskilled workers. Most of the jobs they used to do have been upgraded. One man with a mechanized floor-scrubber does the job of five men with brooms and mops. The operator gets paid twice as much as the old sweeper, but we are still ahead of the game—despite the cost of the machinery.

"I would like to take you on as a trainee for one of our production machines, but I can't. We invest almost three months in the training program, plus another three in specially supervised work, while paying the trainees at the same time. We need some assurance that people will finish this training period. We can't afford to gamble that someone who couldn't stay in school six hours a day can last eight with us."

After the interview, Jim was very depressed and thoughtful. He spent two days locked in his room, not even coming out for meals. At the end of that time, he emerged and announced that he was returning to school. That same day, he saw the guidance counselor and mapped out a program of studies. He is now back in school and determined to finish. Mr. Allen has promised to take him on as a trainee when he graduates.

The Demand for Resources

We have already seen in Chapters 5 and 6 the way in which firms make decisions on how much to produce and how to produce it. As firms make these production decisions, they are simultaneously making decisions about what resources to use. Therefore, in this chapter we will merely look at the same action; but this time we will focus our attention on the other side of the firm's activities—its purchase of resources rather than its sale of the product. All of the reasoning will be quite familiar. As before, we will first look at the case where only one factor of production is variable and all others are fixed. We will then move on to the case of two variable factors.

In Chapter 6, we saw that it is possible to start with the production function, multiply the input by its cost, and then add the fixed cost to obtain a total cost curve, indicating the cost for each level of output. We could, however, have approached the process from the opposite direction. We could have multiplied each output by its selling price to obtain a total revenue curve for each level of input. Because such a curve combines the production function, relating input to output, with the ordinary revenue function, relating output to revenue, it is called a *revenue-product function*.

From this total revenue-product function, it is possible to derive the demand curve for the factor. Just as the competitive firm would want to produce any unit of output whose marginal cost is less than the selling price, it would also want to hire any unit of input whose purchase price is less than the marginal revenue-product. Thus the demand curve for the factor is the marginal revenue-product function which is derived from the total revenue-product function.

For the competitive firm, one can provide this same calculation in a different way. From the total production function, one can calculate the marginal product which results from every extra unit of output, and then multiply this marginal product by the selling price to obtain the marginal revenue product.

For the monopolistic or imperfectly competitive firm, the process is similar, but slightly more complicated. Because such firms face sloping demand curves, one would have to multiply each output by its appropriate selling price to obtain the total revenue-product function. In using the alternate method, one would multiply the marginal product by the appropriate marginal revenue.

In all these calculations involving the resource market, we are merely reflecting the firm's decisions with respect to output. When the price of an input factor rises, the firm's costs rise, so it produces less output and uses less of the resource. In other words, it has a demand curve of the usual shape, indicating greater purchases at lower prices.

The Substitution Effect

If more than one input is variable, a new factor comes into play. Figure 11.1 shows one isoquant of Figure 6.5, along with the equal cost line which was used to derive one point of the total cost curve, assuming a wage of $2.50 per hour for labor and a price of $4.00 per hour for machinery. A separate

Figure 11.1
Output and Substitution Effect

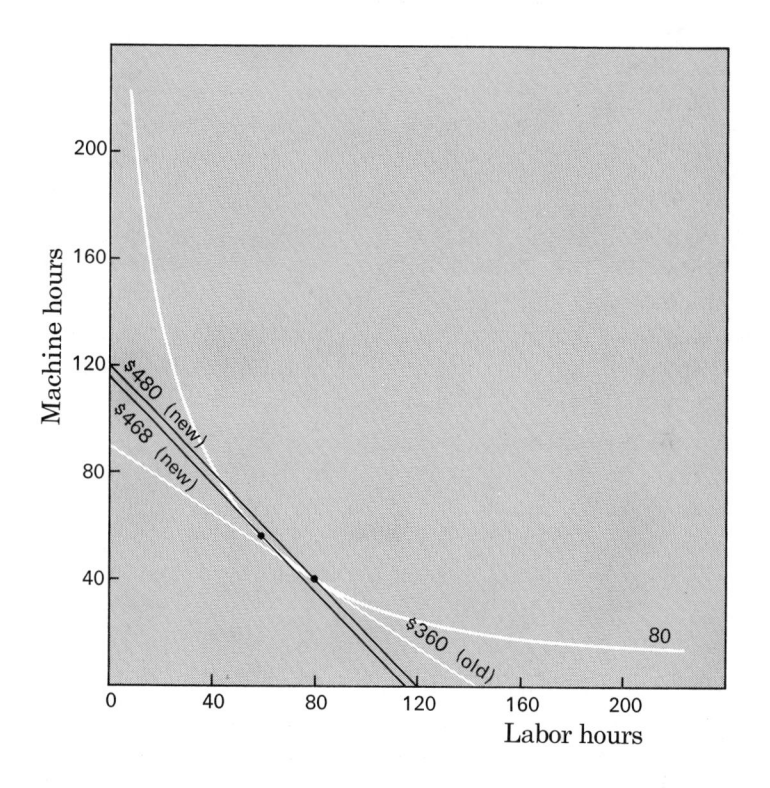

Resource Markets

cost line is also shown, with the same price for machinery but a wage of $4.00 for labor.

Let us examine the differences between the two best positions. At the old costs, the firm would produce its output of 80 units by using 80 hours of labor and 40 hours of machinery, for a total cost of $360. With the new prices, the best combination uses 60 hours of labor and 57 hours of machinery, for a total cost of $468. Notice that if the firm had remained at its old position, the cost would have risen to $480. It has kept its costs from rising that much by substituting machinery for labor. However, it has still not been able to avoid a large cost increase. Since this same effect will occur at other outputs, the entire cost curve will rise and the firm will probably cut back on its output. (The exact amount of the cut will depend upon the demand curve.) Thus there is the same *output effect* as in the case where only one factor is variable: higher factor prices reduce output and decrease the amount of the factor demanded. In addition, there is a *substitution effect* which does not exist in the other case: at every level of output, the firm will use less of the factor which has become more expensive and more of the one that has not. Thus a lower quantity will be demanded for two reasons: less of that factor (the one which has become more expensive) is used at each output, and a lower output will be produced. These two effects are similar, but not identical, to the income and substitution effect for the consumer.

The effect of higher wages on the use of machinery is less clear; the substitution effect leads to more machinery and less labor, but the output effect leads to less of both. When both are combined, the net change may be either an increase or decrease in machinery, depending upon which effect is the stronger.

The Elasticity of Factor Demand

We have seen that the demand curve for a factor of production is derived by combining the demand curve for the product and the production function. We have also seen that where more than one factor of production is variable, the net effect of a change in factor price is the combination of the output and the substitution effects. We can use these relationships to make some observations about the elasticity of demand for factors of production.

1. *The more slowly the marginal revenue product curve for a factor declines, the more elastic the demand for that factor.* Since the marginal revenue product curve is the demand curve for the factor of production, it follows, as a matter of definition, that its rate of decline determines the elasticity of demand for the factor. We state this principle only to emphasize that the rate of decline is a combination of two elements — the technical production function and the market conditions under which the final product can be sold. We can therefore derive two subsidiary principles.

(1a) *The less the curvature of the production function, the more elastic the demand curve for the factor.* If a production function like that of Figure 6.1 is almost a straight line, then the marginal revenue product will be declining very slowly and, consequently, the demand for the factor of production will be very elastic.

(1b) *The more elastic the demand for the product, the more elastic the demand for the factor.* If the demand for the product is perfectly elastic (as in pure competition), the marginal revenue product, which is equal to the marginal product times the marginal revenue, will decline only as fast as the marginal product curve, for marginal revenue is a constant, the price. On the other hand, if the product market is more monopolistic, both the declining marginal product and declining marginal revenue will contribute to the declining marginal revenue product. Therefore, the more competitive the market is for the product, the higher the elasticity of demand is for the factor.

2. *The greater the proportion a single factor is of total cost, the more elastic its demand.* If the entire cost of production consisted of a single factor, then a 10 percent change in the cost of that factor would mean a 10 percent change in the cost of the product. If, on the other hand, the factor constituted only half of the total cost, a 10 percent change in the factor price would lead to only a 5 percent change in the price of the product. The resulting change in output would be only half as large. The decline in output would be even smaller if a particular factor constituted only 10 percent or 2 percent of the cost of the product. For example, suppose that a certain product had an elasticity of demand of 10 and that one

factor of production constituted 20 percent of the cost of making this product. For simplicity's sake, let us also assume that the quantity of this factor used in every unit of output was the same. Then a 10 percent increase in the price of the factor would lead only to a 2 percent increase in the price of the final product. With an elasticity of ten, there would be a 20 percent decline in the quantity demanded. We therefore see that the 10 percent increase in the price of the factor would result in a 20 percent decline in its use, for a factor elasticity of only two. In contrast, if this factor constituted half of the cost, the same 10 percent factor price increase would lead to a 5 percent increase in the product price and a 50 percent decline in output. In that case, the 10 percent increase in price of the factor would result in a 50 percent decline in the quantity demanded, for a factor elasticity of five.

3. *The more easily substitutable a factor is, the more elastic will be its demand.* If a factor has few substitutes, its elasticity will depend only upon the output effect. If, on the other hand, it can be easily replaced by another factor, a small increase in its price is apt to lead to a very large decline in its use. Therefore the elasticity depends upon the ease of substitutability.

The Supply of Labor

Although the demand for different factors of production—labor, land, and capital—is symmetrical, their supply is not. Accordingly, we will discuss them separately, beginning with labor.

We have already seen in Chapter 4 that a household makes its consumption decisions by selecting that combination of goods which maximizes its utility. We can use exactly the same principle and the same logic to evaluate its participation in the labor market. We do this by observing that a household wants both income, which would enable it to buy goods, and leisure, which would enable it to enjoy them. However, under normal circumstances, the only way to obtain income is by working—that is, by giving up leisure. Therefore, the household will choose that combination of income and leisure which maximizes its utility. In Figure 11.2, we have drawn an indifference map for the two goods, income and leisure. (For the sake of simplicity, we have assumed that there is only one worker in this household and that there is only one kind of job at which he can work. Furthermore, we have assumed that he may choose to work whatever number of hours he wishes. We will remove each of these assumptions later.)

The indifference map shown in Figure 11.2 is very similar to those of Chapter 4. The major difference, of course, is that it is impossible to have more than 168 hours of leisure per week. If we wish to measure labor on this scale, we must measure from the right-hand side reading backwards, because each hour of leisure given up is an hour of additional labor service offered. Consequently, if we derive a demand curve for leisure, we will also be deriving a supply curve for labor.

We have already observed that every consumer decision is made by comparing what the consumer would like (his indifference map) with what he can have (his opportunity set). In order to find the demand for leisure, we must examine what the opportunity set would be at different wage rates. No matter what the wage rate, of course, one opportunity which is available to a consumer is to have 168 hours of leisure and no income—that is, not to work at all. Consequently, all opportunity lines will go through that point. For every hour of leisure which the worker is willing to give up, he can increase his weekly income by the amount of the hourly wage. Therefore, each opportunity line is a straight line extending from the point of 168 hours of leisure and no income, with a slope determined by the wage rate. In Figure 11.2, four such opportunity lines are shown. The higher the wage, the steeper the opportunity line. We see that at a wage rate of $2.00, this worker would choose 118 hours of leisure and a weekly income of $100.00. At a wage of $4.00, he would choose 126 hours of leisure and $168.00 of income. We can plot these amounts and some others on the bottom diagram as the demand curve for leisure.

We have already observed that leisure is the time spent not working. Therefore, the demand curve for leisure is the supply curve of labor. The worker who chooses to spend 118 of the 168 hours in a week at leisure has also chosen to spend the remaining 50 hours working. We have, therefore, added the scale for labor, reading from right to left, on the bottom diagram. If we

Figure 11.2
The Supply of Labor

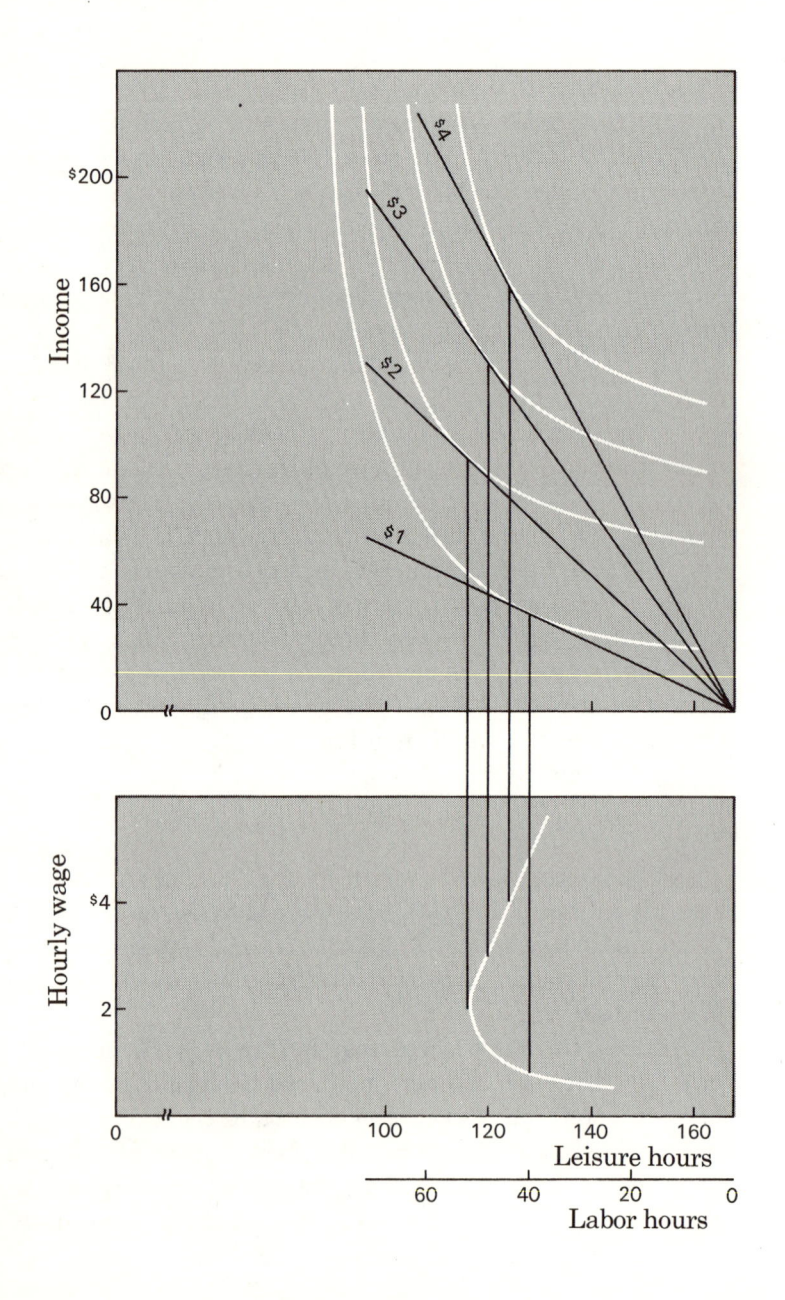

262 Markets

use this lower scale, the demand for leisure becomes the individual's labor supply curve. We could of course reverse the diagram so that the scale could be read in the usual manner from left to right.

We have assumed that the worker has a choice of working only at one particular job. We have also drawn the diagrams in such a way as to imply that the job has certain disadvantages to the worker—that is, he would always prefer to work less if it were not for the income he received. Neither of these assumptions is always true, and therefore we should relax them. Many workers find that they actually like their jobs and would prefer to be working at them rather than doing nothing. In some cases, their utility would actually be decreased if they were forced to work less, even though their income was the same. In such a case, the right-hand end of each of the indifference curves would actually tend to rise rather than decline, indicating that increased leisure would decrease the worker's utility unless it were compensated by extra income. We should observe, however, that even in the case of good jobs, there is a limit beyond which additional work ceases to be desirable. A worker might feel very unhappy if he were forced not to work at all; but he might feel just as unhappy if he were forced to work for 60 to 70 hours a week. We can find many instances in our society which demonstrate that preferences for work are common. The best known of these is the person who finds himself at a loss when he is forced to retire by fixed retirement-age rules. Many times, such retirement leads to a general depression which manifests itself in physical symptoms and a general decline of the individual's health. Often, those who are forced to retire acquire volunteer or low-paid jobs in order to keep working. This phenomenon is especially pronounced in the United States, where medical care has prolonged life and health and where the custom of working is well established. Even those who inherit substantial sums of money are expected to work at something, and people who live solely on an inherited income are quite rare.

Wage Differentials

Just as workers often prefer some amount of labor over leisure, they also often prefer one kind of job over another.

If a job offers nonmonetary satisfactions, workers are often willing to work for lower amounts of money. Among these nonmonetary considerations are the prestige which is associated with the job, the feeling of accomplishment which the worker has, and the value of his surroundings and co-workers. On the other hand, some kinds of jobs are considered undesirable; workers will accept them only for more money or if they have no other alternatives. Such jobs include those of very low prestige or with undesirable or dangerous working conditions. Figure 11.3 illustrates the worker's choice between two different jobs. In this case, there would be two sets of indifference curves, one for each job. We have not drawn full indifference maps, but only a single curve for each job. These two curves represent the same level of utility, indicated by the fact that they both touch the right-hand edge at the same point. (Not working at one job has the same utility as not working at the other.) It can be observed that the indifference curve for the less desirable job, labelled I_U, is higher at all other points than the indifference curve for the desirable job, labelled I_D, indicating that a worker's utility would be kept equal only if he received more money for a given number of hours at the less desirable job. We have also drawn in price lines for each of these two jobs. In this example, the less desirable job is assumed to pay $3.00 per hour, and the more desirable one, $2.00. Since each of these wage lines is just tangent to the appropriate curve at points P and Q, we see that at these prices the worker would be equally willing to accept either job. It is significant, however, that he would be prepared to work more hours at a lower total income at the better job than at the poorer one.

Because the two indifference curves represent the same level of satisfaction, counting the job and money together, we could not say which of these jobs the worker would actually take. If the wage differential were more than $1.00, the worker would choose the poorer job at the higher pay; if it were less, he would choose the better job. One well-known example of this kind of job preference lies in the willingness of teachers to accept positions at less money than they could obtain from other occupations. However, when the wage differential becomes too great, they will nevertheless change from teaching to alternative occupations, even though they like them less.

Figure 11.3
Choice Between Jobs

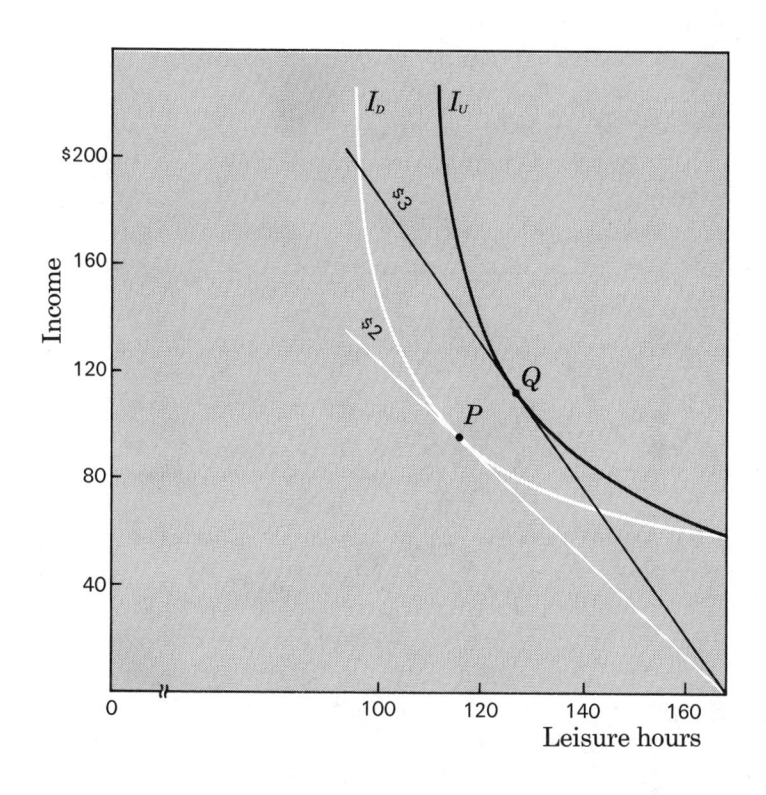

Resource Markets

In the cases which we have been considering, differences in wages make up for differences in the jobs. We refer to such allowances as *compensating wage differentials*. However, there are also *noncompensating wage differentials*—cases where more desirable jobs actually pay more.

One possible explanation for such differentials is a difference in native ability. Few people have the ability to sing grand opera, bat .300, or throw forward passes with high accuracy. Those who have such talents find the bidding for their services quite active. Such bidding has little incentive effect, but it serves to ration the supply among potential bidders. (In sports, the draft system substitutes other kinds of rationing for price rationing, with the usual effect of lowering prices.)

A more common cause of noncompensating differentials, sometimes associated with natural talents, consists of limited access to the training required for certain jobs. Because places in medical schools are limited, many people who would like to become doctors cannot. Doctors' incomes are therefore higher than necessary merely to compensate for the characteristics of the job. (In the illustration at the end of this chapter, we will see that unions sometimes create such differentials.)

Many of these differentials come about because of social institutions which prevent certain workers from having access to certain jobs, thereby decreasing the supply for reasons other than those based upon training or natural ability. To the extent that there is significant discrimination on the basis of race or sex, many of the differentials which we observe are noncompensating in nature. However, it is also true that many differentials which seem to be associated with race or sex do depend upon other characteristics and therefore may not be the result of simple prejudice. As an exercise, consider which of the arguments given in the illustration at the end of Chapter 2 represent simple masculine prejudice and which are genuinely the result of differential productivity.

Another reason for differential wages is the lack of mobility of labor from one job to another. One reason often given for low incomes in agriculture is that for farm workers to move into other occupations requires a change not only in their industry but also in their entire way of life. Consequently, the barriers to such a move are substantial. In contrast, a worker in the city can change occupations without changing the location in which he lives. Consequently, labor mobility is much higher within cities than it is between rural and urban areas. In an international sense, mobility of labor is further restricted by immigration regulations and by language differences between countries. Such barriers are usually so high that workers in different countries can be considered noncompeting groups and the wage differentials are considered entirely nonequalizing.

Income and Substitution Effects

So far, we have been considering the case of a worker whose sole income is derived from the labor market. In some cases, this is not true. Exceptions include not only those who have inherited money, but also wives whose husbands are working. Part—sometimes all—of their income comes from the family pool rather than from direct services in the labor market.

We would expect that workers with outside income would be apt to use that income to buy both more income and more leisure—that is, less work. (We could demonstrate this by drawing new lines on Figure 11.2, higher than the originals but parallel to them.)

The evidence of the choice between leisure and income is all around us. We observe, for example, that wives are more apt to enter the labor market if their husbands' incomes are low. We also see that workers with outside sources of income prefer to work shorter hours and are less apt to accept overtime or moonlighting jobs. However, we must temper both these conclusions with our previous observation about the possibility that the job itself may be desirable and that the indifference curves might actually curve up on the right-hand end. We certainly see many cases of people whose outside income might be enough to persuade them not to work at all, but who do work hard because of the job satisfactions involved. We also see many wives who work primarily for satisfaction and fulfillment, rather than for money. Perhaps the extreme example of this behavior is represented by Governor Nelson Rockefeller of New York, who has spent large amounts of his own money to be elected to a job where he can work long hours at relatively low pay. Obviously, there are other satisfactions in being governor of New York.

We have seen that outside income tends to induce people to choose more leisure and less work. We would therefore expect that the *income effect* of higher wages would also lead to less work. However, there is also a *substitution effect:* as wages rise, the cost of leisure also rises, inducing workers to choose more income and less leisure. The net effect of a change in wage rates, therefore, is a combination of both. The higher wages induce the workers to choose work (the substitution effect) and leisure (the income effect). Whether the net result is that workers will offer more or less labor as wages rise will depend upon which effect is stronger. If the income effect dominates, the supply curve will actually bend backward, so that less labor will be offered at higher wages.

It was a common observation of many businessmen when they first went into underdeveloped countries that it was difficult to find incentives to persuade local workers to work longer hours. In many cases, higher wages produced less labor, because of the backward-bending supply curve. Such a phenomenon is not unknown in advanced countries, however. As real wages have risen in the United States since 1900, the regular work week has steadily declined from 60 hours to a present level nearer 40, and there are some indications that the decline is still continuing.

One way of overcoming this problem is by the use of time-and-a-half payments for overtime. In this way, wages for the extra hours are set high in order to achieve a maximum substitution effect for the extra work; but the basic wage is left unchanged in order to avoid the income effect which would make workers less apt to offer the extra service. During World War II, substantial numbers of women entered the labor force, lured by the combination of high wages for themselves and the low incomes which their husbands received while serving in the armed forces. In this case, both the income effect and the substitution effect led them to take jobs.

In our discussion so far, we have assumed that the workers can always choose exactly the number of hours they will work. This is usually not the case, however, since most firms require that their workers put in a fixed number of hours in order that the entire business may run on a schedule. Still, there are ways in which workers may effectively vary the amount of work which they offer, even within fixed work weeks in the individual firms.

There are many jobs which provide opportunities to work less than the standard work week; some workers use them so they can work more by moonlighting. Workers who carry two full-time jobs are not unknown. Workers who wish to work less than the standard week also sometimes resort to absenteeism. It is significant that absenteeism rises in periods when wages are high or when employers try to lengthen the work week.

If we take the household rather than the individual worker as the unit of labor supply, it is clear that there are even more opportunities for flexibility. Secondary workers, wives and children, move in and out of the labor force. Earnings of the principal worker may often determine whether children will continue their education or go to work. Similarly, retirement of older workers may depend upon the income of younger members of the family.

In order to find the market demand for labor, it would be necessary to add together the demand curves of various firms. Similarly, in order to find the market supply curve, it would be necessary to add together the supply curves of individual households. The final level of wages and employment would depend upon these market demand and supply curves and the market organization.

Rent

In ordinary conversation, rent is used to refer to the payment for the temporary usage of anything, whether it be land, a building, machinery, or an automobile. Economists have traditionally reserved the term for the rent of land, because its supply conditions are quite different from those of other products which are rented. (There is a second category of economic rent which we will discuss presently.)

Firms engaged in renting automobiles or other pieces of equipment are supplying a service to possible buyers. In general, if the rent of this service rises, one would expect an increase in the supply of machinery or automobiles available. In other words, the characteristics of such firms are almost like those of other firms in that they combine materials and labor to provide useful services. When we look at land, however, we see that the conditions of supply are quite different. The aggregate amount of land supplied is fixed, regardless of the price. Higher prices do not induce an increased supply of land in this sense of the term. We saw in the early chapters of this book that price performs two functions: it rations the product among possible buyers, and it provides incentive to possible suppliers to provide the product. Land rent performs only one of these functions—the rationing; there is no incentive effect.

With respect to agricultural land, the observation of the perfectly inelastic supply curve is no longer quite correct. It is true that the amount of land available in a given country is fixed. However, if the land is measured not in terms of its acreage but in terms of its productivity, it is clear that any given piece of property is the result of natural endowment and also of investment of labor and materials to improve its productivity. Applications of fertilizer, arrangements to improve drainage, and many other factors all affect the productivity of the land and its supply. Large scale irrigation projects often increase the supply of farm land by making land which would otherwise be unproductive into a productive asset. The same can be said of many forms of land reclamation. The extreme case occurred in Holland, where agricultural land was created out of what was previously sea. We may thus conclude that agricultural land, which nineteenth century economists often described as the fixed and immutable gift of God, is a produced product almost as much as any other in our society, although the time response of the supply curve may be somewhat slow.

With respect to urban land, the situation is quite different. In this case, the essential characteristic of a piece of property is not its physical characteristics, but its location. A piece of property acquires its value simply by its proximity to other attributes of the metropolitan area. The quantity of land having such characteristics is exactly limited, and therefore the idea of the vertical supply curve applies quite precisely here. It is also clear that the demand for particular pieces of property is largely the result of social circumstances surrounding them and bears slight relationship to the activities of the owner. Consequently, it is often said that it would be more appropriate for society as a whole to reap the benefit of the rent from this land rather than the individual owner, who contributes little or nothing to its value.

Because rent represents a payment which has rationing, but

few incentive, effects, we have come to recognize a concept of economic rent in many other forms of payment which help to ration a given factor among possible buyers but do not affect the supply of that factor. Such rents are especially clear in the wages paid to individuals with particular talents. Thus the noncompensating differential based on talent can be considered economic rent.

Even the ordinary supply curve of labor contains elements of rent. Those persons who would be willing to work for lower prices than the market actually sets can be said to receive a certain rent if the amount that they are paid is greater than the amount required to get them to offer their services. In fact, everyone except the marginal worker receives some degree of rent in his wage. This is because the market price is set to entice those who are least willing into a particular occupation. Those who are more willing to enter the occupation receive more than the minimum amount which would be required. Consequently, a portion of their income may be called rent.

Thus we see that the concept of rent, originally developed to apply to agricultural land, has grown less applicable to such land, but is now regarded as generally applicable to many other circumstances in our economy. In fact, it can probably be said that most incomes contain a rent element of varying importance.

Interest

A full discussion of the rate of interest in the society would require a discussion of the role of banks and other financial institutions and of governmental activities. Such a discussion is primarily the province of macroeconomics. However, one important component belongs with microeconomics: the role of households as savers and lenders of money, and, occasionally, as net borrowers.

Each household normally expects a certain income stream in the future—possibly rising, possibly falling, probably ceasing altogether at some time. By borrowing or lending money, it can redistribute that income stream and also change its total size (by the amount of the interest paid or received). Of all the income streams attainable, one will usually be preferred. Only by a rare coincidence will the best stream be exactly the one the household expects to earn. The household will, therefore, be a borrower or a lender at some point; and, at different times in its life, it may be both.

The process by which a household makes its spending and saving decisions is illustrated in Figure 11.4. On the two axes, we have represented the amount of money which the household will spend this year and next. A set of indifference curves will describe the household's preferences among various ways to divide its spending. Its opportunity set depends upon two basic factors—the incomes which it expects to receive this year and next, and the rate of interest at which it can exchange this year's income for next year's. In this example, the household expects an income of $10,000 this year, and $12,000 next year. The interest rate is assumed to be 10 percent. It can therefore exchange $1.00 now for $1.10 next year. The household would maximize its utility by choosing the combination along the opportunity set which is tangent to the highest indifference curve. (This process exactly corresponds to that of Chapter 4, where the household tried to adjust its purchases of goods so as to reach the highest indifference curve attainable from its income line.) We see that this point is at $10,700 for this year, and $11,230 for next. In order to reach that point from its initial starting position, it must borrow $700, expecting to repay $770 next year. In that way, consumption this year will be raised from $10,000 to $10,700, and next year's consumption will be lowered from $12,000 to $11,230.

In this example, the household is on a rising income pattern. It is therefore led to transfer some of its future income into the present by borrowing. If, on the other hand, the household expected a decline in income, it would be more apt to transfer some of its present income into the future by becoming a saver in the present period. This conclusion corresponds to the commonsense observation that young families are often borrowers, but that they become savers as they get older and approach the low-income period after retirement. The principles which are demonstrated in this simple two-year diagram can be applied to the more general case of the household's decisions over longer periods of time.

If a household is a saver, how will it react to increased interest rates? On the one hand, the substitution effect will increase sav-

**Figure 11.4
Saving Decisions**

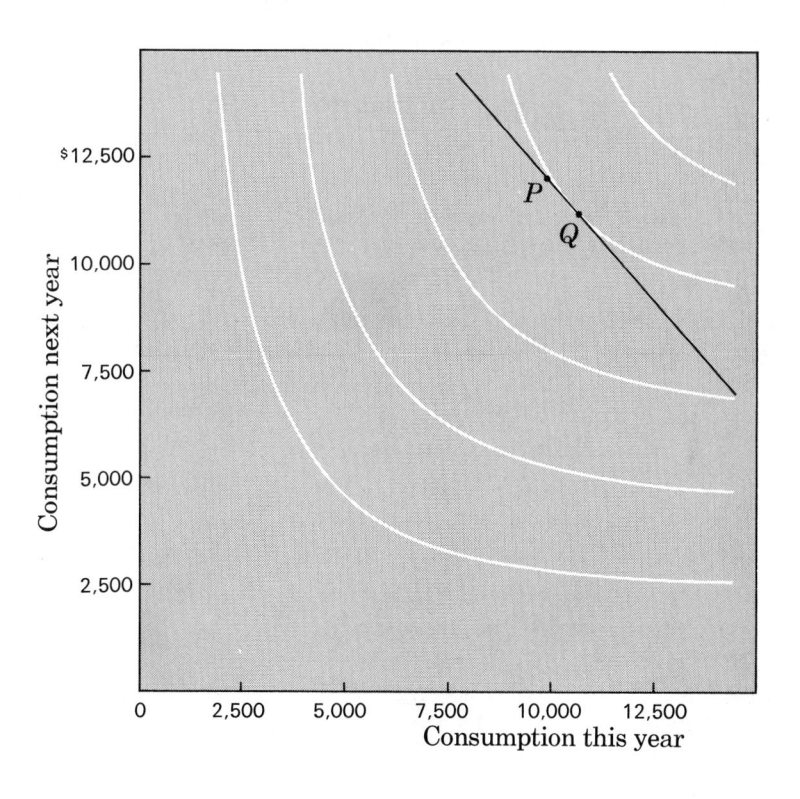

Resource Markets

ing, because each dollar saved will bring more money later. The income effect, however, will tend to decrease saving, since one could save less and still have the same amount or more in the future. Here, as elsewhere, it is not possible to tell whether the income effect or the substitution effect will be more important in particular cases. There is some evidence to show that, in fact, households' net reactions to changes in interest rates are relatively small, indicating that the income and substitution effects tend to balance.

In Figure 11.4, we have assumed that the interest rate is the same, whether the household wishes to borrow or to lend. In fact, this is seldom true. The typical method by which households borrow is through consumer loans, most of which have interest rates above 10 percent. On the other hand, if families wish to save, they often find that the best opportunity available to them is in a savings account or through a savings and loan association where the return is closer to 5 percent. In such cases, the opportunity set is no longer represented by a single straight line but by two different lines which meet at the expected incomes. Because these two so often meet with a slight corner, there is a tendency for the family to choose to stay exactly where it is. There is not enough to be gained by saving, but the costs are apt to be too high for borrowing. The lack of symmetry in interest rates increases the number of households who choose to "neither a borrower nor a lender be" (*Hamlet:* Act I, Scene 3, Line 75).

An Illustration: Unions and Wages

Workers often form unions in order to raise their wages. Such an effect can only take place, however, if unions manage to alter the supply or demand curves for labor.

One device which is often used by unions is to attempt to increase the demand for the labor of its members. Such action may utilize campaigns to buy goods with union labels, but it also may use various kinds of governmental activity. For example, many restrictions which have been written into building codes have the effect of increasing the demand for union construction workers and of preventing that demand from being satisfied by those who have not met the union standards. Similarly, the licensing methods of lawyers and doctors effectively increase the demand for their services and can often be considered to resemble union activities. College professors achieve the same result (without actual licensing) by the customary requirement of the PhD for college teachers.

More commonly, however, unions affect wages by their control over the supply, not the demand, of labor. This takes place in either of two ways. The first is illustrated in Figure 11.5. Unions which are organized along craft lines usually control the apprentice program whereby new workers enter the field. By restricting the number of apprentices, the union can shift the supply curve of that kind of labor to the left, thereby increasing the wages of those who remain in the industry.

Organization of craft unions is usually only possible where there is a significant level of skill which cannot be easily learned except through the apprenticeship program. For production workers, who are usually classified as semiskilled and who can often learn their jobs in a few weeks time, such control over entry into the profession is not feasible. Such workers are usually organized in industrial unions. The industrial union operates primarily by means of collective bargaining, under which (1) a wage is negotiated by the union for all employees of the plant, and (2) all of the workers agree not to work for less than the union wage. Such union activity is illustrated in Figure 11.6. It is significant that an industrial union can only succeed if it has, either as members or as sympathizers, most of the workers available for employment; nonunion workers are a ready source of supply for the employer who does not wish to pay a union wage. Such unions tend to be all inclusive. In effect, they substitute a right-angled supply curve, offering the employer as much labor as he wishes at the union wage, but no labor below it.

An important limitation upon the policy of an industrial union is that while its strength requires it to obtain all potential workers as members of the union, the higher wage it gains is apt to decrease the number of workers actually employed in the industry. Therefore, unemployed workers are both a significant source of discontent within the union and a severe limitation on its strength. Over a long period of time, this weakness can be overcome, because the workers who find no employment as a result of

**Figure 11.5
Craft Union**

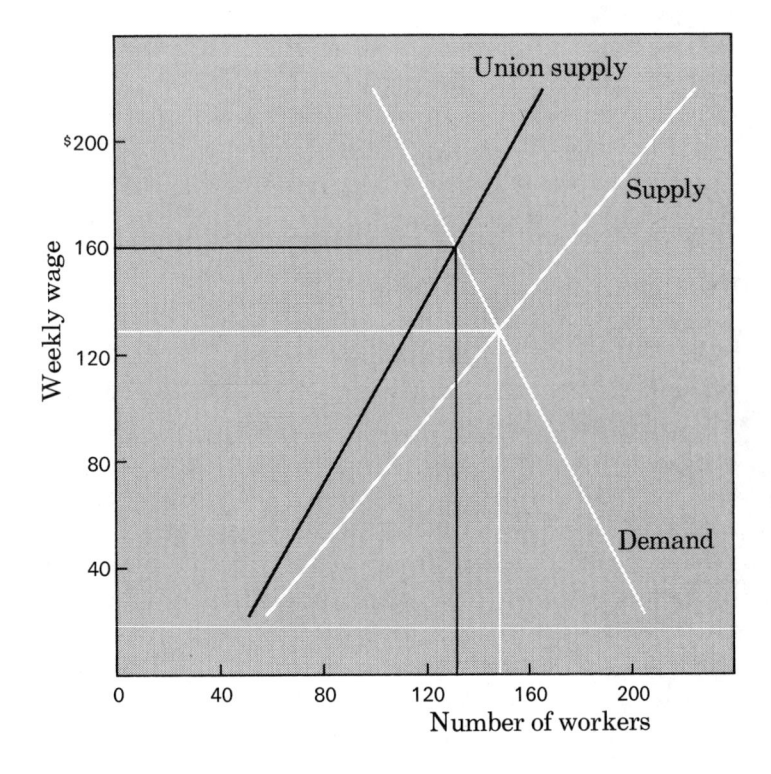

**Figure 11.6
Industrial Union**

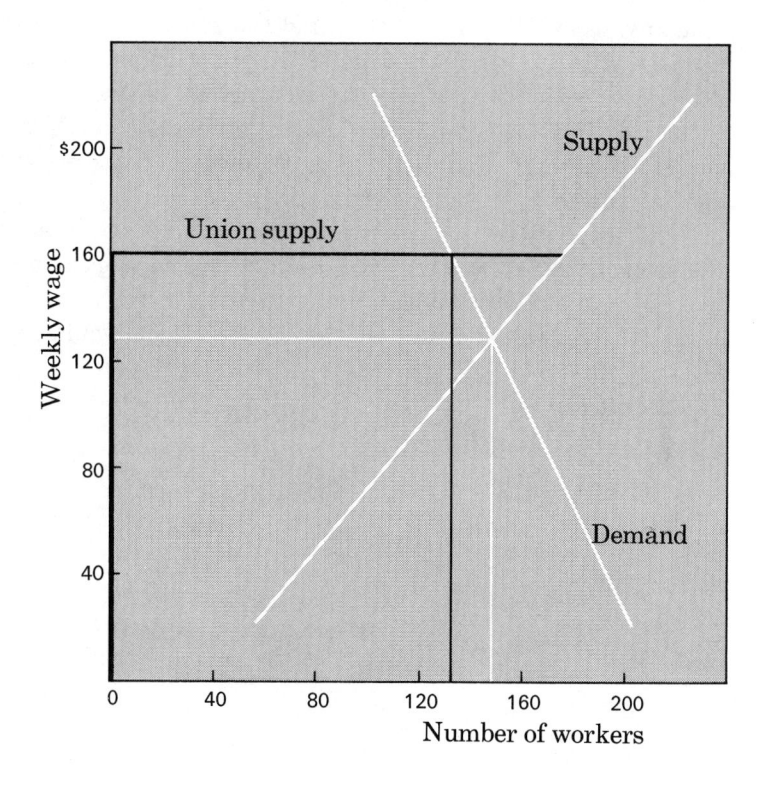

Resource Markets

unionization in the industry tend to move elsewhere. An important effect of unionization in some industries is that the supply of workers in those industries is, in effect, decreased; workers who might have worked there seek positions in other sectors of the economy, especially in the retail and the service trades. Consequently, it is likely that the higher wages of union workers are associated with lower wages for workers in the nonunionized industries. In some nonunionized sectors of the economy, however, wages rise along with union wages, primarily as a method of preventing the growth of union strength.

If the economy were 100 percent unionized, it is not clear what the level of wages would be. The present discussion relates mainly to union wage differentials. If unions were everywhere, the principal problems would center on whether the unions would be willing to settle for a high general level of unemployment in order to force wages up.

Appendix to Chapter 11
Labor Unions

This chapter contains a discussion of the general characteristics of labor unions and of the ways in which they try to raise the incomes of their members. This appendix discusses some of the characteristics of union membership in the United States.

Union membership in the United States is concentrated in construction, manufacturing, transportation, communication, and public utilities — that is, in industries characterized by large establishments and a high proportion of blue-collar workers. The reasons for this concentration come from the nature of unionization. The construction industry is the traditional home of the craft union, where long apprenticeships make it possible to control the supply of labor. To some extent, the same forces are at work in transportation, especially on the railroads. In manufacturing, on the other hand, industrial unions are more common. In these large establishments, workers often feel the need for collective bargaining to enable them to make gains which they can not make individually. It is in such cases that unions can offer significant services to their members.

Table A11.1 shows the industrial distribution of

Table A11.1
Union Membership by Industry, 1966

Industry	Employees over 16 (in millions)	Percent in Unions
Mining	0.6	35.9
Construction	4.3	41.4
Manufacturing	22.6	37.4
Transportation, communication, and other public utilities	4.3	50.3
Wholesale trade	2.7	13.6
Retail trade	11.8	12.3
Personal services	4.9	7.0
Other	13.4	4.8
Total Private	64.6	23.9

Source: *Labor Union Membership in 1966,* U.S. Census, Series P-20, No. 216, p. 16.

workers and the degree of unionization in each major industry group. Notice that unionization is very low in trade and services, where establishments are typically smaller and workers have a closer relationship to their employers. Both because of the size of the firms and the nature of the work, employees often believe that they can do as well for themselves.

Men are more apt to be union members than women. There were, in 1966, 38.6 million men working in the private sector of the economy, of whom 12.1 million, or 31.4 percent, were union members. Of the 26.1 million women working, only 3.4 million, or 12.9 percent were union members. It is not clear why so few women are unionized, although there are several contributing factors. A larger percentage of women are part-time workers, and part-time workers have less interest in joining unions. In addition, women are more apt to have office jobs than production jobs, and office workers are generally less unionized. Finally, women are less apt to work in the kinds of industries which are most heavily unionized. Almost no women work in construction, and only one-third of the labor force in manufacturing is female. In contrast, more women than men are employed in retail trade, and three-fourths of the service workers are women.

Table A11.2
Union Membership by Occupation, 1966

Occupation	Employees over 16 (in millions) Male	Female	Percent in Unions Male	Female
Professional and technical	3.6	1.6	11.6	4.7
Managers	4.2	0.8	9.6	3.9
Clerical	2.6	8.7	24.1	9.0
Sales	2.7	2.4	7.9	6.9
Craftsmen	8.6	0.3	46.7	20.2
Operatives	9.8	5.5	48.7	35.2
Service	2.3	6.2	19.3	4.5
Laborers	3.6	} 0.6	33.1	} 6.1
Farm workers	1.2		0.9	
Total private	38.6	26.1	31.4	12.9

Source: *Labor Union Membership in 1966*, U.S. Census, Series P-20, No. 216, p. 8.

An examination of union membership by occupation, as shown in Table A11.2, indicates many of the same factors. We see that, among men, the most unionized occupations are craftsmen and operatives (production line workers). Among women too, operatives are most apt to be unionized. In contrast, clerical, sales, and service workers have much lower rates of unionization for both sexes, but are especially low for women. Managerial, professional, and technical workers also show low rates of unionization for both sexes, mainly because these workers often prefer individual bargaining and because their employers often consider them part of management. Farm workers show the lowest unionization of all, although the percentage has probably risen slightly since 1966.

One of the continuing questions is whether and how much unions raise wages. Some clue can be obtained from Table A11.3, although those answers should not be considered definitive; the same factors which lead some workers and not others to join unions might be related to their income differences.

In order to increase comparability, the data in Table A11.3

Table A11.3
Median Earnings by Occupation, 1966
(Full-time male workers)

Occupation	Median Earnings Union	Nonunion
Professional and technical	$8,824	$9,514
Managers	9,322	9,590
Clerical	6,541	6,361
Sales	6,831	7,720
Craftsmen	8,288	6,760
Operatives	6,916	5,539
Service	5,183	4,149
Laborers	6,165	4,117
Farm workers	(F)	2,687
Total private	7,419	6,980

(F) Too few for reliable calculation

Source: *Labor Union Membership in 1966,* U.S. Census, Series P-20, No. 216, p. 10.

cover only male workers who worked full time for the full year. We see that nonunion workers had higher median earnings in professional and technical, managerial, and sales occupations. These are three areas where unionization is lowest. It is quite possible that those workers who are most confident of their ability to obtain higher incomes on an individual basis are the ones who are not interested in unions and collective bargaining. In other words, the higher incomes of nonunion workers may be the cause of the low rate of unionization. Other evidence indicates that unionization of workers in these occupations usually takes place where their work is most apt to be routinized—that is, most like that of production workers. If so, this fact would offer another explanation of the lower incomes of union members.

Union members who are craftsmen and operatives have consistently higher incomes than nonunion workers. Again, it is not clear whether it is the unionization which produces higher incomes, or whether unionization tends to be concentrated in larger and more successful establishments. For example, in construction, most firms which build offices and apartment buildings and a large number which build homes are unionized. In contrast, many of the smaller firms which specialize in repair and minor remodeling are nonunion.

Perhaps the most interesting difference is found in the case of laborers, where the ratio of union earnings to nonunion is the highest. Because many of the union laborers work for companies which employ significant numbers of other union workers, there is a high probability that these other workers tend to carry the laborers' income up in the general bargaining.

When incomes of union and nonunion workers are examined in detail, certain other differences emerge. The incomes of union members are more concentrated near the median. In every occupation and every industry, more nonunion workers have very high and very low incomes. Again, it is not clear whether one should conclude that unions help the lowest paid employees at the expense of the highest paid, or whether unionization is most apt to occur among middle-income workers, with low-income workers lacking the power to form unions and high-income workers lacking the incentive.

When incomes are examined by race, we find that black union members are farther above black nonunion members than is the case for whites. In this case, the explanation is probably that blacks who are not members of unions are more apt to be forced into poorer jobs, while union members can get better ones. It is still true, however, that black union members average lower incomes than white union members.

In summary, we may say that about one-third of male and one-eighth of female employees are union members. Union membership is concentrated in construction, manufacturing, and transportation. Workers who are craftsmen and operatives are most apt to be unionized. Union workers in these occupations, as well as laborers, have higher incomes than nonunion workers; but nonunion professional, managerial, and sales workers earn more than union members.

Chapter 12
The Market System and Economic Welfare

Over the last twenty years, the evidence has been accumulating that cigarette smoking leads to lung cancer, heart disease, and various other diseases. Many cigarette smokers quit. Others were too addicted to stop, but felt they should "do something."

Unfortunately, the evidence against cigarettes is primarily statistical, so that it is not possible to identify the exact component of cigarette smoke which causes damage. There is a strong suspicion that the danger is at least related to tar and nicotine.

Cigarette manufacturing is dominated by five large firms, each of them selling almost identical cigarettes at identical prices, and spending large sums on advertising as their only form of competition.

When the health scare first began, the cigarette companies reacted by putting filters on their cigarettes. These filters removed a portion of the tar and nicotine, but also a portion of the taste. The companies then launched new brands of cigarettes, substituting stronger burley tobacco for the milder flue-cured tobacco which had been used for unfiltered cigarettes. The result was that the filters still removed tar and nicotine, but enough was left to produce smoke from filtered cigarettes which was almost identical with that from unfiltered cigarettes.

The new cigarettes were launched with massive advertising budgets, typically over $20 million in the first year. The usual theme of the advertisements was to emphasize both the filter and the flavor. The advertisements were semantic masterpieces, for they manged to imply that the new cigarettes were safe without actually saying so. Smokers were encouraged to persuade themselves that they were doing something about health hazards while avoiding giving up the pleasures of smoking. Filter sales rose as unfiltered sales fell, and tobacco company profits were largely unaffected.

The growers of tobacco were not in the same favorable position. Flue-cured tobacco is grown mainly in Virginia and North Carolina, while burley tobacco growing is concentrated in Kentucky and Tennessee. Soil and climate prevent growing burley in the coastal areas.

The tobacco growers of Virginia and North Carolina faced a serious depression. The demand for their premium tobacco fell drastically with consequent declines in price and quantity. The growers of burley, who had previously sold their product mainly for pipe tobacco, now found demand substantially increased, with consequent rises in price and quantity. The total revenue for all tobacco growers changed little, but it shifted toward the western growers. Unlike the manufacturers, the growers merely reacted to the new situation, without being able to channel it in their own interest.

Interrelated Markets

Our society is not merely a collection of individual markets, but a system of markets, all of which are tied together in various ways. The forms of this relationship are many and varied, and we can do little but sketch a few examples here. The important thing to remember is that every economic action has a wide variety of reactions, not only in its own industry but in others which may be further removed. In the example above, we saw that new medical findings caused changes in the cigarette industry, and that the actions of the cigarette manufacturers in turn had substantial effects upon the tobacco growers. We could also have followed the example further and discovered the repercussions in other agricultural industries, as land which was once used for tobacco was redirected to other crops. Sometimes, as in this example, the relationships work themselves out through the supply side of the market, and in other cases, through the demand side. In many circumstances, there will be repercussions on both sides of the market. The illustration at the end of this chapter traces some of the effects of the development of the automobile. In every case, we must follow different paths of reasoning; but it is safe to say that there is usually more to each than meets the eye.

In recent years, it has become fashionable to talk about *ecology*, the study of the way different factors in the environment interact. One should remember that *economics* has the same root, and has always concerned itself with this process. However, economics has the added implication of management of the interaction process, whereas ecology means merely understanding it.

One very simple form of interrelationship occurs when two markets for an identical product are separated only by geography. In Figure 12.1, we have shown the supply and demand curves for a particular product in two different markets. If these two markets were completely independent, the price in the first would be $0.40 and the price in the second would be $0.85. However, if it were possible to ship some of the product from the first market to the second, many of the sellers would want to do so. The excess supply in the first market—the difference between the supply and the demand curves at each price—would then find its way into the second market. If there were no transportation cost, we could simply add this excess supply from market I to the supply in market II, which is shown as the curve $S_2 + XS_1$. We now see that the price would be $0.55 in the second market, because the excess supply coming in from the first market would lower the price to that level. However, the price in market I would also have risen to $0.55, because no one would sell in market I at a lower price than he could get in market II.

In the more likely case, there will be a transportation cost or other barrier between the two markets. If the transportation cost were $0.15, it would not pay to ship any of the product from

**Figure 12.1
Related Markets**

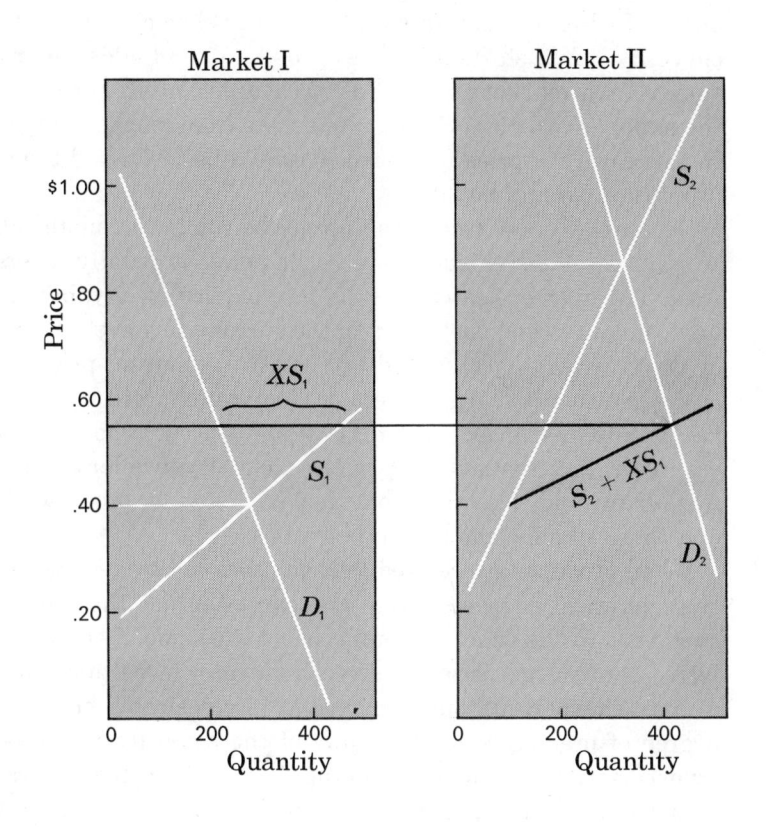

market I to market II until the price were at least $0.15 above the equilibrium price in market I. At that price, the excess supply from market I would appear in market II with a $0.15 differential. In Figure 12.2, this differential is shown. The combined curve $S_2 + XS_1$ starts at the level of $0.55 and adds the excess supply from market I at a $0.15 price differential. For example, the supply at $0.60 is S_2 plus the excess from market I at $0.45. In this case, the price in market II would be $0.65 and the price in market I would be $0.50.

Occasionally, the relationship may be somewhat more subtle. A market seldom exists at one single point; it usually covers an area. The market center may lie in a particular city, but it will have suppliers and customers in the surrounding area. The price in the surrounding area will be the central market price *minus* transportation cost if suppliers predominate; it will be the market price *plus* transportation if customers predominate. Customers in a rural area usually pay less than city dwellers for native fresh fruits and vegetables, but they pay more for processed foods and those which come from other areas.

When products are related to each other not by geography but their physical characteristics, one can often use the same logic even though the exact reasoning is not the same. As certain preferred products get too expensive, buyers may be willing to switch over to cheaper, although somewhat less desirable brands. The degree of preference serves many of the same functions as the transportation cost in the geographic model. In the geographic model, one would expect new firms just starting business to enter market II rather than market I, to take advantage of the higher price; in the case of differentiated products, one would expect new competitors to try to match the preferred product rather than the inferior one.

Economic Welfare

By the time the student has reached this point in the book, he must be aware that there is a close relationship between the working of the market and the satisfaction of the desires of the consumer. He has also seen, however, that there are important respects in which the market does not serve all

**Figure 12.2
Related Markets with Transportation Costs**

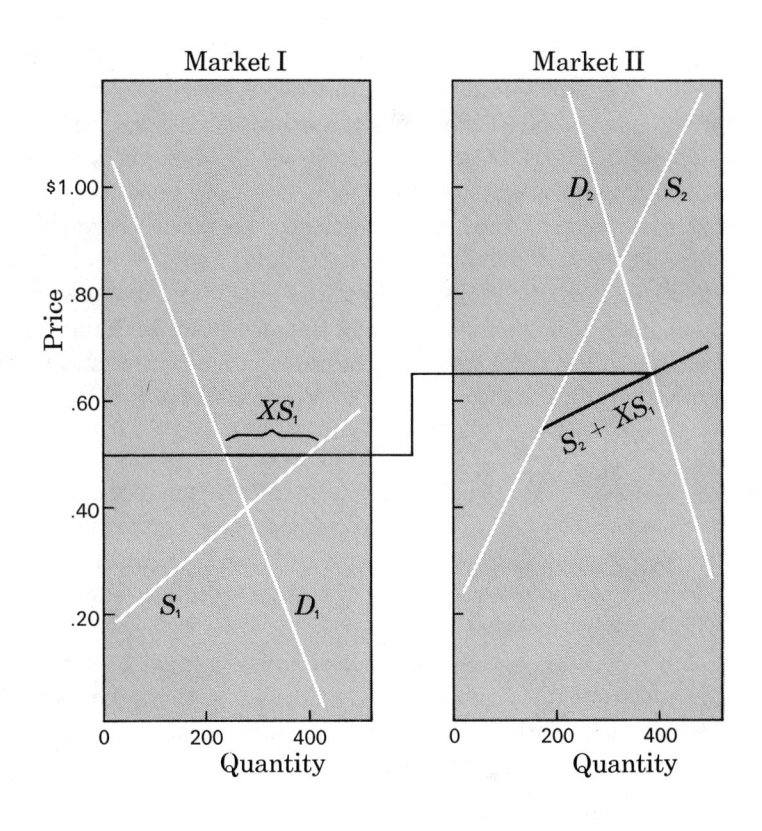

consumer needs. At this stage, it may be well to review both the positive and the negative aspects of the market system.

Efficiency.

Purely competitive markets produce standardized products by known methods at the lowest possible cost. They also produce the goods which consumers want most, as indicated by their willingness to buy them. Less competitive markets, including monopolies, are not under the same pressure to produce at the lowest cost. However, imperfectly competitive markets are often better at developing new techniques and new products than purely competitive ones. Any attitude we may have toward such imperfectly competitive markets usually involves balancing the possible gains from lower prices at the moment against the possible gains from new products or methods of production.

Income distribution.

The market system distributes income in accordance with contributions to the productive process. Accordingly, many people are unable to earn enough to provide themselves with an adequate standard of living, while others often earn amounts which seem excessive.

Traditionally, society has found some method to redistribute income from those who have "too much" to those who have "too little." Part of this redistribution takes place through private charity; but, increasingly, government welfare programs have assumed a greater role. Two problems are associated with the redistribution—the ethical question of who deserves how much, and the economic one of how to keep redistribution from interfering with economic incentives. If people could obtain all they wanted without making a contribution to production, there would be no incentive for them to contribute. Furthermore, if too great a portion of earned income were redistributed to others, the incentives of the givers would be destroyed. The difficulty is to balance this economic problem against the desired ethical distribution.

Social costs and benefits.

The market responds only to those forces which appear in the market. Where benefits accrue to someone other than the purchaser or costs are imposed on others than the supplier, the market will not reflect them, because it matches private costs with private benefits. We have seen that it is sometimes possible —with license fees, fines, or taxes—to convert public costs into private ones, but it is seldom easy. Where there are public benefits, some form of joint purchasing agency or subsidy is apt to be needed.

Other goals.

Even if the market system worked perfectly, we would still not have achieved Utopia; at its best, an economic system provides the goods and services which individuals want. There is no reason to expect that they will all want the right things, or that they will seek the good or the beautiful. The economic system merely provides methods of harmonizing the interests of individuals. If their interests are wrongly directed, the answer lies in better education, philosophy, or religion. While we await personal improvement, there are still advantages to an effectively operating economic system.

An Illustration: The Automobile Century

No product illustrates the far-reaching effects of a single change in the economy as much as the automobile. Before 1914, the automobile was primarily a toy, used by a few wealthy enthusiasts. After World War I, it became a general mode of transportation. The most important factor in this shift was the development of the Ford Model T, the first mass-produced, low-priced automobile in America. Immediately changes in other industries began. The oil industry, which had previously been devoted largely to the production of kerosene for lamps and which was about to face extinction because of electric light, found itself the supplier of fuel for the new method of transportation. (A by-product of the production of gasoline was a large supply of fuel oil, which oil companies sold for heating. Thus one effect of the growth of the automobile was a declining demand for coal.) The rubber industry found a huge new market in tires for automobiles. The steel industry found itself with a rising demand for steel for automobiles at a time when the demand for steel for railroad cars was declining. Consequently, the steel industry managed to retain its same position. By 1929, the twelve largest manufacturing firms in the United States included two automobile companies, six oil companies, and two steel companies; thus only two of the twelve were not primarily involved with the automobile.

Even the changes which had taken place in the 1920s were small compared to the impact which was to come. In the 1930s, new highways (requiring governmental action) were built, which effectively linked most major cities with at least two-laned, paved highways. The number of automobiles increased steadily, although the rate of increase was held down by the depression. During the early 1940s, no civilian automobiles were produced because of World War II; but immediately after 1945 came the great expansion of the automobile. The savings which people had accumulated during the war were available for the purchase of new automobiles, and it was several years before the shortage which had developed during the war could be filled. Furthermore, because of higher postwar incomes, many people who would not previously have bought cars were now able to do so.

The entire shape of urban America changed. Cities which had developed before the automotive era were built compactly, so that people could live within walking distance or, at the very least, streetcar rides from their jobs. The older sections of American cities still contain row after row of small lots, even for fairly expensive houses. But houses built in the post–World War II era were built in the suburbs, often many miles from public transportation. They were also more spread out. Quarter-acre lots were typical, and half-acre lots not uncommon. Another characteristic of the building in this postwar era was that it did not follow simple radial lines. Older suburbs tended to cluster along rail lines which would simplify commuting; but the suburbs created in the '40s and '50s showed no such pattern.

Because housing had developed according to the unstructured commuting of the automobile, it was inevitable that retail areas would also be matched to it. Increasingly, commercial areas to serve the suburbs developed. The stores were either grouped in planned shopping centers or spread along highway strip developments. The most critical part of any suburban commercial development is adequate parking space, because customers arrive only by automobile. In the older shopping areas downtown, customers often use public transportation.

As populations shifted into the suburban areas with their low densities, it was not feasible to follow them with public transportation. No conceivable routes could develop adequate traffic to permit economical operation. Every major city in America talks about public transportation, but a map of where people live and where they work will indicate that it is almost impossible to design a rapid transit system which would carry enough passengers to be economically feasible.

New institutions have developed to serve the automobile-borne customers. Drive-in restaurants, banks, motels, and even churches have appeared.

Nowhere has the age of the auotmobile progressed as far as in southern California, an area which developed after the automobile became common. As a result, Los Angeles spreads widely over the surrounding landscape and is elaborately crisscrossed with freeways, most of which are overcrowded at rush hours. In Los Angeles, it is almost impossible to live without an automobile; whereas in older cities like New York and Boston, many people still do.

In recent years, many writers have increasingly blamed the automobile for much of the pollution and the general disorganization of our cities; and, in large part, these complaints are justified. However, the reason the automobile has this effect is that it provides individuals with flexibility and freedom which they did not have with older transit methods. It would be more precise to say that the difficulties of the automobile result primarily from the fact that private reactions have taken place quite efficiently and rapidly, whereas the public reactions—roads, zoning, and other controls which would make te automobile a civilized member of our society—have been much slower in coming about. The very efficiency of the market system has made the problem more severe than it otherwise would have been.

Index

ability to pay taxation 241
"Acapulco Gold" 69
adaptability and pure
 competition 173
advertising 215
automobile, impact on society 291
average cost 121
average revenue 121

"bandwagon effect" 16
benefit taxation 240
big business 224-230
budget line 87
Bureau of Labor Statistics 96
business taxes 177

capital equipment 155
collusion 213
compensating wage differentials 266
complementary goods and
 supply 20, 85, 93, 46
conglomerate merger 227
consumer incompetence 176
Consumer Price Index 96
consumers and demand 74-99
consumption outlays 106
corporation 129
cost and resources 132-151

cost and supply 45, 110
cost of education 124
cost of living 96
countercyclical taxation 241
craft union 275
cross elasticity of demand 93, 127

demand 7-29
demand and supply 52-73
demand curve and
   time 7-29, 93, 9
demand for leisure 260
demand for resources 255
determinants of demand 16
determinants of supply 43
differentiated oligopoly 204
differentiated products 205
diminishing returns, law of 134
discrimination by race 253, 283
discrimination by sex 48, 280
diseconomies of scale 145, 170
distribution of income and
   government 104, 175, 252, 290, 234
dividends 103
durable goods 106

economic rent 271
economic welfare 288
economies of scale 125, 145, 171
education, and income 102
   and resources 157
   cost of 124
efficiency 290
   and imperfect competition 217
   and pure competition 172
elasticity, of demand 23, 192
   of factor demand 258
   of supply 47
equal-cost lines 140
equal-product curve 138
equilibrium price 53
electricity prices 198
Engel, Ernst 107
Engels, Friedrich 107
entrepreneur 154
expectations and demand 21
explicit cost 112
external economies of scale 169

fair trade laws 219
firms 110, 127-131,
   and supply 109-125
fixed cost 112
fixed factors of production 134
Fortune 224
"free-rider" problem 175
functions of government 232

Gary, Elbert H. 213
Giffen's paradox 79
government 231-253
   and social benefits 175
   and planning 243
grant in aid 237, 248
graph, plotting 3

Homestead Act 244
homogeneous production
   function 140
horizontal merger 226
households 100-108
Hughes, Howard 130

imperfect competition 203-223
implicit cost 112
incentive function of price 34, 57
incentive taxation 242
income, and demand 18
   and wealth 103
   consumption line 90
   distribution 104, 175, 234, 252, 290
   effect 75, 79, 267, 274
   elasticity 90
   taxes 182, 249
   use of 106
increasing cost industry 170
indifference map 80-87
industrial union 275
industry 127, 205
inelastic demand 23
infant industries 171
inferior goods 20, 90
input 111
interest 103, 271
intergovernmental grant 237, 248
intermediate resources 155

internal economies of scale 145
interrelated markets 285
invention 218
inventories 156
isoquant 138

knowledge as a resource 157
labor 152
labor unions 274, 279-283
land 153
land rent 269
law of demand 11
law of diminishing returns 134
law of supply 34
long run 121, 138, 164
   and monopoly 188
   supply curve 37
Luddite riots 149
luxury goods 20, 90

marginal cost 116, 188
marginal factor cost 197
marginal labor cost 197
marginal rate of substitution 83, 140
marginal revenue 116, 188
marginal revenue product 256
marginal utility 78
marijuana 68
market, defined 14
market system 284-293
markups and elasticity 193
Marx, Karl 107, 149
medical care 26
merger 213, 226
minimum wages 56
mobility as a substitute for competition 229
mobility of labor 266
monopoly 185-202
monopsony 197
monopolistic
   competition 204, 207, 212
Morrill Act of 1862 245

natural resources 153
necessities 90
noncompensating wage
   differentials 266

nondurable goods 106
nonprice competition 211
number of consumers and demand 18
number of sellers and supply 43

oligopoly 204, 212-215
Operation Breakthrough 150
opportunity cost 111
opportunity set 76
output 111
output effect 256
overtime wages 268

parking 7
partnership 128
personal income 101
"plucked goose" taxation 242
price-consumption line 94
price control 56
product development 218
production function 134
profit 110
progressive taxes, defined 250
property taxes 182, 249
proportional taxes, defined 250
proprietors' income 101
proprietorship 128
protective tariff 171
public utilities 194
pure competition 161-183

rationing function of price 11, 55
redistribution budget 243
regressive taxes, defined 250
regulated monopoly 194, 198
related goods, and demand 20
   and supply 46
rent 103, 269
rent control 52
resources 152-158, 254-278
   and costs 132-151
Rockefeller, Nelson 267

sabotage 149
sales taxes 177, 249
saving 271
service budget 243

services 106
short run 138, 164
shut-down point 114
size of firms 130
Smith, Adam 173, 212
social benefits and costs 111, 174, 290
social goods, defined 234
stability of pure competition 176
stabilization budget 243
substitute goods 20, 85, 93
  and supply 46
substitution
  effect 75, 79, 256, 267, 272
supply 30-51
supply curve 31
  and time 32
supply of labor 260

tariff 171
tastes and demand 20
taxes 240
taxes, business 177
techniques of production and
  supply 45
"technostructure" 229
technological change,
  and employment 149

and imperfect competition 218
  and pure competition 172
Tennessee Valley Authority 201
three budget system 242
time, and demand curve 9
  and supply curve 32
tools of government 236
transfers 236

unions and wages 274, 281
unit elasticity of demand 23
utility 75

variable cost 112
variable factors of production 134
vertical merger 227
voluntary groups and social
  benefits 175

wage differentials 263
wages and salaries 101
welfare, economic 288
welfare expenditures 234, 252
Women's Liberation 48